Towards a Liberal Utopia?

Towards a Liberal Utopia?

EDITED BY PHILIP BOOTH

The Institute of Economic Affairs

First published in Great Britain in 2005 by
The Institute of Economic Affairs
2 Lord North Street
Westminster
London SW1P 3LB
in association with Profile Books Ltd

The mission of the Institute of Economic Affairs is to improve public understanding of the fundamental institutions of a free society, with particular reference to the role of markets in solving economic and social problems.

A CIP catalogue record for this book is available from the British Library.

ISBN 0 255 36563 2

Many IEA publications are translated into languages other than English or are reprinted. Permission to translate or to reprint should be sought from the Director General at the address above.

Typeset in Stone by MacGuru Ltd
info@macguru.org.uk

Printed and bound in Great Britain by Hobbs the Printers

CONTENTS

PART 2: TIMES PAST

THE AUTHORS

Roger Bate

Roger Bate is director of the health advocacy group Africa Fighting Malaria and a visiting fellow at the American Enterprise Institute. He has a PhD from Cambridge University and has advised the South African government on water and health policy. Dr Bate is the editor/author of ten books, including *What Risk?* (Butterworth Heinneman, 1997), a collection of papers that critically assess the way risk is regulated in society, and *Malaria and the DDT Story* (Institute of Economic Affairs, 2001). He has also written several scholarly papers and over five hundred shorter scientific/policy articles for newspapers and magazines, including the the *Washington Post*, the *Wall Street Journal*, the *Financial Times* and the *Daily Telegraph*. Dr Bate founded the Environment Unit at the Institute of Economic Affairs in 1993 and co-founded the European Science and Environment Forum in 1994.

John Blundell

John Blundell has been Director General of the IEA since 1993. He was educated at King's School, Macclesfield, and at the London School of Economics. He has previously worked at the Federation of Small Businesses, and has been president of the Institute for Humane Studies and of the Atlas Economic Research Foundation. He is a director of Fairbridge and chairman of the executive committee of the board of Atlas and a board member of the Mont Pèlerin Society. John Blundell's previous publications include *Waging the War of Ideas* and *Regulation without the State: The Debate Continues.*

Philip Booth

Philip Booth is Editorial and Programme Director at the Institute of Economic Affairs and Professor of Insurance and Risk Management at the Sir John Cass Business School, City University. Before joining the IEA he was Associate Dean of the Sir John Cass Business School and was a special adviser on financial stability issues at the Bank of England. He has published books and journal articles in the fields of social insurance, regulation, investment and finance, and actuarial science. Philip Booth is editor of *Economic Affairs*, published by the IEA, and associate editor of the *British Actuarial Journal*.

Tim Congdon

Tim Congdon is Chief Economist at Lombard Street Research, the economics consultancy, which he founded in 1989. From 1993 to 1997 he served on the Treasury's Panel of Forecasters, known as the 'Wise Men', and in 1997 he was awarded the CBE for his services to economic debate. Tim Congdon's published books include *The Debt Threat* (1988) and *Reflections on Monetarism* (1992), and he is currently working on *Money in a Modern Economy*. He is an Honorary Fellow of the Institute of Actuaries and Honorary Secretary of the Political Economy Club.

Helen Evans

A former NHS senior nurse with nearly twenty years' experience, Helen Evans is a graduate in Health Management from Anglia Polytechnic University and is currently in the final stages of a PhD at Brunel University. Her doctorate examines notions of government failure in health systems.

Tim Evans

Tim Evans is President and Director General of the free market think tank the Centre for the New Europe. Between 1993 and early 2002 Dr Evans was the Executive Director of Public Affairs at the Independent Healthcare Association in London, where he oversaw political affairs and public relations. In the late 1980s Dr Evans was the Assistant Director of the Foundation for Defence Studies and subsequently became a Senior Policy Consultant at the Adam Smith Institute. In 1991 he was appointed Chief Economic and Political Adviser to the Slovak prime minister – Dr Jan Carnogursky – and was head of the Prime Minister's Policy Unit. In 1993 he was awarded his PhD from the London School of Economics. A political sociologist by background, he has taught at a number of academic institutions over the years, as well as at the Police Staff College at Bramshill.

David Green

David Green is the Director of CIVITAS: the Institute for the Study of Civil Society. Previously he was Director of the Health and Welfare Unit of the Institute of Economic Affairs. He has been a research fellow at the Australian National University and served as a Labour councillor in Newcastle upon Tyne. He has written books about mutual aid, civil society, the development of the new right and the reform of healthcare and social security.

Ralph Harris

Ralph Harris was born in 1924. He was educated at Tottenham Grammar School and Queens' College, Cambridge University, from where he graduated with First Class Honours as Foundation Scholar in 1947. He was then a lecturer at St Andrews University and leader writer with the *Glasgow Herald* before joining the Institute of Economic Affairs as its General Director in 1957. In 1979 he was elevated to the peerage by

Margaret Thatcher, as Lord Harris of High Cross. He sits on the cross benches of the House of Lords and is one of the IEA's founder Presidents.

David Henderson

David Henderson is Visiting Professor at Westminster Business School, and a former head of the Economics and Statistics Department at the OECD. He had previously worked as an academic (fellow of Lincoln College, Oxford, and professor at University College London), as a national civil servant (in HM Treasury and two other government departments), and an international civil servant (with the World Bank). In 1985 he gave the BBC Reith Lectures. His latest book, published by the IEA, is *The Role of Business in the Modern World: Progress, Pressures, and Prospects for the Market Economy.*

John Meadowcroft

John Meadowcroft is Deputy Editorial Director at the IEA and also lecturer in Parliament and Politics on the Hansard Scholars' Programme at the London School of Economics and Political Science. Before joining the IEA he was lecturer in Politics at Queen Mary, University of London, for three years. He has published widely in the field of political economy and the economics of government.

Patrick Minford

Patrick Minford has been Professor of Economics at the Cardiff Business School, Cardiff University, since October 1997. Between 1967 and 1976 he held economic positions in the Ministry of Finance, Malawi, Courtaulds Ltd, HM Treasury, HM Treasury's delegation to Washington, DC, Manchester University, and the National Institute for Economic and Social Research (NIESR). From 1976 to 1997 he was Professor of

Economics at Liverpool University. He was a member of the Monopolies and Mergers Commission from 1990 to 1996 and one of HM Treasury's Panel of Forecasters (the 'Wise Men') from January 1993 to December 1996. He was awarded the CBE for services to economics in 1996.

David Montgomery

David Montgomery is vice-president of Charles River Associates and an internationally recognised authority on the economic impacts of climate change policies. He was a Principal Lead Author of the Second Assessment Report of the Intergovernmental Panel on Climate Change (IPCC), Working Group III, and is the author of a number of studies on climate change policy published over the past seven years. Prior to joining Charles River Associates, Dr Montgomery held a number of senior positions in the United States government. He was Assistant Director of the US Congressional Budget Office and Deputy Assistant Secretary for Policy in the US Department of Energy. He has taught economics at the California Institute of Technology and Stanford University, and was a senior fellow at the environmental research organisation Resources for the Future. Dr Montgomery holds a PhD in Economics from Harvard University and was a Fulbright Scholar at Cambridge University.

Julian Morris

Julian Morris is Executive Director of the International Policy Network (IPN). He is the author, co-author, editor and co-editor of numerous books and papers on the subjects of environmental policy, technology and free markets.

Paul Ormerod

Paul Ormerod is the author of *Death of Economics* and *Butterfly Economics*, and is currently a director of Volterra Consulting. He read Economics at Cambridge, then did postgraduate work at Oxford. Paul began as a macroeconomic modeller and forecaster at NIESR before moving to the private sector and the world of small business. He has published widely in the academic literature. His current interests include understanding economic and social behaviour with models in which agents have low cognition.

Geoffrey Owen

Geoffrey Owen is Senior Fellow, Inter-Disciplinary Institute of Management, London School of Economics. Before joining the LSE in 1991, he had spent most of his career at the *Financial Times*, serving as deputy editor from 1973 to 1980, and editor from 1981 to 1990. He also worked for the Industrial Reorganisation Corporation (1967–9) and for British Leyland Motor Corporation (1969–72). His books include *Industry in the USA* (Penguin, 1967) and *From Empire to Europe: The Decline and Revival of British Industry after the Second World War* (HarperCollins, 1999).

Mark Pennington

Mark Pennington is Senior Lecturer in Political Economy at Queen Mary, University of London. He is the author of *Conservation and the Countryside* (Institute of Economic Affairs, 1997), *Planning and the Political Market* (Athlone, 2000), *Liberating the Land* (Institute of Economic Affairs, 2002), and articles in leading political science and political economy learned journals.

Razeen Sally

Razeen Sally is Senior Lecturer in International Political Economy at the London School of Economics and Political Science and was head of its International Trade Policy Unit. He is Visiting Professor at the Institut d'Etudes Politiques in Paris, and Visiting Senior Research Fellow at the

Institute of Southeast Asian Studies, Singapore. He was also Director of Trade Policy at the Commonwealth Business Council in London. His research has focused on trade policy-making in developing and transitional countries, notably in eastern Europe and east, southeast and south Asia, and on developing country participation in the WTO. Dr Sally has published *Classical Liberalism and International Economic Order: Studies in Theory and Intellectual History* and many articles and chapters in books on trade policy. He is co-publisher of the *Ordo* political economy yearbook in Germany.

Arthur Seldon

Arthur Seldon is Founder President of the Institute of Economic Affairs and was its Editorial Director from 1959 to 1988. He has also been a staff examiner at the London School of Economics (1956–66), a member of the BMA Committee on Health Financing (1968–70) and was vice-president of the Mont Pèlerin Society (1980–86). He has received honorary degrees from University Francisco Marroquin, Guatemala, and Buckingham University and an honorary fellowship from the London School of Economics. Arthur Seldon has published widely on a range of subjects related to the role of markets in solving economic and social problems. He was appointed CBE in 1983.

J. R. Shackleton

J. R. Shackleton is Professor of Economics at the University of Westminster and head of Westminster Business School. He was educated at King's College, Cambridge, and the School of Oriental and African Studies, University of London. He has taught at a number of universities and has worked as an economic adviser in the Government Economic Service.

James Tooley

James Tooley is Professor of Education Policy and Director of the E. G. West Centre at the University of Newcastle upon Tyne. In 1998 he directed the International Finance Corporation's global study of private education, and he has authored several publications, including *Education without the State* (Institute of Economic Affairs, 1996), *The Global Education Industry* (Institute of Economic Affairs, 1999), *Reclaiming Education* (Continuum, 1999) and *The Miseducation of Women* (Continuum, 2002); he co-edited *Government Failure: E. G. West on Education* (Institute of Economic Affairs, 2003).

FOREWORD

F. A. Hayek dedicated *The Road to Serfdom* 'to the socialists of all parties'. It analysed the dire consequences of giving up liberty and showed how the complete loss of liberty can sneak up on a society from an accumulation of apparently minor surrenders.

This book, a celebration of 50 years of the Institute of Economic Affairs, is aimed at liberals of all parties. It is designed to help them have more courage in promoting liberal policies that can lead to the development of a wealthy, free, complex and ordered society at peace with itself. Its purpose is also to help intellectuals, opinion formers and academics develop a vision of a better world and promote that vision.

Those who passionately embrace 'central planning' have lost influence. Happily, today there are liberals across all political parties who believe that liberalism in the economic sphere is desirable or, at the very least, is instrumental in wealth creation. But, beware, there are still serious dangers posed by people who believe that taking yet more power from individuals and centralising it in the state will improve society. So often, academics, intellectuals and policy-makers who pay lip-service to liberalism cannot let go of a tendency to socialism.

Such people come in several guises. First, there are the 'experts', who feel that if only the state were to control things in the way they suggest in their own particular policy area, things would be so much better. Then there are the 'meddlers'. They are so intent on regulating the actions of a free market as to make a mockery of the word 'free'. Others equate freedom with a 'free for all' because they cannot envisage the complex institutions that evolve in a free society to bring order to our lives. Still others believe that, while the market should be the basis for most economic exchange, we need state intervention to protect the weak and the poor and provide health, welfare and education. Yet, if the government is spending 45 per cent of national income already and still we have the squalor, poverty and misery that these people are concerned about, surely more government is not the answer.

The motivation for *Towards a Liberal Utopia?* came from two directions. First, there was a desire to create a lasting reminder of how the IEA's founders and supporters struggled in a harsh intellectual and political climate to shift opinion firmly away from central planning towards a belief in a more liberal economy. Second, we wished to sketch out a vision of a liberal utopia that could be referred to for many years to come. In doing so, the IEA's authors are responding to Hayek's appeal to liberal academics in *The Intellectuals and Socialism.*

The authors of Part 1 of *Towards a Liberal Utopia?* were asked to look forward 50 years, ignore the politically possible, and show how a liberal policy framework should look in their own areas of expertise. They have done that in different ways. Some writers have ignored the current political conjuncture altogether. Others have produced chapters setting out practical solutions, suggesting how the liberal policies they dream about might evolve out of the current situation.

Part 2 looks at what has happened to some of the ideas that have found a forum at the IEA. It shows that radical ideas do not have to remain just that. In the first 30 years of the IEA's life, Ralph Harris and Arthur Seldon drove the Institute forward to numerous achievements. In the 1970s, for example, it was discussing privatisation and how to go about it, reform of labour laws to curb unions, how controlling the money supply would cause inflation to all but disappear, the abolition of exchange controls, selling off council housing, road pricing – all ideas that have turned into solid reality. Ralph Harris looks back at these and many others in Part 2.

No fewer than ten Nobel Prize winners have worked with the IEA. James Buchanan, Milton Friedman, F. A. Hayek, John Hicks, James Meade, Douglass North and George Stigler are all IEA authors: their work will be featured in a special volume, *The Road to Economic Freedom*, to be published by Edward Elgar later this year. Gary Becker, Ronald Coase and Vernon Smith have been long-term friends and advisers to the IEA. Arthur Seldon discovered most of them well before they received their honours. Their work changed the thinking of a whole generation of political philosophers and politicians. An appendix to Part 2 describes, in Arthur Seldon's own words, the process of recruiting the best authors to write for the IEA.

We are grateful too to our current generation of outstanding authors, who write monographs and articles for the IEA's journal, *Economic Affairs*. Many of them have written chapters in this book, urging intellectuals and policy-makers to expand the domain of the individual and reduce the domain of the state.

Towards a Liberal Utopia? is intended as a lasting contribution to both academic and political education and debate, not just in the UK but overseas. It is also intended as a reminder of just how close the UK came to finding the socialist system of central planning overwhelming the country, and how ideas had so much influence in rolling back that system. We hope that a new generation of liberal thinkers, as well as those who are already persuaded by liberalism, will be inspired by the ideas in Part 1 of the book. We hope that Part 2 will give them confidence that their ideas can bear fruit.

As in all IEA publications, the views expressed in this book are those of the authors and not those of the Institute (which has no corporate view), its managing trustees, Academic Advisory Council members or senior staff.

JOHN BLUNDELL
Director General,
Institute of Economic Affairs
January 2005

ACKNOWLEDGEMENTS

I would like to thank all IEA authors and academics who are involved in any way with the IEA, as well as the IEA's other supporters who make its work possible. With regard to this particular publication, I would like to thank Ralph Harris and John Blundell for their very helpful discussions and guidance. I would like to give particular thanks to Dr John Meadowcroft, Research Fellow and Deputy Editorial Director at the IEA, who has given a great deal of assistance in the production of this book.

FIGURES AND TABLES

TO
THE LIBERALS
OF
ALL PARTIES

Towards a Liberal Utopia?

1 INTRODUCTION
Philip Booth

In *The Intellectuals and Socialism*, Hayek challenged liberal academics to:

> ... offer a new liberal programme which appeals to the imagination. We must make the building of a free society once more an intellectual adventure, a deed of courage. What we lack is a liberal Utopia, a programme which seems neither a mere defence of things as they are nor a diluted kind of socialism, but a truly liberal radicalism which does not spare the susceptibilities of the mighty ... which is not too severely practical, and which does not confine itself to what appears today to be politically possible. (Hayek, 1949: 26)

In Part 1 of *Towards a Liberal Utopia?* the IEA's authors have responded to Hayek's appeal.

There is, of course, no such thing as a liberal utopia in the sense of an end point that we can expect to be reached in practice. In *The Road to Serfdom*, Hayek was scathing of the pretended utopia of democratic socialism: 'That democratic socialism, the great utopia of the last few generations, is not only unachievable, but that to strive for it produces something so utterly different that few of those who now wish it would be prepared to accept the consequences, many will not believe till the connection has been laid bare in all its aspects' (Hayek, 1944: 23). The quote at the beginning of the second chapter of *The Road to Serfdom*, from Hoerlderlin, is: 'What has always made the state a hell on earth has been precisely that man has tried to make it his heaven.' Hayek's condemnation of the quest for utopia was unequivocal.

So why did Hayek want liberal economists to sketch out a liberal utopia? Is it that he thought that liberals had found the 'right theory' whereas socialists promoted the wrong theory? That can hardly have been so as the pursuit of utopia is inimical to the whole concept of liberalism. No liberal would pretend to know what a liberal utopia would look like. St Thomas More's Utopia was 'no place'. That is precisely where a liberal utopia is too.

So, what is the purpose of the intellectual task of sketching out a liberal utopia? What is the nature of that task? Are we defining an outcome or an institutional framework? Can we define a liberal utopia precisely enough to be able to know whether we are moving away from it or towards it? If we can, has policy in recent decades moved the UK away from the idea of utopia or closer to it?

The purpose of this exercise is to sketch out a path to a better society to which intellectuals, policy-makers, opinion formers and academics can aspire. One should not criticise the concept of a liberal utopia for not being 'practical' or not being 'politically possible', as one reason for sketching out the vision is to extend the bounds of the politically possible by creating a healthier intellectual climate in which liberal political ideas can be discussed. Also, politicians and opinion formers can use a liberal utopia as a benchmark when judging individual policies and policy programmes: to do so may make them less likely to backtrack and lose sight of their principles when the going gets tough.

In discussing the concept of a liberal utopia, it should be clear that our authors are not defining what society will look like. That is the socialist way. Liberals are aware that, when there are impediments to the market economy, there are undiscovered opportunities for increasing welfare. If those opportunities for increasing welfare have not been discovered, we do not know in any detail what the effect of their discovery would be. We know, for example, that our state-controlled education system has fossilised and politicised the provision of education; we know that it does not respond to parental desire; we know that schools and other providers of education have been prevented from innovating and providing education in so many ways of which we have not yet dreamt; we know that good schools cannot expand and that poor schools 'thrive' and take an increasing share of the educational budget. We might be able to describe the policy framework that will bring about a better outcome. We have a broad idea of how some aspects of that better outcome may look, but we certainly know nothing in detail about how education would be provided if we had a genuinely liberal system of education. All we can do is sketch out a framework for a liberal utopia and infer some of the outcomes from our observations of liberal policies being pursued in other parts of the economy and other parts of the world. Liberalism requires humility and an absence of conceit. Indeed, this is why Hayek argues that liberalism does not come naturally to academics!

Nevertheless, although we cannot know in detail how a liberal society will look if the policies discussed by our authors are followed, we often know enough to be able to determine whether particular policies move us towards or away from a liberal utopia. The features of a liberal policy framework can be identified relatively easily. To continue with the example of education, a system that impedes the supply of education as comprehensively as that in the UK or the USA is clearly not liberal. Also, if we are dreaming of a better, more liberal world – not just trying to implement the politically possible – we surely must go beyond giving parents vouchers to spend at the schools of their choice and restore to parents the freedom to educate their children in ways that suit the circumstances of individual families, and we must restore to them the income taken from them by the state too.

There are areas for debate among liberals – there are ambiguities. We cannot even define the policy framework with total certainty.

That does not undermine the value of the intellectual exercise of sketching out a liberal utopia – indeed, it makes it more important. No liberal academic could suggest that there is a list of policies to which all other liberal academics should sign up. To do so would hardly be liberal! It may be that people working in the policy field have reservations about some aspects of the programme for a liberal utopia on moral grounds: there are many liberal economists who subscribe to the view that there is an objective morality that transcends liberal values and should do so in some respects in the policy field, even if the perspective of such people is, more generally, liberal.

There may be some goods and services that cannot be provided in a totally liberal environment, although, even here, there are more liberal and less liberal ways of proceeding. Defence, for example, might have to be provided by government – although whether the government should employ all the soldiers and own all the ships and aircraft and cook the food is a moot point. Sometimes, even where two liberals agree on matters of morality and the provision of so-called public goods, there is legitimate dispute about what is the most liberal policy. On constitutional issues, for example, some would prefer a hereditary monarch who had some powers to eject the government. Such a monarch can provide a check on the abuse of powers by an elected government, and a monarch does not directly represent interest groups as his or her power arises through an accident of birth. More generally, it can be argued that totally democratic societies put too much faith in democracy as an absolute value and too little faith in liberalism. Other liberals would suggest that hereditary monarchs, not fully answerable to the people they serve, can follow their own interests and abuse their powers. Liberals also disagree about the need for a written constitution. Liberals sometimes come in the purest of forms but, sometimes, liberalism is tempered by, or complemented by, a degree of conservatism.

Have we, in recent decades, moved closer to or farther away from a liberal utopia? Here the record of the last 50 years, discussed in the second part of this book, is mixed. State industries have been privatised; individuals and investing institutions can exchange sterling for foreign currencies, whereas 25 years ago it was forbidden without the permission of the central bank; the purchasing power of money halves only once every generation instead of once every few years; workers' pay is a matter between them and their employer, not a matter for government; and trade union monopolies no longer dictate policy. On the other hand, the financial sector is more heavily regulated than ever before; government policy has ensured that independent schools are increasingly the preserve of the rich; many details of labour market contracts are written by the state; and the European Union intrudes in virtually every aspect of life.

In many areas of economic life, we have moved closer to a liberal utopia – or at least farther away from hell on earth – but in many other areas we have moved backwards. There is much to be done, but one should not underestimate the achievements of those who have gone before us. People reading this book today may not believe that we can return to a liberal education system, a liberal health system or a low-tax economy. But 40 years ago the establishment really did not believe that it was possible to allow individuals and employers to agree levels of pay between themselves. James Tooley's views on education or Tim and Helen Evans' views on health, in Part 1, may seem like anarchy to some, but then the political establishment felt the same way about the idea that individual investors should be allowed to decide whether to exchange sterling for foreign currency.

This leads us on to the question of whether our liberal utopia is anarchy. It certainly is not. Defence, law and order, courts to enforce contracts, the enforcement of property rights and so on may all be functions undertaken by the state – although private institutions can undertake these tasks too. Also, the institutions that make up civil society and help regulate our lives, in the best sense, such as family, Church, clubs and societies, wider social networks, paternalistic institutions set up by companies or groups of companies to which individuals are happy to submit themselves, friendly societies, credit unions, and so on, are, in fact, often undermined by the state. Such institutions go a long way towards providing stability and a genuine sense of community and, in the words of an early IEA publication, ensuring that freedom is not a free-for-all.

The question mark appears in the title of this book for many reasons. A liberal utopia cannot be defined objectively. Thus, precisely what we mean by utopia is itself a matter for debate. We cannot always say whether we are moving towards it or away from it. We cannot say, with certainty, that our country is more liberal today than when the IEA was founded in 1955, although in many important policy areas we have certainly taken some decisive steps in the right direction. Perhaps most importantly of all, even if the policy framework described in this volume is implemented, we will not reach utopia: we will merely have a better society.

The book is divided into two parts. In the first part, IEA authors sketch set out their view of a liberal utopia in separate chapters covering a number of aspects of government service provision, taxation, trade, regulation and the constitution. The purpose of these chapters has been discussed above. We hope that they will enthuse a new generation of liberal thinkers and provide a benchmark against which liberal opinion formers and policy-makers can judge their policies. Policy-makers have a choice: will they help take us forward to allow the creation of what Hayek termed the 'great society' or will they vest more power in functionaries of the state who, in their conceit, believing they know more than they do, wish to subject industry, commerce and all aspects of everyday life to more and more regulation and control by the state?

The second part of the book, written by Ralph Harris, reflects on the first 50 years of the IEA's work. It reveals the emphatic opposition that the IEA had to face in what some would regard as the most unlikely places – the higher echelons of industry and in all political parties. In the end the forces of truth won and no right-thinking politician would reverse the liberal reforms that IEA authors advocated. The second part of the book shows how, in so many aspects of policy, IEA authors, by thinking beyond the bounds of the politically possible, created a climate in which a liberal utopia moved a little bit nearer. There remains much to be done.

References

Hayek, F. A. (1944), *The Road to Serfdom*, London: Routledge and Kegan Paul

Hayek, F. A. (1949), *The Intellectuals and Socialism*, republished in *Rediscovered Riches*, no. 4 (1998), London: Institute of Economic Affairs Health and Welfare Unit

Part 1
Times future?

2 HEALTH 2055
Tim Evans and Helen Evans

Promise and reality: how the NHS failed people

The concept of a free health service for all was first supported in Britain by Beatrice Webb in her minority report of the Poor Law inquiry of 1909 (Timmins, 2001: 15). It fell to Sir William Beveridge, however, to fully articulate such a plan and to lay the foundations for such a service in his 1942 paper, *Social Insurance and Allied Services* (Beveridge, 1942).

Arguing that the state should establish a 'national health service for the prevention and comprehensive treatment available to all members of the community',[1] Beveridge understood the political implications of his proposals. Prior to the paper's publication on 1 December 1942, he told the *Daily Telegraph* that his proposals would take Britain '… half-way to Moscow' (Timmins, 2001: 41).

Significantly, after World War II two papers marked 'secret' and providing a detailed commentary on Beveridge's plan were found in Hitler's bunker. One ordered that publicity should be avoided but, if mentioned, the report should be used as '… obvious proof that our enemies are taking over national-socialist ideas' (ibid.: 25). The other provided an official assessment of the plans as no 'botch-up': 'a consistent system … of remarkable simplicity … superior to the current German social insurance in almost all points'[2].

In February 1944 the British government published a White Paper entitled *A National Health Service*. It proposed that everybody '…

---

1   Much of this paper was reproduced in Fraser (1973: 265).
2   Fritz Grunder, *Beveridge Meets Bismarck*, York Papers, vol. 1, p. 69.

irrespective of means, age, sex or occupation shall have equal opportunity to benefit from the best and most up-to-date medical and allied services available'; that the service should be 'comprehensive' for all who wanted it; that it should be 'free of charge'; and that it should promote good health 'rather than only the treatment of bad' (Foot, 1966 [1973]: 131).

In 1948, just weeks before the appointed day of the National Health Service's launch, the government issued a leaflet to every home in the country. It promised that the NHS '… will provide you with all medical, dental and nursing care. Everyone – rich or poor – can use it'.[3] Today, more than half a century on, it is clear that the NHS has never delivered on its promise.

While the NHS was created to treat the whole population in an equitable manner and according to need, in practice the historical evidence suggests that its impact has been otherwise. Julian Le Grand has shown that, relative to need, people in the professional and managerial classes receive more than 40 per cent more NHS spending per illness episode than those in the lower semi-skilled and unskilled classifications (Benzeval et al., 1995: 104).

At the dawn of the twenty-first century, the NHS has more than 1 million people on its waiting lists and another 200,000 trying to get on to them.[4] Each year in its hospitals, more than 100,000 patients pick up infections and illnesses that they did not have prior to being admitted.[5] And according to the Malnutrition Advisory Group up to 40 per cent of NHS hospital patients are under-nourished during in-patient stays.[6]

---

3   Department of Health leaflet announcing the NHS, June/July 1948.
4   This was the estimate of the Independent Healthcare Association in early 2002.
5   'Hospital infection rates in England out of control', *British Medical Journal*, 26 February 2000.
6   'New screening tool for malnutrition', *The Pharmaceutical Journal*, 265(7,128), December 2000, p. 909. Also, see the Malnutrition Advisory Group report on UK hospital malnutrition at http://www.bapen.org.uk/pdfs/newsletters/bapen_news08.pdf.

The political economy of health rationing

Back in 1944, Bevan's White Paper, *A National Health Service,* estimated that the service would cost taxpayers £132 million per year. This was revised upward, however, to £152 million in 1946 and again to £230 million just before the act came into force in July 1948. In its first year of operation, 1949/50, the NHS actually ended up costing the taxpayer £305 million and required a supplementary estimate of £98 million (Klein, 1989: 35).

The inaccuracy of the estimates can be attributed to a number of factors. The first was that the early projections of cost assumed that demand would remain roughly constant despite there being no price constraints on demand – the service being 'free' at the point of use. Second, contemporary social and medical developments exacerbated the problems created by an absence of any price constraints on demand, not least because medical advances at the time meant that there was a dramatic expansion in the type and range of health services that could be made available.[7]

To keep demand in check the service deliberately rationed supply – through scarcity rather than price. While doctors who worked in NHS hospitals had been encouraged at first to treat their patients according to need, the imposition of cash limits soon turned them into allocators of scarce resources. More than minimal care was denied in cases where there was little chance of successful recovery, particularly with young children or the elderly with serious conditions. Indeed, healthcare for everyone else was provided sparingly by international standards.[8]

---

7   In many ways, the NHS was designed to provide a style of healthcare that was more appropriate to the nineteenth century than the twentieth. Previous improvements in health had been brought about through large-scale immunisation and better sanitation. These measures had been relatively inexpensive, easy to administer and subject to large economies of scale. Nevertheless, many of them had been introduced by private sector companies and organisations.

8   In the late 1970s, for example, coronary artery bypass operations were performed about ten times more frequently pro rata in America than in Britain. And where these did not increase life expectancy, they tended to reduce adverse symptoms such as pain. While American doctors responded to complaints about pain, British doctors have tended to

The supply of healthcare has been rationed still further by queuing. Crowded waiting rooms are common in most general practices and out-patient departments. And queues have become a fact of life for in-patients, often with long waiting periods for those operations given priority.

Certain health services have never been provided by the NHS, thus artificially restricting the demand on its resources still further. Most forms of cosmetic surgery have rarely been available, and face lifts, lipo-suction, hair transplants and sex change operations have never been provided except where they have been deemed necessary for reasons of health or as part of some other form of treatment. Other services have been provided on a minimal basis too. Much psychiatry, the treatment of infertility and substance misuse services remain cases in point.

More than half a century on since the NHS's inception it is clear that in reality people have never had a meaningful right to free and equal treatment on demand. What they have had – in the main – is an unlimited right of access to a waiting list from which – with a few exceptions – they will not be excluded.

Tiptoeing back to market

As such, in an age of growing consumer awareness, one cannot open a newspaper today without reading about the pressures, strains and failures of the service. Higher expectations, new technology and the manifest failings of a politically run service mean that its masters are eager to move away from the past. As a recent Secretary of State for Health, Alan Milburn, commented:

> For fifty years the NHS has been subject to day-to-day running from Whitehall. The whole system is top down. There is little freedom for local innovation or risk taking ... A million strong

---

pay more attention to the probable increases in life expectancy, or the improvements in a 'quality of life' not always synonymous with an absence of serious discomfort. For more information, see Aron and Schwartz (1984: 67).

health service cannot be run from Whitehall. Indeed, it should not be run from Whitehall. For patient choice to thrive it needs a different environment. One in which there is greater diversity and plurality in local services, which have the freedom to innovate and respond to patients' needs.[9]

Since 1992, most capital investment in the NHS has been arranged under a scheme ironically known as the private finance initiative (PFI). Under its auspices the private sector can design, build, finance, own and even operate key areas of NHS provision – including some clinical services. Although this policy was initially adopted by John Major's Conservative government, it was actively embraced by Tony Blair's Labour administration.

Indeed, in recent years, under the more general rubric of Public Private Partnerships (PPPs), the government has championed a whole raft of market-oriented reforms. In 2000, Milburn signed a concordat with the representative body of Britain's resurgent independent health and social care sector, the Independent Healthcare Association (IHA). Under this agreement, the NHS could send its patients to independent hospitals and clinics for treatment and care (Vaizey, 2002: 88–9). Between 2000 and 2003 more than 250,000 NHS-funded patients received treatment in the independent sector, and others were sent to private hospitals in France.

Then, in 2001, the government made it clear that it wanted to establish a new generation of 'Independent Foundation Hospitals'. As such, it wanted all NHS hospitals to be 'set free' from Whitehall control by 2008 and to have a greater say over how they developed and from where they raised their capital.

In 2002, the government made it clear that it wanted the private sector to design, build and operate a new generation of Diagnostic and Treatment Centres (DTCs) specialising in acute surgery. As such,

9   The Secretary of State for Health, the Rt Hon. Alan Milburn, MP, speech to New Health Network, 15 January 2002.

ministers drew up a list of private companies that would be allowed to bid for the contracts, and when the winners were announced all of them were foreign new market entrants – thereby underlining the stress being placed on competition.

When it comes to the question of health funding, many people's attitudes have already changed. Today, some 7 million people have private medical insurance and another 6 million are covered by private health cash plans.[10] Millions of others have no formal coverage at all, preferring instead to self-fund as and when the need arises. In 2000, more than a quarter of a million people chose to self-fund for independent acute surgery without any insurance at all.[11] In dentistry, more than a third of the population has abandoned the NHS and instead prefers to rely on the independent sector.

At the dawn of the twenty-first century, more than 8 million go private for a range of complementary therapies.

According to research published in the *Daily Telegraph*,[12] more than 3.5 million trade unionists – more than 50 per cent of the Trade Union Congress's 6.8 million members – now enjoy the benefits of private medical insurance or health cash plan schemes.[13]

A real market

Today, the healthcare debate has two characteristic sides. On the one hand there are those who believe that government should continue to

---

10 Some schemes offer private medical, permanent health or critical illness cover. Others offer private health cash plans that pay for services that include items such as dentistry, ophthalmics, physiotherapy, chiropody, podiatry, maternity services, allergy testing, hospital in-patient stays, nursing home stays, hospital day case admissions, convalescence, home help, mental health and psychiatric treatment, and even the use of an ambulance.

11 This information was obtained from the Independent Healthcare Association.

12 Daniel Kruger, 'Why Half the Members of Trade Unions Have Private Health Care', *Daily Telegraph*, 11 September 2001.

13 For a sound history of trade union and friendly society involvement in independent healthcare, see Green (1985).

provide healthcare free at the point of delivery, irrespective of problems and failures. On the other hand, there are those who believe that the NHS is simply another nationalised industry and that, as it has all the characteristic failures of such an institution, it should be opened up to more privatisation of provision and funding.

For classical liberals and libertarians the truth, however, lies somewhere well beyond (see Rothbard, 1965, 1973; Friedman, 1989). As far as genuine believers in a free market are concerned, the root of the problem is that British medicine, *all* British medicine (be it state or independent), is ultimately a government-sponsored monopoly (Gladstone, 1993). For to be a doctor one must be accepted by the General Medical Council (GMC) and all its attendant legislative favour. If you are not a 'doctor' (as the government, advised by its preferred group of doctors, understands that word), then there are three things you are precluded from doing. You cannot sign a death certificate, prescribe medicines or (in general) take medical risks. In other words, medicine is a government-sponsored monopoly. Today, no country in the world has a medical market that is un-interfered with by the local state (Micklethwait, 1991).

A real free market would be very different.[14] The very process of defining who is and who is not a doctor would be negotiated voluntarily between the people offering themselves as doctors and those deciding whether to submit themselves as patients. At the heart of the medical issue is the right of the individual to take whatever risks he wants and to make deals on that basis (ibid.).

For the British libertarian Brian Micklethwait, a genuine market would mean that people would be able to consume whichever medicines they wanted and that medical practitioners would be able to openly advertise their services. Over time, a new and much better consumer-driven market, reliant upon reputation (not state regulation and monopoly), would emerge.

Far from being obvious to me that a truly free medical market

---

14 For an interesting review of genuine markets, see Cowen and Crampton (2002).

would be disastrous, I believe on the contrary that such arrangements would be of huge benefit to mankind, and that the sooner medicine is done this way the better. Things would not, inevitably, be perfect. Some fools would make crass blunders, by ignoring manifestly superior medical services for the most frivolous of reasons, and by patronising the most notoriously incompetent. Some such fools would perish from their foolishness. Others would merely be unlucky. No law can prevent either stupidity or bad luck, although the world is now filled with the particular stupidity which consists of refusing to face this truth, and with the many luckless victims of this stupidity ... Given that for most people the avoidance of suicide rather than suicide is the objective, a truly free medical market would enable them, for the first time ever, to purchase steadily improving medical advice and medical help, and at a steadily diminishing price. (Ibid.)

In a real market, patients would come to truly value their healthcare, as a commodity working in accordance with the language of price. This would encourage people to face the costs of their actions in ways that the state currently precludes. In a real-time market of advanced diagnostics and nano-screening, individuals would be presented with much greater incentives to better manage and value their health than is currently the case.

Questioning the role of a state

In questioning the role of the state in healthcare, Micklethwait similarly points out that one of the most pernicious restrictions currently imposed on medicine is the restriction on advertising. In a free market, rival medical procedures, rival medical philosophies, rival views on the relative importance of confidentiality, hygiene, speed of treatment, riskiness of treatment, and so forth, would all battle it out in a real and ever improving market.

'Alternative' therapists would be allowed to prescribe potentially dangerous drugs, as only government favoured therapists may

> now. It would be up to the patients to pick therapists who seemed to know what they were doing and their look out if they chose badly. The already thriving medical periodical press would assist with voluminous comparative advice, praise and criticism. In such a free market, any number of different medical styles could be practiced, and patients would make their choices. (Ibid.)

Although in 2005 such an opinion remains utopian and radical, the fact is that politicians of all persuasions are now prepared to countenance various forms of private provision, funding and competition in healthcare that only a generation ago would have seemed unthinkable.

Today, there is every good reason to suppose that, as the twenty-first century progresses, there will be more opportunity for private sector input and choice. One can even imagine direct-to-consumer advertising for medicines and healthcare services – and by 2055 a real culture of consumer empowerment emerging.

While some things might well be moving in the right direction, however, there is also good reason to believe that they will not go far or fast enough. For in reality, ever since Roman times, political elites in Britain have always sought to plan, control and regulate the provision of health services. First through the military, then the Church, the Royal Colleges, Parliament and the timeless granting of legislative favour, the state has always sought to empire-build and to control people's access to healthcare and medicine.

Today, just as there is evidence that a more liberal direction is being charted when it comes to the ownership of hospitals and the role of the independent sector, there is also a new threat to human freedom looming on the horizon.

Rise of the therapeutic state

As politicians try to get themselves off the hook of past promises by continuing their incremental and 'market-oriented' reforms in health, so the state is slowly reinventing itself under new rubrics to legitimise control and intervention.

Just as definitions of national security have widened to encompass an ever greater array of areas over the last century (Hoppe, 2003), so notions of public health are becoming ever broader and more intrusive. Today, most people accept that the government has a right to outlaw tobacco advertising. People accept that pubs can be redefined as 'public spaces', and that the Department of Health can consider active measures to curb what its experts define as an obesity epidemic.

Fed for years on a daily diet of health scares and moral panics, people are now beginning to accept a therapeutic state which, at the behest of its allies and experts in the regulated professions, is justifying an erosion of personal lifestyle choice, liberty and responsibility – as never before (Anderson et al., 1991).

In moving away from the twentieth-century experiment of full-blown health nationalisation, politicians of all persuasions are slowly making pronouncements on the need for the state to underpin human happiness and medical well-being. Indeed, in 2005 it is difficult to imagine a future in which personal lifestyle choices will not be increasingly monitored and controlled by the state.

For example, in the dying days of the last parliament (2001) the government laid the foundations for the nationalisation of patients' health records. While the Health and Social Care Act covered many aspects of healthcare, one particular section allowed the government to open people's newly computerised records to any organisation they consider to be in the public interest – requiring neither the consent nor the knowledge of the individual.

The highly respected Conservative peer Earl Howe warned the House of Lords that the measure 'more than any other clause in any other Bill that I have ever dealt with, has incurred the alarm, anger and condemnation of virtually the entire medical community'.[15] Counselling against the

---

15   House of Lords debate, *Hansard*, 22 March 2001, col. 1,679.

act's erosion of patient confidentiality, he warned against a system that will cause 'irreparable damage to the relationship between clinicians and their patients'.[16]

Today, at the hands of all departments of state, people's liberties are being undermined not so much by Big Brother, but by Big Mother. The Establishment's desire to control, categorise, profile and investigate ordinary folks' every action chimes with a deep-rooted human desire to be mothered and mollycoddled.

Under the recent Regulation of Investigatory Powers Act,[17] agents of the state can now investigate people's private financial affairs in a way that the Soviet secret police could only have dreamed of. Under other legislation, the National Criminal Intelligence Service has now placed duties on lawyers and accountants to spy on their clients and pass on information without them being informed.[18]

If the authors thought such measures would help in the fight against crime then they might support them. If the authors believed the government's version of electronic patient records would help provide better health information, and thereby outcomes, they might be persuaded. But instead, they believe the opposite.

In the years ahead, a parallel universe will be created. As is already the case in many other places, two types of conversation will become the norm when dealing with professionals – the truth and the official version.

In future, the person who goes to the doctor with depression might well be worried about how this information will play out in other arenas.

---

16 House of Lords debate, *Hansard*, 3 May 2001, col. 1,994.

17 The Regulation of Investigatory Powers (RIP) Bill was introduced in the House of Commons on 9 February 2000 and completed its parliamentary passage on 26 July 2000. The bill received royal assent on 28 July 2000. The Regulation of Investigatory Powers Act 2000 (RIPA) updates the law on the interception of communications in the age of the Internet. It puts many intrusive investigatory techniques on a statutory footing for the first time and provides the police and other agents of the state with new powers to combat the use of strong encryption.

18 For more on the sweeping powers of the National Criminal Intelligence Service and the legislative environment in which it is empire-building, see Carr (2001).

How will it be used in terms of career development or even a court of law? Will it stop them becoming a care worker? Might it persuade a potential employer to go with another candidate? On being prescribed amitriptyline, the patient might well want the official health record to read 'headache' – not 'depression' (it can treat both).

For all the private hospitals, private funding, new medicines and medical technology that the next 50 years will hopefully bring, so long as government remains involved in granting medical professionals legislative favour and continues to build a highly regulated therapeutic state, healthcare will not be as efficient and as effective as it could and should be.

Instead of an ambulance crew arriving at the scene of an accident in 2055 and immediately swiping a patient's bar code to reveal an accurate health record and thereby make sound clinical judgements, the data will increasingly be unreliable and dangerous. If an individual has diabetes, epilepsy or is receiving anti-coagulant therapy that is not shown on their health record, treatments might be initiated or surgery undertaken that could cause further complications or even death. Again, unrecorded allergies or intolerance to antibiotics and even substances such as latex could entail unacceptable risks.

In a world where joined-up government increasingly means joined-up Big Mother the incentives for people to connive and avoid the truth become immense. In a society that erodes consent and confidentiality, people go out of their way to defend their profiles and reputations – as never before.

The unintended consequence of uninvited monitoring is that, over time, individuals debase the public record. A huge feedback loop is created whereby the 'garbage in, garbage out' axiom really begins to bite.

In health, the more information that is gathered and utilised without patient consent, the more people will find they live in a world where the incentives to avoid the recording of the whole truth become overwhelming. Lies, obfuscation and partial truths become common currency in any culture that replaces consent with coercion.

At the time of the break-up of the Soviet Union, the secret police held vast amounts of information on citizens, most of it increasingly inaccurate and therefore meaningless. As official records progressively failed to match reality over the decades, so state plans and projections came to be based on a cycle of ever weaker analysis.

In health, the argument for privacy is not simply about people's liberty. Liberty is a prerequisite for accurate information and good decision-making. As Big Mother pries into every corner of our lives, slowly people will rediscover an urge to leave the nursery. Just as today people are slowly beginning to rediscover and accept various forms of independent healthcare, so in another 50 years they might again value privacy. As people die as a result of clinical decisions being made on the back of bad health records, so people will again begin to rediscover and value the benefits of consenting confidentiality.

In the longer term, the authors believe, experience will be the best teacher. As regards the short term, they are not optimistic. Just as in 2001 Earl Howe condemned the coming 'Sovietisation of British medicine',[19] so, in 2005, the prospect of Big Mother's brave new world should cause all friends of the IEA the gravest concern.

For just as the IEA has spent decades highlighting the manifest failings of the NHS, and offering a range of positive market alternatives, so now, over the next 50 years, it must go on to defeat the therapeutic state and its attendant monopoly experts with all their rent-seeking legislative favour.

In the process of 'waging the war of ideas' (Blundell, 2003) over the next 50 years in this field of healthcare, the objective must be to create in Britain, and for the first time ever, a genuine market – a market built on real competition, reputation and the libertarian principles of non-coercion. After all, people's healthcare is so important that nothing less will suffice.

---

19   House of Lords debate, *Hansard*, 22 March 2001, col. 1,680.

References

Anderson, D. et al. (1991), *Health, Lifestyle and Environment*, London: Social Affairs Unit

Aron, H. J. and W. R. Schwartz (1984), *The Painful Prescription: Rationing Hospital Care*, Washington, DC: Brookings Institution

Benzeval, M., K. Judge and M. Whitehead (1995), *Tackling Inequalities*, London: Kings Fund

Beveridge, W. (1942), *Social Insurance and Allied Services*, London: HMSO

Blundell, J. (2003), *Waging the War of Ideas*, London: Institute of Economic Affairs

Carr, D. J. K. (2001), *Don't Trust Me, I'm a Lawyer: The Operation, Scope and Possible Effects of the Government's War on Money Laundering*, Legal Notes no. 35, London: Libertarian Alliance

Cowen, T. and E. Crampton (2002), *Market Failure or Success – The New Debate*, Cheltenham: Edward Elgar

Foot, M. (1966 [1973]), *Aneurin Bevan: A Biography*, London: Four Square

Fraser, D. (1973), *The Evolution of the British Welfare State*, London: Macmillan

Friedman, D. (1989), *The Machinery of Freedom*, Open Court

Gladstone, D. (1993), *The British Medical Monopoly: How It Was Created, the Harm It Causes and What to Do about it*, Political Notes no. 79, London: Libertarian Alliance

Green, D. (1985), *Working Class Patients and the Medical Establishment – Self Help in Britain from the Mid-nineteenth century to 1948*, Aldershot: Gower

Hoppe, H. H. (2003), *The Myth of National Defence: Essays on the Theory and History of Security Production*, Alabama: Ludwig Von Mises Institute

Klein, R. (1989), *The Politics of the National Health Service*, London: Longman

Micklethwait, B. (1991), *How and How Not to Demonopolise Medicine*, Political Notes no. 56, London: Libertarian Alliance, p. 3

Rothbard, M. (1965), 'The Anatomy of the State', *Rampart Journal of Individualist Thought*, 1(2), summer

Rothbard, M. (1973), *For a New Liberty*, New York: Macmillan

Timmins, N. (2001), *The Five Giants: A Biography of the Welfare State*, London: HarperCollins

Vaizey, E. (2002), *The Blue Book on Health*, London: Politico's

3 EDUCATION RECLAIMED

James Tooley

A dream of education without the state

Having eaten and drunken too heavily at the Institute of Economic Affair's 50th anniversary dinner, I fell quickly into a deep sleep when I retired. Dreams often reflect what has happened during the day; not surprisingly, having spent the evening in high-spirited debate about the past 50 years of education and how it should be reformed, I found myself flung forward 50 years to witness the future of education. Here is a summary of what I found.

By 2055, much had changed. The sceptics I had spoken to over dinner, who had pointed to the difficulty of genuine market reform in education, were wrong. The reasons for the dramatic changes would have surprised them, however.

In 2055, according to my semi-structured interviews and focus groups with key stakeholders in education, people looked back on our obsession with *schooling* with a mixture of horror and bewilderment. They thought it only folly to imagine that all the diverse aims of education – to prepare young people for adult life, for citizenship, careers and family life, and to initiate them into the best that had been thought and known – could be sensibly realised in one venue – the school or college – and by segregating young people away from adult life. They described schools and colleges as 'youth ghettoes', creating an alienated youth culture, miserably cut off from adulthood, forcing young people into compulsory idleness and irresponsibility. 'The prolonged agony of adolescence' was one term that was used to describe the result. And they thought our views on teachers were odd, too. Why, they asked, were inspirational teachers given not only the same pecuniary rewards but also the same *number of children* to teach as teachers who lacked motivational ability? 'Even back in 2005,' it was pointed out to me, 'you had the technological capability to allow inspiring teachers to reach millions of young people, but instead you forced all teachers into an egalitarian straitjacket.' The only exception, it was suggested, seemed to be when we had stimulating history teachers (the specific names they mentioned were Dr David Starkey and Professor Niall Ferguson, both of whose work apparently was still valued, even in 2055!), who did make powerful contributions to popular awareness of their subject; but although their offerings were available, schools perversely eschewed them, instead forcing all children to learn from teachers who generally lacked any relevant talent at all.

Three principles

I probed my focus groups on the underlying principles governing education in 2055, but they were uncomfortable with my terminology. However, after I told them a little joke about our own guiding principles ('Tony Blair's motto,' I said, 'when leader of the opposition, was that his principles in government would be the "three Es": "education, education, education". Prime Minister John Major had rejoined that his principles were the same, but in a different order!'), one of the stakeholders suggested that their principles were the 'three Fs':

- family
- freedom
- philanthropy.

It was obvious, she pointed out, where the *family* fits in. It is 'the core educational institution' around which all others in society are built, crucial to early development, and to the promotion of a thriving civil society.

Freedom was required, she said, first, to enable families to choose educational opportunities. It was also needed so that the whole range of entrepreneurs attracted to education could have the freedom to invest their energies and to raise investment wherever they thought they could best tackle educational problems. They need freedom to be able to devise student loan schemes and methods of cross-subsidisation. And they need the freedom to devise methods of inspiring and motivating young people to want to learn.

Finally, there is *philanthropy*. This, she assured me, had a key part to play, to help those families who were dysfunctional, providing substitute families if necessary or mentoring for those who needed it. And it has a part to play in finding funds, administered with discretion and discernment, to those who need help to fund their own or their children's educational opportunities.

The end of 'school'

What did these ideas mean in practice? I was fortunate to engage, in my dream, in a small number of field visits to educational sites selected opportunistically, where I observed, interviewed and examined written artefacts. For those who were hoping for details of a large range of institutions such as our schools, colleges and universities, however, the results, I am afraid, are disappointing. There were only two places that were anything like schools as we know them now – the 'learning centres' and 'places apart'. But apart from these, my requests to visit educational settings were met by my eager hosts taking me on trips to places that we wouldn't usually describe in such terms: to family homes, workplaces, sports centres, town halls, reading rooms in pubs, debating chambers, bookstores, and so on. 'Education pervades the whole of society,' I was told, and people did eventually grow impatient when I kept querying this.

Mastering the brief

When I asked to see where preparation for the world of work took place, however, I did strike lucky at first. The dedicated learning centres were the equivalent of our primary and middle schools, where children of about six to twelve or thirteen went to study. But differences were immediately obvious. For instance, I was told that the punishment for anti-social behaviour in one place was that the child would not be allowed to come in on the weekends. There was laughter when I told the children that our equivalent punishment would be to make the child stay longer in school. 'That would be a pleasure for us,' one said. Another difference was obvious in terms of management and funding: the centres were run by large, competing chains, and were funded entirely by parental fees and, for those too poor to afford these, there was philanthropy or selective cross-subsidisation. Outside some of the centres, I recognised a distinctive bright orange logo: these were part of the 'EasyLearn' chain. I also recognised the characteristic red 'V' of 'VirginOpportunity'.

Within the learning centres, I was told, the key activity was called 'Mastering the Brief'. One young girl showed me the problem that she was working on: 'I'm trying to help a company in Albania modify its marketing strategy,' she said. Another small boy said he was raising finance for a borehole scheme in Zimbabwe. 'What is needed', said one young manager of a learning centre, 'is for young people to have acquired the ability to learn, in whatever situations they find themselves in, to "master the brief".' For younger children, he said, this could mean conducting projects that were contrived. But as soon as children became capable of 'mastering the brief', they were moved to genuine problems, to give them an exciting engagement with adult life. Indeed, 'keeping children stuck in artificially contrived and pointless tasks', he said, 'could accomplish the almost impossible: getting children to lose interest in learning!'

These learning centres were attached, either physically or virtually, to workplaces and research and development laboratories, so that children could see how real projects were carried out, and could use materials and expertise from these, and solve problems relating to them. But they also had 'quiet' areas – Quiet Zones – where children could step back from the hurly-burly of the project and have access to learning resources to help them acquire the knowledge and skills necessary for these projects.

Where are the secondary schools?

So far so good. But when I asked to see the secondary schools, I met with a blank. 'You know,' I said, 'where children are further prepared for the world of work …' They understood, and took me on tours of work-places again – and although some of these had the equivalent of learning centres within them, they had all sorts of people, young and old, busily engaged together in tasks; there were no places where there were only children. 'So there is no secondary education?' I asked. 'But what about places where children and young people are taught the habits, values and dispositions for children to become democratic citizens? What about the inculcation of personal and social education, for learning isn't just about preparation for work?' In response, I was only referred again to the same list of family homes, workplaces, sports centres, town halls, etc., etc. And it was while I was pursuing this subject that my focus groups came up with their responses to our ideas on schooling which I've quoted above.

Education for its own sake

Apart from the primary/middle schools, then, the only other insti-tutional setting that had education as its sole function was the 'places apart'. Some were run by chains, apparently, but I saw only places that seemed rather like monasteries, run as charities or trusts, dependent in the main on donations, subscriptions and patronage, and charging very low, if any, fees. In these places apart, there were younger and older people together, engaged in a variety of seminars, group discussions and individual reading and study. Here, I was told, were places where people wanted to acquire knowledge for its own intrinsic value, without worrying too much about its applicability (although some of the sponsorship for these places did apparently come from big business, aware that ideas with commercial potential were sometimes developed within them). People came here for weekends, during the day, in the evenings, or for prolonged sabbaticals. Some people came and never left. Some people dipped in and never came back. But all were welcome, young and old, if they were prepared to embrace the somewhat austere surroundings, and to engage in work such as preparing food, cleaning and the minor tasks that helped support them, such as growing vegetables, tending animals or repairing vehicles in the workshop.

The journey

Having discovered how they viewed education in 2055, the most important question I had to explore was how they arrived there from where we are today. I told my focus groups the problem I foresaw. What they had – they had told me – was a genuine market in education, where there was no state intervention of any kind, in funding, provision or regulation. But people in my time of classical liberal persuasion were pessimistic about the potential of reform towards a true market. For whenever a market reform had been mooted, I told them, it had met with trenchant opposition from vested interests such as the teacher and student unions and government departments, who were able to capitalise on people's fears, and so either nothing had been accomplished, or the proposals had been so watered down that they often led to the exact opposite of what had been proposed! I told them of the Conservative government's reforms of the late 1980s which were supposed to bring in a qualified market in education, and had simply led to the most onerous government regulation of education that we had ever seen, with the National Curriculum, national testing, national league tables, and bureaucracies burgeoning all over the place – all in the name of the market!

People power, not vouchers

How had we managed over time to change the system so radically, given the vested interests that must have tried to prevent it? Did we manage to introduce vouchers in the end, against all opposition? I asked. My innocent question was met with hoots of laughter: 'Vouchers were certainly not the way forward,' one respondent exclaimed, 'given that they entail government taxing you, then giving you back some small portion of your own money, to spend only within the constraints that they set you!'

No, the changes didn't happen that way: 'It was nothing to do with politicians at all.' The explanation for how change emerged surprised me. The first time I heard it, I thought perhaps it was some idiosyncratic view. But I heard it from all my focus groups, so I began to believe it. Change began in the world's two most populous nations, India and China, and among the poorest people there. Even before 2005, I was told, although not many knew about this, 'poor people were already reclaiming education for themselves, from the state'. Apparently, in the slums and villages of these two countries, poor people were leaving the state system en masse, migrating to private schools that were set up by a variety of local entrepreneurs, community groups, churches, mosques and ashrams. They were fleeing government schools, I was told, because conditions for them there had become unbearable, partly because of poor facilities, but mainly because of the teachers. Well before 2005, I was told, surveys showed that only half the teachers in government schools turned up for work. The unions were so strong that they had negotiated not only all the school holidays but weeks and weeks of 'casual' leave, mandatory 'sick' leave, 'optional' leave. And if teachers did turn up, they didn't teach, because they were accountable to no one, could never be dismissed, and were promoted simply through time-serving. And parents recognised all this and entrepreneurs responded to their needs, and created this alternative private sector. By 2015, I was told, the government sectors in these countries had more or less collapsed. Those who could afford the low fees paid for their children to attend private schools, and those who couldn't usually received scholarships either from the schools themselves, or from outside philanthropy.

The power of competition

But, I pointed out, these parents may have 'privatised themselves', but their children were still in schools – so nothing much had changed, even though the ownership of education may have moved from one sector to another. But that, I was told, missed the fundamental 'magic' of the system: for competition within it changed everything. With so many competing schools catering for the people, how did the entrepreneurs maintain and expand their market position? They experimented to improve what they offered to children and parents, and slowly innovations that one school adopted, which led to improvements in outcomes or satisfaction, were relentlessly copied by other schools. Meanwhile, while some schools went out of business, others developed into large educational chains. These chains could afford, through economies of scale, to fund dedicated research and development (R&D) centres to ensure that they kept ahead of pedagogical developments and introduced more efficient and effective ways of learning. And if one company introduced developments that were effective, again these were shamelessly copied by others, until the market became saturated with beneficial innovation.

I was given one concrete example of how this happened, and from this I could discern the general principles. Even before 2005, there was a large Indian computer education company, NIIT, which had over a thousand franchises across India and had expanded into 25 other countries to promote its R&D-based education, including (a neat spin on global capitalist imperialism) the UK and USA. An educational inventor working for the company had experimented with children teaching themselves how to learn through the Internet. The results were surprising to many – even illiterate slum children had been found to teach themselves easily how to access the Internet, and to teach others how to do it too. (One of their favourite sites, the children told the inventor, was where they could play the 'Rat Game'. Upon investigation, this turned out to be the Disney website, and the rat none other than Mickey Mouse!) This was disconcerting to the inventor's company – which charged hundreds of dollars to teach adults how to do the same – but nonetheless he persisted, found some investment capital and created the Hole in the Wall Company (so named because his first experiment was built in a hole in the wall of his company's headquarters, which conveniently bordered a slum area). As part of his experimentation, he took his computers into some of the private schools for the poor, and explored how children could teach themselves English, including good pronunciation, using interactive programmes. Being an old-fashioned researcher, he shared his ideas with the schools, and didn't mind that one or two started to copy them. But after a couple of years, other schools soon realised that this self-teaching method was far superior to any that they had tried, and copied it too, sometimes bringing in appropriate modifications. Software companies – including NIIT, bringing the system back full circle to where it was invented – now became interested in this market, and started to finance the development, and expand it on a franchise basis to thousands of these private schools. And as these consolidated into chains of schools, it became the standard way of learning English in the poorer, then the not so poor, parts of India.

Apparently, it was this process of experimentation – successful outcome; copying; further success and innovation; investment; further copying – which began to pervade the whole system. 'In a state system', I was told, 'there is no way such innovations could be taken on. In the privatised system, it happens all the time.' Slowly, parents and entrepreneurs realised that what was going on in schools much of the time was the result of an earlier system becoming ossified and counter-productive. If you want to acquire knowledge for its own sake, school is not necessarily the place to do it. Ditto knowledge and skills for work. Ditto upbringing in general. Ditto education for citizenship. All the functions that we now combine in schooling became slowly disaggregated by this combination of inventors, enthusiastic to experiment, entrepreneurs and investors, greedy for a return on their investment, and parents, eager for the best for their children.

Educational innovation moves from East to West

I could see how all this might lead to massive social change in India and China. But that didn't explain how change happened here, in Britain. That was simple, I was told. It was exactly the model that companies such as NIIT were following back in 2005, expanding their purview to the markets of the West, able to keep costs low because all head office functions, including research and development, operated from the low-cost environments of India and China. Exactly the same thing happened with the chains of educational centres that were now developing in those countries. It was true, even before 2005 there were already some developments along these lines in Britain – four of the early pioneers, I was told, were GEMS (Global Education Management Systems), Cognita, CfBT (Centre for British Teachers) and the New Model School Company, all of which were creating embryonic chains of budget, 'no frills' but educationally effective private schools. These were soon supplemented by the foreign chains, with venture capitalists eager to support them, sensing a lucrative, largely untapped market, based on the low-cost environments back home, and the market expanded and consolidated some more.

And slowly, the situation that had arisen in India and China began to arise in England too; and then in America. Slowly, almost imperceptibly at first, then with a gathering momentum, parents began removing their children from state schools. And slowly, almost imperceptibly at first, schools were transformed through the dialectical exchange between entrepreneur and parent, parent and entrepreneur, beginning to disaggregate education into its multiple functions, to pervade all of society.

That was what I saw in my dream, anyway. One senior fellow at a place apart had put it succinctly to me, and on his comments I end: 'In your time, education subsisted under what we call the "Two Tyrannies", of the state and schooling. Within fifty years, by reclaiming it first from the state, we successfully reclaimed it from both. That's liberation.'

References

Mitra, S., J. Tooley, P. Inamdar and P. Dixon (2004), 'Improving English Pronunciation: An automated instructional approach', *Information Technologies and International Development*, 1(1): 75–84

Tooley, J. (2000), *Reclaiming Education*, London and New York: Continuum

Tooley, J. and P. Dixon (2003), *Private Schools for the Poor: A case study from India*, Reading: CfBT

4 POLICING A LIBERAL SOCIETY
John Blundell

Introduction

In many ways, the inclusion of this chapter illustrates the paradox of the title of this book, *Towards a Liberal Utopia?* If we had utopia we would not need police. But this paradox is resolved in the discussion in the introduction of this volume, and the reality of imperfectibility means that the task of sketching a vision of a liberal utopia for policing is a task that remains to be undertaken. It is important not to confuse the particular practical methods of policing suggested here with the wider vision. Some methods will be more appropriate in one age than in another; others will be enduring. However, if the political structures are appropriate, we are more likely to see the adoption and dissemination of the best methods of maintaining law and order in a free society.

The growth of crime

Crime in the UK is growing. From time to time there are downturns, but looking back over the past 50 years both crime and the fear of crime have grown massively. Some of the blame for this might be due to the undermining of individual responsibility, with the welfare system and the education system – issues dealt with in other chapters. A large part of the blame, however, rests squarely with the police's approach to tackling wrongdoing. Law-breakers know there is a good chance of getting away with it. The public knows it too and has little confidence in the police.

So far, so depressing. But there are American models for improving crime rates that could inspire both police policy in the UK and hope in the public. Key to these innovations is the fact that American forces are freer to experiment, while the UK, in common with many other countries, operates national strategies that deny experimentation.

The control of the state over law enforcement is a relatively recent development. The London Metropolitan Police, the first modern force, was not created until 1829, and the development of organised, publicly funded police forces was much slower in other countries (Davies, 2002: 152–3). As in many areas of public policy in Britain, there is still little clear consensus on how best to police a free society, or even on the number of police we need to the nearest 20,000 or 30,000 officers.

In the meantime, crime figures speak volumes. In 2003, one survey suggested that 60 per cent of the public feared that crime would continue to get worse, while 78 per cent had little or no confidence in the police.[1] Even the then Home Secretary, David Blunkett, admitted that, despite the record number of police officers currently employed, fear of crime was at an all-time high in 2003.[2] Any reduction in crime or the fear of crime in the last few decades has proven to be a short-term cycle within a long-term worsening trend, not a reversal of the trend itself.

The public's fear is well founded. The number of violent crimes in this country has topped a million for the first time.[3] Robberies of personal or business property in England and Wales rocketed from 53,000 in 1992 to 121,000 by 2001/02. And 5,500 of these robberies were committed using weapons (Dennis et al., 2003). The total number of crimes reported in 2002 was 5.8 million, compared with 1.7 million 30 years previously. This contradicts the Home Office's assertion that the chance of being a crime victim is historically low.

---

1 www.mirror.co.uk, 7 July 2003.
2 Cath Lee, 'Crime in the High Street', *Greater London Voice of Business*, November/December 2003. According to the mayor's office, the total number of police and police community support officers will have reached 31,000 by March 2004. See http://www.london.gov.uk/londonissues/crimepolicingandemergencies.jsp.
3 Bob Roberts, 'Lawless UK', www.mirror.co.uk, 22 July 2004.

Better policing

How do we best address that fear, bring crime down, restore confidence in the police and work towards a safer society consistent with liberal principles?

Across the Atlantic, where big-city police chiefs have more freedom, a number of highly effective police chiefs have emerged over the past decade or so. Common to all of them is first a willingness to question fundamental issues and expose myths and, second, an ability to recast their whole effort into preventing crime rather than solving it long after the deed has been committed. And their work shows that it is not necessary to recruit more officers to achieve a reduction in crime.

These ideas are not new. They echo London Metropolitan Police founder Sir Robert Peel's vision for police conduct, as outlined in his famous Nine Principles of Policing. Peel believed that the police's primary goal should be to 'prevent crime and disorder' and that the 'test of police efficiency is the absence of crime and disorder, not the visible evidence of police action in dealing with it'.[4] Reported crimes are a fraction of the actual total, if a recent survey of Londoners is to be believed: so the denominator of the clear-up rate is artificially deflated. A disturbing 38 per cent don't report crimes, half of them because they believe the police will do nothing.[5] But, in any case, figures detailing crimes solved are no guide to effectiveness – rather the opposite, as the basis of a clear-up is an initial failure to prevent a crime.

Exploding myths
Myth 1: 999 policing is the best way to fight crime

This is perhaps the most surprising myth of all. The speedy response of emergency services to 999 calls can be valuable for road accidents

---

4   This example of Peel's Nine Principles was taken from www.safe-nz.org.nz/Articles/peels.htm. An astonishing and growing number of police department sites around the world now feature Peel's Nine Principles very prominently.

5   See Hugh Dougherty, 'Third of Crime Not Reported', *Evening Standard*, 29 April 2004.

or fires when it is imperative that trained fire or ambulance personnel arrive quickly. In the case of the police, however, its usefulness is questionable.

It's easy to see why 999 became so attractive: when it was introduced, it used what was then modern technology – radios and fast cars – in an attempt to 'keep up' with the criminal element. The message to the public from 999 services is that the police can be virtually omnipresent. The reality is that officers race from scene to scene, while the public feels frustrated at the lack of immediate results and the necessarily rushed, even brusque, dealings with officers. The average target response time is said to be twelve minutes, so any wrongdoers are usually long gone.[6] When every local criminal knows the response times you might as well not bother.

Emergency-response policing does nothing to allay fear of crime.[7] One study reveals that less than 3 per cent of reports of serious crime lead to arrest resulting from emergency response (Kelling and Coles, 1997). It is perhaps the worst modern example of reactive, 'warrior' approach policing that fails to *prevent* crime. Emergency response is crucial, but basing a force's whole strategy on it, as now, is not a viable approach to law enforcement. It means officers have already lost the battle; all they are doing is picking up the pieces after crime has happened.

Another drawback is the overuse of 999, and some police forces in the UK are beginning to realise this. London police estimate that 70 per cent of all 999 calls are not emergencies and have been pushing for a non-emergency hotline number to alleviate the strain on their resources.[8]

---

6   See 'Emergency Response Time Below Average,' www.walthamforestguardian.co.uk, 23 February 2004.

7   Ed Davis, former Superintendent of Police in Lowell, Massachusetts, in a speech to the Institute of Economic Affairs, 6 November 2001 (hereinafter, the Davis Speech). By 1999 Lowell had experienced the biggest decrease in crime of any large-sized US city during the 1990s.

8   See Martin Wainwright, 'Non-emergency Police Line to Ease 999 Strain', www.guardian. co.uk, 1 January 2003.

This new number, either 222 or 333, would help the public get in touch with police over non-life-threatening concerns, such as suspicious activity in the neighbourhood or minor traffic accidents.[9] In Scotland police have adopted a prioritisation system for 999 calls in an attempt to improve their response time to real emergencies. They are attempting to implement a national service number that will offer advice or send an officer later for such issues as vandalism or non-violent theft.[10]

Myth 2: Private burglar alarms save police time

In fact, responding to false private sector alarms is an enormous waste of police time. Once an alarm is activated the call goes to a distant call centre. An operator there then phones the household and, should nobody respond with the correct password, officers are immediately called. The burglar alarm will generally cause any burglars to flee before police arrive. Thus, the burglar alarm has done its job and the police time devoted to responding to the alarm is wasted.

Just how much police time burglar alarms waste is evidenced by figures from Los Angeles. There, it is estimated that as much as 15 per cent of police patrol time is lost responding to false call-outs to such alarms and that the chances of apprehending anyone are close to zero. The Los Angeles Police Department (LAPD) responds to about 136,000 such alarms a year and 90 per cent of them are false.[11] To correct this, the force now plans to ignore most private residential and business burglar alarms unless a third party – for example, a home owner or neighbour – can verify that the alarm is valid.[12]

---

9   Ibid.
10   Ian Johnston, 'Police Plan to Put Most 999 Calls "On Hold"',
     http://news.scotsman.com, 11 January 2004.
11   Mariel Garza, 'Alarm Plan: Police May Quit Reacting', www.dailynews.com, 13 December
     2002.
12   Ibid.

Thames Valley officers have adopted a similar policy. If the force receives two false alarms from the same source in a year, further calls will not get priority treatment, and the police will not respond at all if there have been five false alarms in the same period.[13]

Myth 3: Police cars on random patrol are a valuable deterrent

Urban areas are often sprawling, and for years police authorities have argued that cars are the best way to cover the most ground, make arrests and provide a viable, visible deterrent. A US experiment, however, proves the opposite. As far back as 1972, the Kansas City, Missouri police department gave one area of the city the standard amount of car presence, one had double and sometimes triple the amount of car attention, while the third had virtually none. The results sent shock waves through police and criminological circles: the crime levels in these three areas remained almost identical (see Sparrow et al., 1990). Random police patrols do nothing to make the streets safer, reassure the public or improve trust between community and the authorities. Rather, cars keep the police from being out in the open and interacting with the public. Cars are cocoons; they block information flows.

Myth 4: Hiring more police reduces crime

Most people would accept in good faith that hiring more officers results in a safer public environment. If there were no police, then crime would go up. Above a certain number, however, the overall impact of extra officers on crime is negligible (Skolnick and Bayley, 1986: 4). As Skolnick and Bayley explain, 'Variations in crime and clearance rates are best predicted by social conditions such as income, unemployment, population, income distribution, and social heterogeneity. We have learned

---

13   www.thamesvalley.police.uk/business-crime/alarms.htm.

that you can't simply throw money at law enforcement and expect proportionate results' (ibid.).[14]

Yet hiring more and more police officers has become the enduring quick fix of law enforcement. Politicians endorse such a policy to court public favour; they are seen to be committed to the 'war on crime'. In turn, senior police and their officers can be guaranteed to line up behind all such demands for extra resources. The need, however, is not for more police, it is for better strategies for approaching crime (Sparrow et al., 1990: 14).

Myth 5: The police fight crime

Both the police and the public cherish this assumption. Thanks to the treatment of law enforcement in popular culture from *Dick Tracy* to *Dirty Harry* to *NYPD Blue*, police forces enjoy a public perception that is as far from reality as Clint Eastwood is from PC Plod. Few police officers have the chance to make high-profile arrests or get into shoot-outs. Officers rarely encounter directly the crimes that scare us most, notably homicide and rape (Skolnick and Bayley, 1986: 4). Most importantly, arrest is rarely the result of Sherlock Holmes-style deduction, with policemen working forward from a set of clues to a suspect the identity of whom is always a surprise. In 99 per cent of cases police make an arrest when a friend or relative tells them who committed the crime.[15] They then work backwards, usually to a known villain. Most police work is about routine and administering emergency care or service.

The idea that police are engaged in a war against criminals allows the public somehow to relieve itself of its own duty in preventing criminal activity. It also enables police officers to adopt an 'us versus the bad guys' approach to their job which in turn sees the ordinary citizen as removed from the process, or even as slowing them down.

---

14 The authors base this argument on the work of Morris and Heal (1981) and Clark and Heal (1979).
15 Davis speech.

This attitude can be traced back to O. W. Wilson, the pre-eminent police theorist of the twentieth century. Wilson and his peers believed that policing should shift its focus from prevention to criminal apprehension. They were responsible for moving policing away from its earlier, community-driven vision, adopting a more militaristic approach. As a result of this so-called 'reform' model, police officers had less and less contact with the public and forces became more bureaucratic (Kelling and Coles, 1997).

Wilson's 'scientific' approach to police work gained popularity all over the world. Rapid response became more and more important until it was the standard practice. Clear divisions of rank and command became the norm. Street officers were seen as being similar to line workers in a factory. They were trusted with the simple, residual work, and could be changed or moved around to another part of the 'factory' whenever it suited command.[16] Parallels can be drawn with the work of Frederick Taylor and his scientific models of management in industry. Just as many in industry have in recent decades turned their backs on Taylor, so we shall see below that the more successful police forces are now turning away from Wilson.[17]

Successful ways of preventing crime

Despite the long-standing influence of Wilson's ideas, and the assertion by some criminologists that crime is a social problem and therefore unassailable by officers, there has been real and practical progress made in policing in recent years. Chiefs and commissioners in the USA have dramatically reduced crime rates and, as a result, reinvigorated cities and rebuilt the public's trust in their officers. Not surprisingly, their methods owed little to 'scientific' policing or criminological trends.

---

16 Ibid., pp. 77, 80.
17 For a full discussion of 'Taylorism' and the new challenge of market process management, see Cowen and Parker (1997) and Parker and Stacey (1994).

Getting out and about

Ed Davis achieved a 70 per cent drop in crime in the late 1990s as head of the Lowell, Massachusetts Police Department thanks to three major initiatives.[18] First, he decentralised his police force, opening small and highly visible police shops on city main streets, rather than having one massive and imposing police building. Second, he gave his officers control over their own 'turf': officers were regularly assigned to the same areas and were expected to take responsibility for those areas. This is in contrast to many police forces that rotate officers from area to area, thereby taking away their chance to build rapport with local citizens or even understand the layout of the streets. He took them out of their cars and put them on the streets solo on foot and on cycles. He reports that the amount of low-grade but vital intelligence coming into his department exploded. Finally, he committed his officers to being preventive rather than reactive. Lowell's officers were taught not only to see crime but also the conditions that allow it to flourish.[19] He explains:

> Problem solving is the process we teach line level police officers to engage in when adopting the community policing policy. It teaches them to be observant of crime but also to look for those conditions that lead to criminal activity. Disorder is their main focus. Graffiti, obstreperous youth, abandoned cars, family dysfunction all fall into this category. We teach our officers to employ the SARA method that is familiar to many professions, especially social service agencies. Scanning, analysis, responding and assessing the response are the methods that our police use in determining the best way to deal with the issues that confront them. It is a very powerful model that gets the officers out of the mindset of arrest and prosecution. Prevention is key to this process. It also empowers officers to use city services, for instance, giving them official blessing to go across boundaries that existed before.[20]

---

18 Information about Davis's success in cutting crime can be found at www.iea.org.uk/record.jsp?typ=article&ID=11.

19 Davis speech.

20 Davis e-mail to the author, January 2004.

Devil in the detail

William Bratton, now head of the Los Angeles Police Department, enjoyed success leading the Boston Police Department and New York's Transit Authority Police Department before coming to national and international renown as the commissioner of the New York Police Department (NYPD). During his 27-month tenure, felony came down by almost 40 per cent and murder by 50 per cent. Bratton, along with former Mayor Rudolph Giuliani, is largely credited with restoring New York's reputation as a top-class world city. Bratton taught his officers to attack the little things, from 'squeegee merchants' to fare evasion, from vandalism to graffiti, believing that it was these petty, so-called victimless crimes which encouraged larger crime in the long run. This radical policy was variously known as Broken Windows, Zero Tolerance or Community Policing. Bratton also dismantled the old-boys'-club approach to promotion and instead rewarded hard work, talent and creativity (Bratton with Knobler, 1998).[21]

His Compstat system, however, was an equally famous innovation. Bratton held twice-weekly meetings with precinct commanders and other key staff built around computer-collected crime statistics. These meetings became instrumental in New York's rejuvenation. Many high-ranking officials had never previously been called on to discuss or defend in public their records and their tactics. The flip side was that these same commanders and their officers were being allowed to follow their own discretion and professional instincts. Police commanders were being trusted with more and more responsibility for their areas, but were expected to produce results – both in terms of crime prevention on the streets and ideas and strategies that could be shared with peers (ibid.: 223–9). Along with the assignment of permanent turfs or beats, such a model of management is akin to giving property rights in the private sector and then expecting a return.

---

21 This text is also an excellent account of how politics (in this case, Bratton's difficult relationship with Rudolph Giuliani) can derail police progress.

No nonsense

The first black police chief in Charleston, South Carolina, Reuben M. Greenberg, became a media regular thanks to his straightforward, down-to-earth approach to crime and punishment. Greenberg's tactics helped to turn around the city, and he relied on simple principles such as consistent police presence, respect for the community, and a preventive approach to criminal activity.

Unlike many of his fellow chiefs, Greenberg does not believe that arrest is the key to lowering crime rates. For example, simply by taking some minor preventative steps, such as reducing motorcycle parking and cleaning up a diner favoured by bikers in Charleston, he was able to remove the potential threat of a Hell's Angels gang moving in. Greenberg succeeded in defusing a potential criminal situation without violence or any dramatic confrontation (Greenberg, 1989: 106–7).

Graduate opportunities

When, twelve years ago, Chief T. Bowman of Arlington, Texas, announced that every officer had to have a full four-year university degree, he was told that women and ethnic minorities would be hard hit. Interestingly, Chief Bowman is black. Despite criticism, he pushed through this all-graduate approach tenaciously. Masters degrees are encouraged and Chief Bowman himself has a PhD. Now, with nearly 17 per cent of its officers being women, Arlington is above the national average of 12 per cent of female officers. The police department's sworn staff is more than 28 per cent ethnic-minority, making it one of the most integrated departments in the USA.[22]

Hand in hand with this went an emphasis on moving decision-making downward and giving officers effective decentralised 'property rights'. Bowman broke his department into four separate geographical areas, giving teams 24-hours-per-day, 365-days-per-year responsibility

---

22   Arlington Police Department figures as at 31 March 2004.

for their allocated area. Lower-ranked but highly qualified officers are making decisions normally made higher up, and he is attracting a calibre of young graduates who would probably not join a department with lower educational standards. Indeed, national agencies regularly raid his department for staff. While crime is falling in Arlington (by 4 per cent in 2002), it is rising in neighbouring Dallas (up 1 per cent in 2002) and soaring in Fort Worth (up 11 per cent in the same year).[23]

Applying these lessons to the UK

These four examples have a number of common characteristics. First, they show leaders who trusted the professionalism of their officers, giving them more and more discretion as to how they handled crime in their area. Second, the officers were expected to foster better relations with the community and move away from the idea that they were the ones tackling crime and that citizens were merely potential victims. Finally, and most crucially, all these forces, not just Bratton's, were committed to 'zero-tolerance' policing. Police were trained to prevent and address all crime in their areas, not merely serious offences. This is the opposite of, say, the London approach to policing, where major crime is the focus and smaller crime is expected to sort itself out (Dennis et al., 2003: 7, 16). The US experience teaches that taking care of small matters seriously impacts on the big issues.

What these officers and their men accomplished is not a distant pipe dream. Our own police, both in the capital and elsewhere, can learn from and take advantage of their successes, and they can begin now by introducing the following simple measures.

Increase the police presence sensed by the public

This does not have to mean hiring more officers. It could mean relying

---

23 Based on a personal visit by the author to the Arlington, Texas Police Department in January 2003, for which he thanks Chief T. Bowman.

less on squad cars and putting officers in regular contact with the people, either on foot or on bikes. Officers could be given the chance to work in areas for longer periods of time, and thus establish a solid rapport with the local community. This type of police presence is far more immediate, personal and helpful. It is also a far greater deterrent to crime than anything else.

The author's experience in Westminster shows how detached many Metropolitan Police officers are from the areas they patrol. When, one day, I asked two policemen on my local beat whether there were any demonstrations planned that day, one of them replied: 'Dunno, mate, we're from Catford.'

Officers must patrol alone wherever possible

A US study has proved that solo car patrols are no more dangerous than working in pairs, possibly because police feel braver and are more inclined to take risks while partnered. Police departments that have adopted this measure have improved their response time to officers who need assistance (Skolnick and Bayley, 1986: 101). In many areas in the UK dangers to police are negligible, even if there is anti-social and low-grade criminal behaviour, but officers still patrol in pairs, effectively halving the police presence.

Foot and bike officers can be sent on solo patrols too. The immediate benefit is that these officers, without the temptation of a fellow officer to talk to, now talk to the public. In Westminster officers are often seen walking in pairs, deep in conversation. When police are patrolling together, talking to each other, three problems arise: they are looking at each other, not at their surroundings; they are not interacting with the public; and the effective police presence is reduced. Concerned local residents in Westminster, who have seen crime rocket, have turned to private security guards who work alone and interact with the public.[24]

24 Harriet Sergeant, 'The Police Have Failed Us – So We've Hired a 6ft 6in Security Guard', www.telegraph.co.uk, 5 April 2004. The author's experience of police foot patrols in

Solo patrols establish communication and trust, and the public not only feels more comfortable with a consistent and visible police presence, but also is more inclined to share information and tips that can lead to crime prevention and arrests.

Foot patrols also raise officer morale (ibid.: 216). Davis in particular recognised the importance of this and, early in his command, made the Chief of Patrol his official number two, sending a signal to his whole force that patrol is a route to the top and not some chore you do for three years before being assigned to more challenging and prestigious work. Indeed, many officers prefer the beat to being in a squad car or inside, saying it allows them to feel better about their jobs while feeling closer to the community.[25]

Eliminate as much paperwork and court time as possible

A recent study showed that the average beat officer spends only about 17 per cent of his time on the street – the other 83 per cent is spent dealing with bureaucracy.[26] If all we did was to increase that figure of 17 per cent to 34 per cent and put officers who now patrol in pairs out on the streets solo, these two measures alone would provide a fourfold increase in police presence.

But who would do the paperwork? A solution attempted by some US police departments is civilianisation. It is controversial because many officers resent the idea of people coming off the street to do their jobs, and fear that lower-paid civilian assistance may eventually lead to lower police salaries (ibid.: 219). It has, however, proved effective. In Houston, Texas, civilian aides help lessen police red tape and take on smaller tasks such as traffic accident follow-up reports, freeing up officers' time.

Westminster endorses this. They are often seen heads down, leaning towards each other, talking about issues such as pensions and pay, holidays and partners, or their superiors.

25 Ty Klassen, 'Beat Cops in West Broadway', www.westbroadway.mb.ca, August/September 2003.

26 Alan Travi, 'Laptop Revolution to Keep Officers on the Beat', www.SocietyGuardian.co.uk, 2 November 2001.

Also key to this idea's success is that many of these civilians are insiders in their community, and can be valuable sources of information and liaison (ibid.: 217–20). Many police report a higher level of job satisfaction since they can focus on the parts of the job they originally thought they were signing up for. By enlisting civilians as volunteers or lesser-paid employees to deal with much of the administration, we let our officers be officers – an idea surely behind the recent advertising push for special/volunteer constables with the Met. Indeed, such has been the success of Sir Ian Blair's initiative that, after proper checks and training, some 500 volunteers have recently reopened seventeen closed London police stations. And this quickly growing phenomenon of volunteer civilians helping carry the load is not limited to London or to manning desks. Volunteer accountants are reportedly helping the Fraud Squad.[27]

Open one-stop cop shops

The Met is selling off large, outdated station houses and investing the projected £900 million to be released by the sale into smaller station buildings, street kiosks and booths in supermarkets such as Tesco's. The move is primarily motivated by financial considerations, but officers also point out that many of the new outlets will be in known 'hot spots' of criminal activity and all will be far more visible and accessible to the public.[28] Such a move shows a refreshing commitment to police decentralisation and inclusion.

Admit failure

Police officers in Britain have to acknowledge fully the failure of their past crime-reduction strategies. Dealing with serious crime in the fragile hope

---

27 'Volunteer Spirit Gives Blue Lamps a Chance to Glow Again', *Daily Telegraph*, 29 November 2004.

28 John Steele, 'Met to Sell £900m of "Outdated" Buildings', *Daily Telegraph*, 24 February 2004.

that smaller crime would naturally drop has not worked (Dennis et al., 2003: 7–8). Conversely, the results from so called zero-tolerance policing speak for themselves. Aggressive begging, graffiti, verbal abuse, physical aggression and so on are less serious crimes which upset the public and have been proven to lead to higher levels of overall crime. When people see the little things being let slide, it is a natural progression to more serious and violent wrongdoing. It establishes a lack of trust in the social structure that maintains order (Wilson and Kelling, 1983).[29] This will require more than mere lip-service to ideas of 'community policing'.

Conclusion: Major institutional change

Crime may be inevitable but it can be dramatically reduced. Altering the approach of the British police and their political masters to their work is a long-term commitment, but the precedent for such success exists. In London the Metropolitan Police has taken some positive steps, and the immediate past Home Secretary has appointed Paul F. Evans, whose successful strategies as Chief of the Boston Police Department – one of the largest in the USA – helped cut violent crime by 34 per cent, murder by 68 per cent and burglary by 40 per cent since 1995, to head his Police Standards Unit.[30]

Heads of police authorities must stop pushing the more-money-and-more-officers agenda. Britain can be a much safer place to live with the resources available to its police now. What works is insightful leadership, a willingness to trust the officer on the street while holding commanders accountable, and a commitment to involving the community being protected. It is all about incentives, property rights and personal accountability.

---

29 This now-famous article helped popularise the idea of zero tolerance, or what is some-times called 'Broken Window' policing. It is based on the idea that a single broken window in a neighbourhood can invite further crime problems by creating an air of social uncertainty and enforcing an idea of few active authorities.

30 'Police Forces Face Shake-up', http://news.bbc.co.uk, 9 September 2003.

The required change will come about only sporadically unless there is major institutional change. Policing may always take place in a 'second best' environment as far as liberal economists are concerned. So we have to develop the structures that, as far as possible, use market-type incentives, to ensure the development of effective policing strategies. Most liberal economists share the view that services that have to be provided by the state should be provided by the lowest level of public authority possible. In the case of policing that should be district or city councils or unitary authorities under our current local government structures. If structures that provide even smaller areas of meaningful local government can be developed, all the better.

Local authorities should have responsibility for raising their own finance for the police, for setting the pay and conditions of their police service (including pension benefits) and for developing their own policing strategies. In such an environment innovation will be copied more effectively and the local electorate will understand exactly who is responsible for policing and cast their votes accordingly.

Parish councils could have the option of levying supplementary policing charges in return for extra policing – or have the option of providing their own additional arrangements. There will be straightforward competitive comparison of crime reduction strategies, costs and success rates between similar and adjacent localities. Of course, there may be some forms of crime for which regional and national police forces are necessary. Just as there are hypermarkets and corner shops, we need different kinds of police forces to deal with different kinds of crime. There should also be cooperation between neighbouring forces – in a competitive environment, where failure is punished and success rewarded, the optimal degree of cooperation pays.

Private policing should be a major part of the solution too. Even today, private security firms provide a very significant proportion of security services. The benefits of policing can often be confined within the boundaries of particular estates or areas that are privately owned or controlled by housing associations. Gated communities could negotiate with local authorities to provide some or all of their own policing, in return for a reduction in local taxes. Indeed as 2004 ended, the Royal Institute of Chartered Surveyors reported a 'mushrooming' in the use of private security firms to police everything from wealthy areas and gated communities to council and social housing.[31] Alternatively, local authorities could provide grants to housing associations or private estate owners who provide their own policing (see Johnston, 2004). Better development of property rights would enable private solutions to policing to develop which we cannot yet envisage.

Governments will need to rid themselves of the conceit that they can impose the best methods and organise the best way of doing things. Governments will have to accept 'postcode policing'. In some areas policing will be undertaken in more effective ways than it is in other areas. But constructive innovation and competitive pressure will ensure that the better policing methods prevail and those that fail will be consigned to the dustbin: a far cry from the current situation. Policing – both private and public – will always be necessary. However, only radical reform of policing will ensure that the police return to their proper role of effectively preventing crime.

References

Bratton, W. with P. Knobler (1998), *Turnaround*, New York: Random House

Clark, R. V. G. and K. H. Heal (1979), 'Police Effectiveness in Dealing with Crime: Some Current British Research', *Police Journal*, January, pp. 24–41

Cowen, T. and D. Parker (1997), *Markets in the Firm*, Hobart Paper 134, London: Institute of Economic Affairs

---

31 'Private Security Firms Join Battle on the Streets', *Daily Telegraph*, 2 December 2004.

Davies, S. (2002) 'The Private Provision of Police in the Eighteenth and Nineteenth Centuries', in D. T. Beito et al. (eds), *The Voluntary City*, Ann Arbor: University of Michigan Press

Dennis, N. et al. (2003), *The Failure of Britain's Police*, London: Civitas

Greenberg, R. (1989), *Let's Take Back Our Streets!*, Chicago, IL: Contemporary Books

Johnston, P. (2004), 'Additions to the Bill', *Search*, 41, summer, Joseph Rowntree Foundation, pp. 7–9

Kelling, G. L. and C. M. Coles (1997), *Fixing Broken Windows: Restoring order and reducing crime in our communities*, New York: Touchstone

Morris, P. and K. Heal (1981), *Crime Control and the Police: A Review of Research*, Home Office Research Study no. 67, London: HMSO

Parker, D. and R. Stacey (1994), *Chaos, Management and Economics*, Hobart Paper 125, London: Institute of Economic Affairs

Skolnick, J. H. and D. H. Bayley (1986), *The New Blue Line: Police Innovation in Six American Cities*, New York: Free Press

Sparrow, M. K. et al. (1990), *Beyond 9/11: A New Era for Policing*, New York: Basic Books

Wilson, J. Q. and G. L. Kelling (1983), 'The Police and Neighbourhood Safety', *The Atlantic*, March, pp. 29–38

5 PENSION PROVISION IN 2055
Philip Booth

Introduction

It is arguable that the state should not be involved in pension provision at all. Some forms of private insurance (such as health and disability insurance) do have certain features that would lead some economists to propose varying degrees of government intervention although, in practice, in such cases government provision may still be less effective than private provision. It is not difficult, however, to envisage a fully private market in pensions without any government intervention at all, and this chapter will propose moving to such a situation.

The long-term nature of pensions policy creates a dilemma for policy-makers. Unless policy changes are made today, they will not make their full impact before 2055. If the agenda proposed here is implemented in 2055, it will not be fully operational until 2105. A transition from one system to another can also be difficult. Thus, after the initial critique of government pensions systems, there are three strands to the analysis. First, a policy for a liberal utopia is outlined. Then a more pragmatic approach is suggested – this could be implemented in the next five years and be fully operational by 2055. Finally some transition arrangements are suggested for people who have accrued a pension under the current system to help us get to our ideal position more quickly.

State involvement in pensions

During most of the 80-year lifespan of state pensions in the UK there have probably been three major arguments against state pension provision. To a degree these problems were anticipated at the time the state systems were developed (see, for example, Bartholomew, 2004). The first argument is that state pensions undermine fundamentally the ability of people, particularly the poor, to plan with foresight and make provision for the future through saving. Second, state pension provision replaces private sector capital accumulation by a system of government-controlled income redistribution between generations. Third, the nature of state pension schemes is such that they are generally unfunded so that current pensions are paid out of the taxes of current taxpayers. This means that, if the demographic profile of the population changes, the government's tax take can fall at the very time pension payments are increasing. Since the late 1980s, much of the debate about pensions in the UK has related to whether 'funded pensions' are better than 'pay as you go' pensions provided by the state. Policy in the UK has been compared favourably with that in continental EU countries. Whole libraries of material have been published on this subject, following work undertaken by the OECD;[1] the debate on the pensions system has broadened again in recent years, however.[2]

The feelings that these three arguments generated are effectively summed up by the following quote:

> There was at the existing time great political pressure from the Governments to adopt or maintain ambitious programmes of so-called social security, with perhaps too little understanding of their ultimate effect on the social and economic structure. A sound social insurance and superannuation programme could sustain and strengthen a nation; on the other hand, a sufficiently unsound one could destroy it. Furthermore, once such a programme was put into effect it became politically impossible to discard it or to

---

1 There is a full discussion of different countries' pension schemes and the unfunded pensions problem in *Economic Affairs*, 18(1).

2 See, for example, the report of the government-appointed Pensions Commission, chaired by Adair Turner.

reduce benefit scales which it was beyond the ability of the nation's economy to support.[3]

It is certainly true that government pension systems have involved huge unplanned and inequitable inter-generational transfers. They have also led to extremely high labour market taxes that may well have reduced labour force participation dramatically.

Early state pension schemes were simple in structure, providing a very basic income, from a given age. For some people this would form the whole of their retirement income whereas for others it would provide a basis upon which to build private saving. In a society in which full retirement at a specific age was common, long careers in stable jobs were common and the demographic profile of the population was stable, such schemes, however undesirable, may have caused only limited damage. These schemes then grew, however, to encompass 'earnings related' elements. Demographic change then led to state schemes becoming a much greater burden than was anticipated. This led to the unfunded versus funded pensions debate which preoccupied pensions economists for much of the 1980s and 1990s and led to pragmatic proposals, involving compulsory private saving, which have been adopted in Chile and Australia, for example. In addition, as the brief period of stable demographics, hierarchical labour markets with standard terms and conditions of employment and more uniform family structures with single-earner couples with dependants, which dominated the early post-war period, has come to an end, compulsory state pension schemes look rather like the compulsory provision of horses and carts as a means of free transport for pensioners.

Time to move on

Whilst economic developments have led state pension schemes to become outdated and inappropriate, they have also become more complex and

---

3   Edward Marshall, former President of the US Society of Actuaries, speaking at the First Business Meeting of the Centenary Assembly of the Institute of Actuaries, 22 June 1948.

meddlesome. State pensions include an earnings-related element but, also, 'supporting' the state pension system are extensive means-tested cash payments, council tax benefit, housing benefit, free television licences, winter fuel benefit, special pensions payments that depend on age, and a special tax system for the old with a complex method of withdrawals of reliefs. Remarkably, there is a 'married couples allowance' for those over 70, but not for those under that age who are more likely to have children to support. Surrounding private pension systems there are also detailed and complex regulations relating to tax, solvency, product sales and contracting out of the state scheme. The state is involved in every nook and cranny of pension provision – not just in relation to the payment of state pensions. Why is this situation increasingly inappropriate?

It is important, as individuals' and families' working patterns differ more, that pension provision can reflect differing preferences and also that individuals are able to take account of the information provided by price signals in labour and capital markets. A uniform state pension system and a highly regulated private pension system cannot cater for the widely different needs and circumstances faced by individuals and families: people are working in a number of different countries during their lives; individuals take career breaks to retrain, to look after family members or for leisure; increasing numbers of people work part time for at least a proportion of their lives; large numbers of people now retire abroad. Furthermore, people are living longer and increasingly, for at least some of these extra years of life, in good health.

Individuals may want different arrangements to reflect their different working patterns. Different pension ages, different annuity patterns compatible with a pattern of partial retirement, the use of equity from a main residence to supplement or replace pension income are just a few examples of the different kinds of pension arrangements that may be appropriate. It is also important that individuals face the price signals relating to their decisions. As populations age, the relationship between the quantity of capital and the quantity of labour in an economy changes, sometimes rapidly. Typically, the capital-to-labour ratio rises as a baby-boom generation comes of age. It may then fall again as a baby boom generation spends its savings. Relative prices, wages and investment returns may change quite rapidly. In this situation, investment returns might fall and wages rise. Any government policy that institutionalises a given pension age, whether through its pensions system or through other aspects of the social security or tax system, makes it less likely that individuals will respond to these price signals by delaying retirement and pension age. This is perhaps particularly pertinent at the current time. Returns on investment seem relatively low, and there seems to be tightness in the labour market. In a free market for pensions, we would expect people to respond to lower investment returns, reflected in higher annuity prices, by retiring later. Such decisions would also work with the grain of the labour market by increasing labour supply. There would be significant overall welfare benefits from allowing people to respond to changes in price signals in this way.

The problem of the size of the workforce reducing as the population ages is clearly understood by politicians. As would be expected, they propose political meddling to deal with a problem caused by earlier political meddling. This meddling comes in various different guises, such as anti-age-discrimination legislation; increases in the minimum retirement age; changes to the state pension scheme; clamping down on the abuse of disability benefit; and various government strictures and special measures. None of these measures would be necessary, however, if the government took a number of actions to reduce policy interference in income provision for the aged. Such actions could include: ending the compulsory purchase of annuities; the removal of restrictions on the forms that pension annuities can take; ending the rigid nature of state occupational pension schemes – it is extremely rare for a teacher or a nurse to continue working after the 'normal' retirement age in those professions; abolishing public sector labour monopsonies; ending preferential treatment for the over-65s in the means-tested benefit system; privatising the state pensions system; and privatising the disability insurance system. If these actions were taken, individuals would face the social and private costs of retiring at their chosen age given the choices available to them in the labour and capital markets. The government would not have to encourage flexible retirement, it would happen naturally.

The difficulty of moving on

In anticipation of the development of public choice economics, Edward Marshall noted how difficult state social security systems would be to change (see page 87). This is true for two reasons. When it comes to decreasing the extent of current state pension systems, the size of the interest groups in receipt of pensions would make it very difficult for politicians to vote for change. With regard to the accrual of future pension rights, the situation is even more problematic. Part of the electorate (for example, those aged 20–50) could vote for policies that would lead to increased pension accrual rates so that they would receive higher pensions on retirement. Those who would pay the cost of that accrual in an unfunded system do not yet vote or are not even born. There is no interest group that can organise on behalf of those not yet born to protect themselves against increases in the future cost of state pensions! The mechanism of contracting out does ease this problem somewhat (see below).

The combination of these problems makes state pensions systems both undesirable and unsustainable. The nature of the problems is such that there is little likelihood that the government will take action to alleviate them until a crisis is reached. This gives rise to another problem. Prospective pensioners cannot know when they will suffer from a policy change and how extensive that change will be. Such policy changes may be fundamental (for example, scaling back benefits) or subtle (for example, by means-testing benefits). Those in state pension systems thus have 'policy-induced risk'. Unlike the risk that arises from private investment, this policy-induced risk is extremely difficult to quantify and impossible to manage.

The minimal state in pension provision: an outline proposal

It is not entirely clear why the state needs to be involved in pension provision at all. There are certain categories of insurance that, it could be argued, are subject to some kind of 'market failure' or 'information asymmetry' that prevents markets working properly. For the sake of argument, let us assume that these problems exist with regard to long-term care, health, disability and unemployment provision[4] and so the state gives assistance to people in need of these benefits. When considering pension benefits, therefore, we are simply considering the provision of an income to those over a typical pension age who are, more or less, fit and well – this is the fundamental nature of a pension benefit. It is paid contingent only upon the individual being alive. There is no serious information asymmetry or potential market failure here – it is not difficult to assess whether somebody is alive whereas it is very difficult to assess whether somebody is genuinely off work as a result of disability. It is not difficult for the insured to know whether he should be paid a benefit, unlike with health insurance, where the individual relies on the opinion of 'experts' and we need the development of intermediary bodies, such as health maintenance organisations, for the health insurance market to work efficiently.

With regard to pensions provision, individuals face a simple problem – how do they arrange their working life and their savings in order to get the income pattern they want over their fit lifetime? The first thing to note is that this is an individual problem. The answer to this question depends on individual preferences and circumstances and cannot be anticipated by the state. The second point to note is that problems of 'poverty' are irrelevant to this question. If the state wishes to help the poor, at any stage in their lives, it can. The poor in receipt of that help can then decide how to use the assistance to provide them with the retirement income they wish to have from the age they want to receive it. In other words, the poor can use private vehicles for retirement income provision, just like everybody else, in the same sense that they can use

4   It is certainly clear in the author's mind that disability and long-term care insurance would be far better provided by the private sector: see, for example, Booth and Dickinson (1997).

the same food shops as their better-off counterparts. In practice, the state pension scheme is used to provide a proportionately bigger income to the poor for a given level of contribution (although Beveridge did not necessarily intend this – see Booth in Deacon, 2002). Whatever degree of income redistribution occurs within the state pension system, however, can be achieved in other ways, whilst allowing the poor to provide for their own pension in the way they prefer.[5] A third point to note is that the decision about how much to save is not a technically complex one. It is also one that can be easily managed. Within reason, if poor investment decisions are taken or insufficient income is saved, this does not lead to financial ruin but to a requirement to work longer than expected or save more later in one's working life. None of the usual arguments to justify government intervention in the insurance of contingencies applies in the case of pensions.

In the long term, there should be a complete deinsitutionalisation of pensions policy as far as the government is concerned. There is no legitimate role for the government in pensions provision. Individuals and families would determine the form of saving they wished to undertake in order that they could optimise their consumption pattern over their lifetimes. The concept of a state-determined, uniform 'pension age' should seem in the future as quaint as the idea of asking the Bank of England permission to purchase foreign currency for a holiday does today. Individuals may well sign up to paternalistic pension arrangements or other contractual arrangements that prescribe particular retirement ages. Conventions might develop across groups in society, in different industries or in different regions of the country, but the government would not need to be involved.

The government would also have to address other issues. For example, all means-tested and non-means-tested benefits should be independent of age and the tax system facing old people should be the same as that facing younger people. Government interference in the tax

---

5   See the pragmatic proposals below.

system surrounding private pension provision should also end, although it is a moot point whether this would mean that all saving or no saving was subject to tax relief (see Booth and Cooper, 2002). The government could dispose of a huge number of general pensions regulations, national insurance regulations and tax rules.

The proposal to remove the state from pension provision altogether may seem a radical proposal but it has clear merits. There would be reduced costs, increased choice, no government interference in the decision as to when and how to stop work, and individuals and families would have much lower taxes and a secure planning framework. Government income provision for the elderly is a relatively recent invention and it is difficult to argue that it has been successful. It would still be necessary for individuals to obtain an income during periods of unemployment, disability, illness and so on, and for many people a proportion of their old age is a period of ill health and disability. Whether such contingencies are covered by the state or privately is an important issue but not the subject of this essay. No compulsory pension provision should be necessary because means-tested benefits for those with no income would be at the same level regardless of age, and there would be a work test before individuals would be allowed to receive means-tested benefits.

A more pragmatic approach

The minimal state proposal effectively suggests that the government should have no role in old-age income provision. Most of the benefits of that proposal, however, could be achieved by a reform that could easily be enacted in the next parliament. The transition might take us to 2055, such is the long-term planning horizon for old-age income provision. The following adjustments would have to be made to government arrangements for income provision for the elderly:

- The government would abolish all future accrual in the earnings-related part of the state pension scheme (S2P, formerly SERPS).

- The government would reduce means-tested benefits paid to over-65s to their level at other ages (if this seems radical, it should be noted that this would approximate to the situation that prevailed as recently as 1997).
- The basic state pension would be changed to the level of income that is paid as the basic means-tested benefit, and it should be offered on the accrual principle so that every year for which an individual paid national insurance contributions (or was otherwise deemed entitled to the accrual of the pension – for example, if they had caring responsibilities) they would receive an entitlement to 1/45 of the level of the state pension, linked to future price increases.
- Housing benefit and council tax benefits would be abolished and appropriate adjustments made to general cash means-tested benefits.
- The free television licence, the winter fuel allowance and all other 'gimmicks' paid to pensioners would be abolished.
- The government would set a particular expected number of years for which it would like the basic state pension to be paid and set up an independent committee to adjust the basic state pension age every ten years to ensure that the average life expectancy at state pension age remains the same (for the sake of argument, at ten years, so that if life expectancy at age 71 were 81, the state pension age would be 71).
- All forms of different treatment of older people through the tax system would be removed.
- All accrued rights in the earnings-related pension scheme would remain (but see the transition arrangements below).
- If people wished to choose to receive a state pension beginning after the set state pension age, they would receive an appropriate actuarial enhancement.

To facilitate the return of power to the individual, the following changes would also have to be made to private sector pension arrangements:

- Tax relief on pensions contributions in general would remain but the tax-free lump sum would be removed (this would ensure that the special tax advantages for pension saving were reduced so that they would not be abused; this would enable the removal of several chapters of regulations surrounding both personal and occupational schemes that are designed to prevent abuse of the tax position).
- Both occupational and personal pension schemes could contract out of the new basic state pension and receive an actuarially neutral rebate of national insurance contributions. If an individual was not contracted out via an occupational scheme, he or she could maintain a personal pension scheme in which the contracted-out rebate would be invested. Any individual entitled to state pension accrual but not paying national insurance contributions (for example, women caring for children) could also contract out of the state pension system and receive a rebate to be invested in a private scheme.

These arrangements might seem complicated. This is because we have described how to get from where we are now to the new arrangements and the current position is appallingly complex. But, in the end, we would have something stunningly simple. The government would set a state pension age so that, on average, people would expect to receive a pension for ten years. Today that age might be, say, 70. The state pension would be set at subsistence levels so that even those who remain in the state system would have received no more than a foundation on which to build. Anybody who wished to do so could contract out of the state system altogether and obtain a refund of the national insurance contributions equal to the actuarial cost of purchasing the state pension benefit. For the first time, people could choose to have no state pension at all and receive an appropriate refund of their national insurance taxes. Also, for the first time, individuals accruing state pension rights who are not paying national insurance contributions could become completely independent of the state for their retirement income. The distortion to work and savings incentives in the economy would be minimised by the fact that the state would simply be providing, at worst, a given (small) income for a short period of time. All redistributional aspects of the current state pension system could be maintained: this is because any rebate of national insurance contributions paid to individuals would not depend on the contributions actually paid but the actuarial value of the pension benefit they have chosen to forgo.

Transition arrangements

Individuals who have accrued entitlements in the existing state pension scheme would be allowed to keep their entitlement. The state could facilitate the transition, however, by offering to 'buy out' state pension obligations. If, for example, a 40-year-old individual has accrued the right to an index-linked pension of £40 per week under the existing state pension system, the individual could exchange the right to that benefit for a cash sum equal to the actuarial value of the benefit. The cash sum would have to be invested in an appropriate pension scheme. The state would be privatising its pensions liabilities in the same way as, in the 1980s, it privatised its assets. It could finance this by borrowing. This would not increase the state's overall debt because obligations to meet the costs of explicit borrowing would simply replace future pensions costs. Preferably, though, the state could meet the cost of this privatisation of pensions liabilities through the privatisation of state assets – roads, television stations, radio and telephone spectrum, housing stock and so on. These transition arrangements would allow large numbers of people to become independent of the state pension scheme even if they had accrued entitlements within it under existing arrangements.

Conclusion

Most Western economies are in a public-choice-reinforced, self-inflicted spiral of decline. The state provides a high level of retirement benefit from a young age and, in many countries, provides early retirement benefits too. The state finances much of the cost of education, at least to the age of 18 and often to the age of 21 or older. In some countries, the state also finances childcare. In some EU countries, up to 50 per cent of people between the ages of 21 and the state retirement age do not work. There is therefore a small section of the population working and paying taxes in order to finance the upbringing or the retirement of the rest of the population. This situation is not stable, as the majority being supported has no incentive to reduce the burden on the minority paying for the support. As working becomes less attractive, the number of taxpayers then falls further. Pensions must be reformed, not just in Britain, but in the whole of the Western world. There is a strong economic case for the state having nothing to do with pension provision at all. At worst, the state should provide a subsistence income for a few years but allow people to make alternative provision and receive a refund of the cost of providing a state pension if they prefer to make their own private arrangements. This policy is not only essential to ensure economic welfare. The end result of the alternative of a public-choice spiral of decline will be ever increasing inter-generational conflict which, in many countries, may be played out on the streets rather than through the ballot box.

References

Bartholomew, J. (2004), *The Welfare State We're In*, London: Politico's

Booth, P. M. and D. R. Cooper (2002), 'The Tax Treatment of UK Defined Contribution Pension Schemes', *Fiscal Studies*, 23(1): 77–104

Booth, P. M. and G. Dickinson (1997), *The Insurance Solution*, London: European Policy Forum

Deacon, A. (ed.) (2002), *Debating Pensions: Self-interest, citizenship and the common good*, London: Civitas

6 SOCIAL SECURITY IN A FREE SOCIETY
David G. Green

Introduction

What sort of cash benefits should be provided in a free society, if any? During the 1960s and 1970s we came to identify concern for disadvantaged people with transferring money to them. The more you cared the more you transferred. The Blair government questioned this doctrine of welfare rights and argued that we had both rights and responsibilities: if you can work, you should. And in the first year or so after 1997 there was talk of 'springboards' rather than 'safety nets', implying a major break with past beliefs, which rested on the idea that most people are victims of circumstance.

But what have the results been? In reality, welfare dependency has increased. Despite a huge fall in unemployment, there were 240,000 more people on benefits and welfare tax credits in 2003 (6,383,000) than in 1997 (6,143,000).[1] The trend is a little harder to discern than it used to be because the government has renamed the main in-work benefit twice and treated it as a 'tax credit' rather than a welfare benefit. But throughout its transformation from family credit to working families tax credit and then to working tax credit, its character has remained the same.

How does welfare dependency today compare with recent history? In 1951 just over 3 per cent of the population received national assistance or unemployment benefit. In 2002, not including the state pension, 26

---

1   Department for Work and Pensions, *Client Group Analysis: Quarterly Bulletin on the Population of Working Age on Key Benefits*, August 2003; Inland Revenue, *Working Families Tax Credit Statistics, Summary Statistics*, February 2003.

per cent of households relied on means-tested benefits (22 per cent) or working families tax credit (4 per cent).[2] The government's estimates of the number of 'workless households' tells a similar story. Workless households are those of working age with no one aged sixteen or over in employment. In 1998 3.1 million households were workless and in 2003 2.9 million. This was a fall of only 137,000 households from 16.8 per cent of all households to 15.6 percent.[3]

Nor is this dependency a matter of 'topping up' largely private incomes. In 2002, 30 per cent of households received half or more of their income from the state and 60 per cent of households with at least one adult over the pension age relied on the state for half or more of their income. Family breakdown is one of the main causes. Only 8 per cent of couples with two children receive income-related benefits, compared with 65 per cent of lone parents with two children.[4]

The current strategy of the government is to 'make work pay', but it is very unlikely to achieve its declared aim of reducing benefit dependency. Its continuing paternalism has led the government to encourage claimants to take a job by paying them additional in-work benefits. This subsidisation reduces the number of people *wholly* reliant on benefits by increasing the number *partially* reliant on welfare. Consequently, it is creating a new kind of in-work dependency, and I will advocate instead measures that encourage self-sufficiency.

Two main proposals are made in this chapter. First, I argue that we urgently need to redefine the social contract between the community and its members. The safety net should always be there to prevent hardship, but we need to reconsider what the members of a society can reasonably expect of benefit claimants. I propose a different method of combining an ever present safety net with a stronger focus on self-sufficiency.

Second, we should abolish all entitlements to benefit and, instead,

---

2   Department for Work and Pensions, *Family Resources Survey 2001/02*.
3   National Statistics, *Work and Worklessness among Households, Autumn 2003*, January 2004.
4   *Family Resources Survey 2001/02*, op. cit.

place a two-part obligation on the government: to provide assistance sufficient to prevent severe hardship for all who need help; and to do so in a manner most likely to lead to self-sufficiency.

The significance of a high degree of welfare dependency is that many people will look to the government – in practice to one political party – for part or all of their standard of living. This creation of 'client groups' in the population undermines the independence of public opinion and invites political manipulation. Before the 2001 election the party in power claimed to have given a million people a pay rise in the form of the minimum wage. Having increased the number of recipients of working tax credit it can now make a similar appeal to them. In November 1997 there were 766,000 recipients of the old family credit. By February 2003 there were 1,427,500 recipients of working families tax credit (now working tax credit).

What is the alternative? An opposition party cannot easily disregard the presence of a block of beholden people and, if it wants to win elections, will have to be equally or more 'generous'. Hence, a cycle of electoral bribery is encouraged and no strategy can afford to ignore its power.

How could welfare dependency be reduced? One approach is to understand welfare dependency as the outcome of too much government – implying that the solution is less government. A pure libertarian policy would 'scrap the lot' to allow philanthropy and mutual aid to flourish, but this approach is not realistic. In any event the problem is not 'too much government' as such, it is the wrong kind of government. A free people with shared sentiments and living under the same laws should offer all its people cast-iron safeguards against serious hardship as a sign that everyone belongs.

Does this sound suspiciously like the solidarity associated with collectivism? There are two very different kinds of policy associated with the term solidarity. The first is redistribution from rich to poor. In truth it creates division. The resulting politics involves conflict between factions and organised groups seeking advantage at the expense of another group

– the rich. The second type of solidarity unifies people: we all do our best to be self-supporting and to do what we can for the common good, but if things go wrong the wider society will always be there to lend a helping hand. Such a policy creates a common bond based on reciprocity.

The aim of policy-makers, therefore, should not be less government for its own sake. It should be to discover policies that unify rather than policies that divide.

The safety net

The underlying problem is that at any one time some people are not able to support themselves. The conundrum is how to help without causing a counter-productive reduction in work effort or creating still worse problems. Legislation has a long history. In 1536 Henry VIII made begging by people able to work punishable on a first offence by whipping, on a second by cropping the right ear and on a third by execution.

Since Tudor times policy-makers have grappled with the problem that having a safety net, of itself, tends to reduce work effort. The 1834 new poor law was based on a 'self-acting' test – that is, help was provided on workhouse terms to all who asked, without a means test. Life in the workhouse, however, was intended to be less attractive than the life of the independent labourer.

The ethos had changed by the end of the nineteenth century. Typical of thinkers at the turn of the century was Helen Bosanquet, an influential member of the 1909 Royal Commission on the Poor Laws, who urged a 'positive' rather than a deterrent approach. Many different types of people needed help, she said, and the underlying causes of their immediate problem should be discovered and help given to restore independence wherever possible. The choice was not between help or neglect; the challenge was to find the best way to restore independence.

During the twentieth century commitment to personal responsibility weakened gradually. By focusing on the 'poverty line', studies by Booth and Rowntree, for example, directed attention towards the symptom of an underlying problem. By the time of the 1942 Beveridge Report, however, the sense of mutual obligation and the commitment to family self-sufficiency, though weakened, remained intact.

Theories of social exclusion and victim status, following what many have called the 'rediscovery' of poverty in the 1960s, led to the abandonment of personal responsibility as a guiding principle of welfare reform. By the 1970s public policies were influenced by a doctrine that can be called 'egocentric collectivism'. It embraced four main ideas: *social determinism*, according to which individuals were seen as powerless and 'the system' dominant, from which it was concluded that holding individuals responsible was 'blaming the victim'; *egalitarianism*; *welfare rights*, or the view that individuals have one-sided claims on the public purse, with little or no acknowledgement of corresponding obligations; and *cultural nihilism*, which insisted that individuals should be released from moral and cultural restraints.

The high point of this doctrine came during the 1970s, and over the next decade a counter-movement developed which might be called the 'rediscovery of independence'. Led by writers such as Charles Murray and Lawrence Mead, it rejected the egocentric rights culture and asserted the importance of a two-sided ideal of community and self-sufficiency. The community should always maintain a safety net and individuals should work, if at all possible.

The alternative

The emerging counter-view was that we should reform social security based on the assumption that there is a contract between the individual and society. All entitlements to benefit should be abolished and a twofold obligation placed on the government: to provide assistance sufficient to prevent severe hardship to all who needed it; and to give only help that would lead to self-sufficiency. To that end, means-tested income replacement benefits should be cancelled and transitional assistance introduced in their place.

Welfare policy should be based on high expectations of human potential. In a free society, individuals can be expected to make provision for the normal expenses of living, periods during the life cycle when expenditure will be high (such as child-raising) or income low (especially retirement), and to provide against possible misfortunes (such as ill health or accident). Moreover, individuals can reasonably be expected to choose a family structure that will allow them to support and care for children.

Policy options for people out of work

Workfare schemes of the form that has been used in Wisconsin have been successful. Between 1994 and 1999 welfare dependency in the USA fell from 14 million to 7 million people. The essential elements of the strategy that led to this result were: scrapping the idea of giving people an incentive to work and laying down a firm rule that there are no benefits without work; if one is disabled, one's capabilities are assessed and appropriate work assigned (people in wheelchairs, for example, can often answer the telephone); and benefits are subject to time limits. Unmarried parents should be treated as a unit regardless of whether they live together. If they choose to live under separate roofs that is up to them. The government will treat them as a self-supporting unit of mother, father and child. The father must support himself and the child; and the mother must support herself.

Work should be a requirement of the benefit system. For the able bodied, full-time work is a reasonable expectation. Where there are two living parents, one-parent families should also be self-sufficient. Absent lone parents should be expected to pay sufficient maintenance to keep their children, and custodial lone parents should be required to work as many hours as necessary to keep themselves off benefits. Disabled people should try to be as self-sufficient as their disability allows.

New applicants for benefit should be subject to strict requirements before any benefit is paid. All new applicants should meet a personal adviser to determine their capacity for self-sufficiency. It is reasonable to expect people to have sufficient savings to cover two weeks without income and so anyone wanting cash assistance should be required to take part in two weeks of job search before benefit is payable. Any emergency cash assistance required during that time should be treated as a repayable loan. A graded series of alternatives should also be provided for people not yet ready for full-time work. But unsubsidised work should always be the first choice, with other options only temporary until the ultimate objective of unsubsidised paid employment is met.

Policy options for those in work on low pay

Should there be in-work benefits to make work pay? Ideally, there should not be. The dangers of providing such benefits have been apparent for a long time. In the 1830s in Berkshire and Wiltshire 'bread money' was a regular payment and a distinction was made between 'bread money' and 'going on the parish'. The lesson to be drawn from the Speenhamland system was that in-work benefits were not effective but, despite this, reliance on in-work benefits has been growing. But it will be too difficult in the short run to scrap the working tax credit. One precept deserving of investigation is that of 'No one who works hard should be poor'.

This does not mean that everyone who has a low income should be given money. But if a person works full time and is still unable to command a 'living wage', an in-work benefit may be defensible. Nevertheless, working tax credit has damaging side effects. It requires only sixteen hours' work a week, with the result that many reduce their work effort to qualify. This defect could be avoided by defining full-time work as 40 hours a week for 50 weeks a year. Certainly, parents with dependent children, whose income was still very low after putting in that amount of effort, would be considered by most people as deserving of assistance.

Such a system would reward hard work. There are now over 1.4 million people on working tax credit and, based on the current proportion of claimants who work full time, a 40-hour requirement would reduce this figure to about 400,000.

Provision for old age[5]

Pensioners have the minimum income guarantee and a system of tax credits intended to encourage private saving. About 60 per cent of pensioners depend on the income-tested elements of the scheme. What sort of strategy would be both compatible with a society of free and responsible people and likely to be acceptable given the high degree of electoral bribery? The current system of saving for old age is dominated by the tax break for private pensions. Free marketeers often defend two alternatives: a funded state system like that in Singapore; or a compulsory private system, like Chile's.[6] Such a policy amounts to compelling people to invest in a bad bet.

The better alternative is tax neutrality for all methods of saving, including cash saving, property and shares. It would be possible to invest in any of them with after-tax income, but there would no further tax on interest, dividends or capital gains. Inheritance tax should also be scrapped.

But wouldn't the loss of the pension tax break be resented? One approach would be to let people take the cash benefit early. At present 25 per cent of a pension fund can be taken in cash at retirement. If people were allowed to take it earlier, it might seem like a fair swap. It may be necessary to limit the amount that can be withdrawn in any one year to avoid having a dramatic impact on the economy.

What would be the result? A family could build up assets – property, durable goods, shares, cash – with the intention of handing them on from generation to generation. When you purchase an annuity the insurer takes the risk that the capital will run out, but members of a family might

---

5   The subject of pensions is also covered in the chapter in this volume by Booth, which focuses on retirement income provision.

6   Although Booth does not propose such solutions.

prefer to take that risk themselves. If the oldest surviving generation, for example, opts to live on its capital rather than to buy an annuity, the risk of their capital running out before they die gives their children an incentive to diminish expenditure, perhaps by caring for their parents themselves. They might use the capital to build a 'granny annexe', so that their parents are close at hand. Such a property-based strategy offers considerable flexibility for families of quite modest means.

This approach could be further encouraged by income tax reform. In some countries couples are allowed to apportion their family earnings as they believe best. They can agree a 50/50 split, or apportion all of it to the wife or the husband. If we were to introduce this system, perhaps we should allow income to be assigned to any adult living at the same address. This could also help to solve the problem of caring for the elderly. Families who took responsibility for caring for their elderly parents could assign their income to them and pay less tax to reflect the saving to other taxpayers.

Tax allowances permit people to keep their own money and thereby encourage a sense of personal responsibility. Benefits tend to have the opposite effect. The chief argument against tax allowances is that people who have no tax liability (because their income is below the tax threshold) do not benefit. The counter-argument is that the existence of the allowance gives people an incentive to earn more so that they do qualify.

Conclusion

The present government is creating a group of people who will look with gratitude to one political party for their income. The alternative approach should be built upon independent individuals who look first to their own efforts in the confidence that the wider society will always be there to help if things go wrong. The end result would be a property-owning democracy, based on government that unifies, not government that divides.

7 LIMITS ON THE TAX BURDEN
Tim Congdon

What is the limit on the tax burden?

High taxation does not mix well with political freedom and economic efficiency. Despite this, the second half of the twentieth century – the years when the Institute of Economic Affairs was making its vital contribution to the public debate – was a period of extraordinarily heavy taxation by long-run historical standards. Before World War II it was unusual for taxation to exceed 25 per cent of national output; after the war very few significant industrial countries had a lower tax burden. Instead the ratio of tax to national output ('the tax ratio') varied in the nations of the industrialised West from a low of about 25 per cent to a high of 60 per cent.[1] Indeed, a large state sector, and a powerful and omnipresent fisc, are widely regarded as among the defining features of the modern industrial state.

At the start of the post-war period economists raised questions about the viability of the tax burden implied by the welfare state, then at an embryonic stage. In 1945 Professor Colin Clark wrote a paper for the *Economic Journal*, presenting evidence that a tax take above 25 per cent

---

1 Table 27 at the back of the 2003/04 issue of the OECD's *Economic Outlook* publication shows the values of the ratio of tax and non-tax receipts to nominal gross domestic product in 27 nations between 1985 and 2002, with projections for 2003 and 2004. Some values are missing, but in total there are almost five hundred values. All are between 25 and 60 per cent, with two exceptions. First, the ratio exceeded 60 per cent in Sweden between 1986 and 2001, apart from one year (1992); but it never exceeded 65 per cent, even in Sweden. When allowance is made for non-tax receipts, the ratio of tax to GDP would have been under 60 per cent in Sweden in this period. Second, the values for Korea were under 25 per cent from 1985 to 1996, but Korea was not an OECD member (i.e. 'a significant industrial nation') at that time.

of net national product would be inflationary. This paper became widely quoted and was still being discussed in an Institute of Economic Affairs pamphlet over thirty years later (Prest et al., 1977: 21–3). In Clark's view anything above the 25 per cent figure carried such serious inflation risks that it must be an upper bound. Keynes – as editor of the *Economic Journal* – endorsed his position, opining that 25 per cent was 'about the limit of what is easily borne'. Given Clark's and Keynes' warnings, the surprise must be that economic performance has been so good over the last 60 years. Output growth has been continual, so that living standards today are vastly better than in the late 1940s. It seems that Clark and Keynes were wrong. The facts suggest that considerable economic dynamism can be achieved even with tax levels far above the quarter of national income that they regarded as the maximum.

There is, though, another way of looking at what has been happening across the industrial world since the 1940s. It turns out that tax is subject to a limit, an absolute upper bound, just as Clark and Keynes thought. But the limit is 60 per cent of national output, not 25 per cent. On what evidence is this assertion based? The answer lies in the simple and plain facts of experience: *no nation in peacetime has had a tax ratio above the 60 per cent figure*. In the post-war period – the period when the state sector has been more extensive than at any other time in history – several nations have had long periods with a tax ratio above 50 per cent and the majority of advanced nations have had at some time or other a tax ratio above 40 per cent. But no nation has exceeded 60 per cent for any noticeable length of time.

Somehow a few nations – virtually all of them in Scandinavia – have coped with a tax ratio of about 60 per cent. But their economic performance has hardly been encouraging and taxpayer resistance has become a major political force. No government in these nations has dared to breach the 60 per cent figure for long. A tax ratio of 50 or 60 per cent may be viable, in the sense that everyday economic life proceeds more or less as normal and national income is stable or even growing slightly. But it is very far from ideal. In fact, an increasing body of evidence argues that the level of and growth rate of national output are inversely related to the tax ratio. An important study on the subject by Andrea Bassanini and Stefano Scarpetta appeared in the OECD's *Economic Studies* in 2001. The numbers depended on the specification adopted, and allowed room for judgement and debate (Bassanini and Scarpetta, 2001: 9–56, in particular p. 35). But in one particularly ambitious formulation, where the tax ratio affected investment and, at a further remove, also influenced the capital stock, a rise in the tax ratio of 1 per cent reduced national output by 0.6–0.7 per cent. In other words, the equilibrium level of output in a nation with a tax ratio of 50 per cent is 12 to 14 per cent lower than in one with a tax ratio of 30 per cent, and the equilibrium level of output in a nation with a tax ratio of 60 per cent is no less 21 to 25 per cent lower than in one with a tax ratio of 25 per cent.

Unsustainability of very high tax rates

The existence of a limit to taxable capacity can hardly be unexpected. If a tax rate of 100 per cent ends voluntary economic activity altogether, a tax rate of 70 per cent or 80 per cent must have drastic adverse effects on incentives. A nation could in theory levy taxes equal to national output without having any tax rate at 100 per cent, because it could combine very high rates of both direct and indirect taxes.[2] This nation might also have a large private sector, with the state handing back enough to the citizens in the form of transfer payments for the bulk of their expenditure still to be on privately produced goods and services. But in practice a nation with a 100 per cent tax ratio – or even a 70 or 80 per cent tax ratio – would be impractical and unsustainable, for three reasons.

---

2   This may seem surprising, but if direct and indirect taxes were both 50 per cent of national income tax revenues would equal 100 per cent of national income, and yet the average rates of direct and indirect taxation would be 50 per cent of national income. Note that an important constraint on indirect taxation is the risk of diverting economic activity into the very small-scale tax-exempted sector, into cash or even barter transactions, or into illicit activities such as smuggling. As far as the author is aware, there is no example of indirect taxation amounting to 50 per cent of national income.

Disincentives and labour market participation

First, the nation would suffer from disincentives to work and save, and from discouragement for people to seek employment and for companies to offer it, even on the assumption that collection and compliance costs were nil, and that taxpayers were wholly honest and paid their taxes in full. This statement should hardly need proof, but the admirers of modern European societies with their large state sectors – such as Adair Turner in his book *Just Capital: The Liberal Economy* – sometimes appeal to economic theory for a counter-argument. The counter-argument needs to be noted and rebuffed.

A tax change can be regarded as a kind of price change. As is well known, the effect of a price change on the quantity demanded depends on two effects, a 'substitution effect' and an 'income effect'. The substitution effect of an increase in price is always to reduce quantity demanded, but the income effect is ambiguous. If the income effect of an increase in price is significantly to increase quantity demanded, it may – in certain special circumstances – outweigh the negative substitution effect. In such a case an increase in price is followed by an increase in quantity demanded. When applied to the labour market, this argument leads to the claim that an increase in tax rates sometimes causes people to work *longer* (Turner, 2001: 250–3).[3]

But in today's conditions it is most unlikely that this sort of response would be common or general. In modern industrial societies people are cushioned against the loss of income from not working by social security payments and the apparently 'free' supply of certain so-called 'public services' (health, education and low-quality housing). The existence of these benefits reinforces the negative substitution effect of high taxation. For many millions of low-skilled or unskilled workers there is no point in working. A prevalent tendency across the industrial world in the last 30 years has been a decline in the proportion of working-age men

---

3   But Turner concedes that 'The case for avoiding very high marginal rates, say above 50 per cent, is strong.'

who actually work. This tendency has been most pronounced in some European countries, such as France and Italy, where the rise in the tax ratio has been greatest.

Fortunately, the decline in male participation in the labour force has been offset by an increase in female participation. Two further prevalent tendencies across the industrial world since the 1960s have been an increase in female participation and a sizeable reduction in the pay differential between men and women. It is clear that without the entry of more female workers into the job market economic growth would have been much lower in recent decades than has actually been the case. But as this mobilisation of the female working-age population can happen only once, the associated output gain will not be repeated.[4] Further, an argument can be made that one of its by-products has been a sharp decline in fertility. Disturbingly, the decline in fertility has reached the point where the populations of nearly all European countries are no longer replacing themselves. The long-term sustainability of the high taxation associated with the welfare state can therefore be questioned from a wider demographic perspective.[5]

Costs of collection and compliance

There can be no doubt that – even in societies where tax payment is frictionless – an increase in the tax ratio reduces the equilibrium level of national income. But tax payment is not frictionless. The second way in which a high tax ratio lowers national output is through the increased

---

4   In the USA the proportion of working-age women actually at work climbed from just over 42 per cent in 1960 to almost 72 per cent in the early years of the current century. It plainly cannot rise to 102 per cent in the next 40 years. Assuming that the maximum proportion is about 75 per cent (and only one OECD country much exceeds this), the USA cannot enjoy the same output boost from extra female participation in future. The same is true in most industrial countries.

5   See Congdon, 'Does the Eurozone Face 50 Years of Economic Stagnation?', *World Economics*, April/June 2002, Henley-on-Thames: NTC Economic & Financial Publishing, pp. 47–60.

costs of collection and compliance. The cost of collection is ostensibly borne by the government, but of course 'the government' is a legal fiction. Ultimately the cost has to be borne by the taxpayer. Further, the compliance costs – of filling in long and difficult forms, of preparing correspondence with accountants, of learning about the tax system and seeking advice on how best to structure one's affairs – fall directly on the taxpayer. They must rise with the tax ratio, particularly if an increase in the tax burden is associated (as is invariably the case) with a higher number and a greater complexity of taxes. Gordon Brown, the Chancellor of the Exchequer since 1997, has tried to counter the disincentive effects of the UK's tax and social security arrangements by elaborate 'tax credit' schemes, in which tax is reduced as incomes rise. These schemes may have encouraged formerly unemployed workers to take up a job, but they have added to employers' costs and have been accompanied by large increases in the tax and social security bureaucracy.

Avoidance, evasion and avoision

Finally, the higher the tax rates, the greater the incentives both to avoid tax (i.e. to find legal means not to pay tax) and to evade it (i.e. not to pay tax, regardless of whether the law is being broken). Different people respond to these incentives in different ways. Of course, the dishonest and unpatriotic have less compunction about avoiding or evading tax than the majority of the population. If they 'get away with it', citizens with a strong sense of civic responsibility feel cheated and angry. The long-run effect is to undermine respect for law and civic institutions. In these conditions illegal tax evasion may be widely regarded as no more despicable than legal tax avoidance. As Arthur Seldon warned in the 1970s, the resentment caused by excessive taxation led to 'tax avoision' in a 'new twilight of law-breaking' (Seldon, 1980: 178).[6]

---

6   See also Arthur Seldon's comments in *Tax Avoision: The Economic, Legal and Moral Interrelationships between Legal Tax Avoidance and Illegal Evasion*, London: Institute of Economic Affairs, 1979.

Tax 'avoision' is often thought to be the preserve of low-income fringe operators, such as building contractors or minicab drivers, in or close to the black economy. But when confronted with true tax rates of possibly as much as 70 or 80 per cent of income even high-income professional people and members of wealthy families structure their assets to escape the attention of national revenue authorities.[7] Favourite strategies are the registration of personal assets in bogus companies to exploit the better tax treatment of corporate entities, the transfer of assets from companies with a transparent pattern of beneficial ownership to nominee companies where beneficial ownership is opaque, the movement of wealth from heavily taxed jurisdictions to tax havens, and the relocation of individuals with the deliberate intention of exploiting tax residence rules (which differ considerably between nations).

All these devices take up an immense amount of time and effort, both for the wealthy people themselves and their armies of professional advisers (lawyers, accountants, brokers of various descriptions). Even so, there is often considerable uncertainty about whether a particular course of action is 'tax efficient' or not. Much of the activity is a ridiculous zero-sum game, as governments both impose heavy taxation on their own long-standing citizens (in the UK's case, those deemed to be 'domiciled' here) and have advantageous tax arrangements for wealthy people of foreign origin who come to live within their borders. Rich French people live in the UK to take advantage of the low tax on people with foreign

---

7   The UK has a 40 per cent top tax rate on income from work, income from assets and inherited assets. So it may appear that the highest 'tax rate' is 40 per cent. But that is not so. Suppose that a wealthy individual saves out of income, receives income from his saved assets during the rest of his life and passes on the assets to children. Then all three activities (working, saving and dying) are taxed at 40 per cent. The true tax rate is (1 minus [0.6³]) per cent, which is just over 78 per cent. No wonder wealthy people want to locate themselves in jurisdictions with no income or inheritance taxes. John Stuart Mill was the first economist to notice – in his *Principles of Political Economy* – that, when a system of income taxation levied taxes on both income from employment and income from assets, it involved double taxation of the income from assets accumulated from taxed income. If allowance is also made for inheritance tax, the system would be better characterised as treble taxation.

domicile and rich Britons live in France to take advantage of the favourable taxation of pension income; rich Americans come to live in the UK and set up artificial companies which masquerade as 'foreign investments' and rich Britons live in the USA to establish exemption from UK capital gains tax, and so on.

Understandably, the national revenue authorities try to catch up with the fiscally motivated peregrinations of the rich. But decisions by their officials are sometimes arbitrary or downright vindictive, which ends the citizen's sense of loyalty to the state and utterly destroys taxpayer morality. It is striking in this context that a large chunk of European saving is now held in portfolios of bearer securities (so-called 'eurobonds'). Because these securities are not registered, it is difficult, or even impossible, for revenue authorities to determine the location and identity of their owners. Regrettably, but unsurprisingly, when the owners receive the income (by handing over a coupon detached from the bond to a paying agent in Luxembourg or New York), they do not report it to their tax inspectors. Most governments in the European Union want a withholding tax to be levied on the income from such securities, but the UK (where most eurobonds are arranged and underwritten) and Luxembourg (because of the importance of paying-agent activity to its economy) have resisted its imposition.

When the IEA was founded, eurobonds had not been invented. At the end of 2003 the value of the outstanding stock of such bonds was about $11,000 billion, up from $2,000 billion a decade earlier. No one knows the proportion of total eurobond issuance owned by citizens of European Union states, but it is almost certainly over half and may be more than two-thirds of the total. This figure has become harder to estimate as the concept of 'the citizen of a nation' has become increasingly complex: as has already been explained, many wealthy Europeans live in – or, at any rate, have residence status in – tax havens or nations with congenial tax regimes for 'foreign investors'. If 60 per cent of all eurobonds were owned by citizens of EU countries this would amount to $7,000 billion. That would imply that the average holding for the citizens of the EU would be almost $20,000 and that it had risen dramatically, by four, five or six times, in the previous decade. There could hardly be a better illustration that high tax, at the levels seen in the modern European state, corrodes taxpayer morality and undermines efficient tax collection: it is an almost perfect example of Seldon's tax avoision.[8]

To summarise, high taxation reduces economic efficiency, because of

- the disincentive effects on the amount of work in any particular employment, on the level of employment and on savings;
- the cost of collecting taxes and of complying with tax codes;
- the erosion of the citizen's loyalty to the state and taxpayer morality.

Tax policy over the coming generations

Given the combined power of these three damaging effects of taxes on production and saving, it is hardly surprising that the rise in taxes in the OECD area since the 1960s has been accompanied by a decline in the rate of economic growth. This decline has been particularly marked in Europe, which is also the continent in which countries have a greater tendency to have tax ratios of over 45 per cent. So far economic growth has continued, if at increasingly trivial annual rates of 1 per cent or so. But the demographic situation is certain to worsen sharply in the 2010s when the working-age population of such nations as Germany and Italy will start to fall. If productivity growth comes to a halt under the weight of further increases in tax and regulation, and if employment contracts in line with the working-age population (typically projected in the nations affected at 0.5 to 1 per cent a year), then significant European nations could experience a trend decline in output. It is not inconceivable that living standards could fall over extended periods, such as five or ten years.[9]

---

8   The data on the issuance of international bonds (or eurobonds) are given by the Bank for International Settlements on its website.
9   Again, see Congdon, 'Does the Eurozone ...', op. cit.

At this point attitudes towards the big-government, high-tax modern European state may change. Leading politicians and high-ranking civil servants may recognise that tax burdens of 40, 50 or 60 per cent of GDP are the main cause of the economic malaise. They may look more favourably on radical proposals for reducing the size of the state and the burden of taxation.

What policies should they consider in order to cut the size of the state? First, they could privatise the supply of health and education, cutting taxes by the full cost of public expenditure on these items and suggesting to their citizens that they use their much enhanced post-tax incomes to pay for them directly. Of course, hospitals and schools would charge for their services, and the market would establish an efficient equilibrium between supply and demand.[10] The privatisation of health and education would reduce the ratio of government spending to GDP by about 12 to 15 per cent of GDP in most advanced countries. That would allow the tax ratio to fall correspondingly.

Income and corporation taxes represent about the same share of GDP as spending on health and education in many countries. Income and corporation taxes could therefore be abolished, ending both their adverse effects on incentives and the destructive nonsense involved in their current methods of collection. The case for market freedom will become more compelling in the early twenty-first century, as the nations of Europe find themselves crippled in an increasingly competitive world by an excessive burden of tax.

References

Bassanini, A. and S. Scarpetta (2001), 'The Driving Forces of Economic Growth: Panel Data Evidence for the OECD Countries', *OECD*

---

10 The idea is not new. In his book *Charge*, Arthur Seldon (1977) argued that the so-called 'public services' should be privatised, and that people should pay for education, health and housing from increased post-tax incomes.

Economic Studies, 2, Paris: Organisation for Economic Cooperation and Development

Prest, A. R. et al. (1977), *The State of Taxation*, London: Institute of Economic Affairs

Seldon, A. (1977), *Charge*, London: Temple Smith

Seldon, A. (1980), *Capitalism*, Oxford: Basil Blackwell

Turner, A. (2001), *Just Capital: The Liberal Economy*, Basingstoke and Oxford: Macmillan

8 BRITAIN'S RELATIONSHIP WITH THE EUROPEAN UNION
Patrick Minford

Introduction

I think it is fair to say that the politics of the European Union have never been particularly popular in this country. That is why the European Union has always been sold here as an economic proposition – often the proposition that the 'economic dangers of being left out are greater than any costs of membership'. The political intrusion involved is generally regarded as unwelcome. This chapter will therefore focus purely on the economics of the European debate.

Much debate on the EU in the last few years has centred on the issue of whether the UK should join the euro. The economics of going into the euro are very negative – a point that was well appreciated by HM Treasury when carrying out the recent five tests. Of course, on the Continent the euro was launched as a political project designed to boost the prospects of close political union and the economic problems it would create were sidelined; that, as we have just argued, could not be done here.

Much ink has been spilt on the single currency; I wrote a short account of the arguments in IEA Occasional Paper 126, *Should Britain Join the Euro?*, and I will not repeat them here. The main argument against joining the euro is that it would involve sharply increased economic volatility because we would lose the ability both to pursue a monetary policy that suited the UK and to steer our (floating) currency between the mutually gyrating currencies of our dominant trading partners, the euro and dollar areas. Those problems are not going to disappear in the foreseeable future, and therefore the issue of our euro membership is dead for the time being.

But the wider economics of the EU have taken a new and dangerous turn with the appearance of the draft new constitution produced by M. d'Estaing's convention. This constitution embodies tendencies that have long been quite apparent, not merely in the actions of the Commission but also, and perhaps more importantly, in the judgments of the European Court, which have favoured the centralising and socialising objectives written into the previous EU treaties' vague preambles. By including the Charter of Fundamental Rights, the constitution has handed these judges the power to extend this agenda very extensively.

My aim in the rest of this short piece is to go through five ways in which the EU is now prospectively a very costly organisation for the UK to belong to. I am, in doing so, interpreting the thrust of future EU policy in the light of recent policy actions by the EU (for example, the decision by France and Germany to scrap reform of the Common Agricultural Policy, the CAP) and of the general thrust (in favour of protectionism and social rights) of the constitution. I must emphasise that the EU does not have to be this way; one can envisage an alternative, liberal set-up in which the CAP would be drastically reformed, free trade announced as the EU's commercial objective, and market forces as its guiding light in internal economic policy. But that is not the EU we are currently asked to contend with, unfortunately. The main sections of this essay take the EU as we find it but, in the conclusion, we then seek to suggest how Britain's relationship with the EU might look in a more ideal world.

Agricultural protectionism

First of all, there is the well-known cost of agricultural protectionism in the form of the Common Agricultural Policy. I would estimate this cost to be about 0.5 per cent of national income – a fairly typical estimate from the range available: 1 per cent of national income is £10 billion per year; so 0.5 per cent of national income is £5 billion a year. Just to get this into perspective, the NHS costs us £70 billion per year – but then at least we get something for this spending! Of course, the costs involved vary with the state of the world market in agricultural products. But this estimate would correspond to an average year for relative world prices of food.

The way in which the Common Agricultural Policy works is that it boosts the prices paid to farmers by consumers from across the EU by about 50 per cent above world prices. The CAP is an example of a customs union in which the common tariff surrounds the protected zone (the EU in this case), but allowing producers from each country within it free access to other member countries' markets. The result is that prices inside the union rise above the world price by the amount of the common tariff; also, member producers can benefit from these high prices and will pay no tariff. Therefore, since we are big net importers of food in this country, this means that our consumers are not only paying a lot more for their food than they need but also that they are paying this excess not in the main to UK farmers but rather to Continental farmers, especially French ones. This creates a burden to the UK of transfers (from us to Continental farmers) on top of the burden of resource misallocation (too little food is consumed because internal prices are too high and too much food is produced, at the expense of other products, because prices to farmers are above world prices).

Manufacturing protectionism

The second cost is not so well known: the protection of manufacturing industries. From time to time we have been told that it is very important for us to be in the European Union because it is good for our manufacturing industry. Again, the truth of the matter is that we import more manufactures from the European Union than we export, and therefore what is happening in manufacturing is very much like what is happening in agriculture.

Manufacturing is a declining industry in the West: it is uncompetitive for obvious reasons, because we have emerging markets such as China that undercut it so massively. What is left is in specialised, high-tech and niche areas. In our economy we have largely let market forces take effect, with generally favourable results for employment and growth; as a result manufacturing has declined in terms of employment wherever it was essentially uneconomic. That has not happened to the same extent on the Continent. As a result we find that there is a great deal of protectionist pressure. The EU is accordingly a customs union in manufacturing as well as in food: it raises tariffs and other protective devices externally on manufactured imports, so that prices for manufactured goods are kept up inside the European Union. In addition to tariffs, the European Union protects manufacturing, in certain areas such as textiles, through quotas, but mainly through anti-dumping rules. Anti-dumping rules operate both through explicit duties and through the threat of levying duties, which often results in importers raising their prices instead. The latter action is more costly to us because not only do our consumers pay higher prices, but the excess revenues resulting do not go to EU governments including the UK's but rather to foreign non-EU producers.

Since, again, we are net importers of manufactures, this protectionism is costly to us in just the same way that the CAP is; it is, if you like, a 'Common Manufacturing Policy'. Our net imports are larger than they are for food, which means the transfer cost is much higher than for food; and the size of our consumption and production is massively higher than for food, so that the misallocation cost is also much higher. Between food and manufacturing EU commercial protectionism appears to cost us some 3 per cent of national income.

Services: a regime of internal protectionism

We now come to trade in services. British service producers are generally efficient and the UK has a comparative advantage in services, of which we are net exporters. These are industries such as insurance, banking, commercial aviation, ground transportation, communications and electricity. It is often argued that the UK therefore stands to gain from the single market in services that is one aim of the EU. At present the services environment in Europe is one of national protection, mostly very high. According to available estimates of services protection the UK and the USA both operate fairly unrestricted regimes, whereas EU countries operate highly restrictive regimes at a national level, presumably to protect their national companies. The argument goes that if this national protection is replaced by an EU-wide protective regime of a customs union type, then Britain would gain greatly, in a mirror image of its losses on other trade.

Unfortunately there is a great difficulty with this argument. Why should the continental EU countries participate in a customs union for services that would retain high prices for their consumers while transferring service production from their own companies to UK companies that are more efficient? For these countries this would be like the UK opting for a CAP; they would be foolish to do it. (We only opted for CAP in the early 1970s because it was the price of joining the EU and our politicians at that time felt there would be compensating benefits.) It seems that, instead, other EU countries would be rational to opt for one of two alternative outcomes: either full deregulation in service industries or no change. No change would keep their own producers' privileges while continuing to penalise their consumers; the difficulties of achieving service liberalisation bear testimony to the tenacity of these producers' lobbying. If, on the other hand, liberalisation, as in the single market agenda, is effective, then full deregulation would give each country large gains to their consumers that would more than offset the losses of their producers. These countries would then, if they so chose, be able to sweeten the pill for their producers by some programme of compensation, at least for a transitional period.

From the UK viewpoint either outcome means that UK service firms would make no gains. Given no change they are in the same situation as now: they cannot trade except at world prices. There is no attraction in trading in the EU relative to any other world market. Given full deregulation the same applies; EU prices would then drop to world levels so our producers would again be no better off.

The whole point about the single market in services, if it were ever to happen, is that it gives a great benefit to consumers by dragging down prices of services across Europe. This would be very good for the rest of Europe because consumers there would enjoy competition. But it would not benefit British consumers because there is already a highly competitive market in UK services; and it would not benefit British producers of services because they would not get better profits in Europe than they can get anywhere else in the world. Therefore, there is no prospective benefit to the UK from the single market in services. Services therefore will not provide an area of gain that can offset the losses we make in our other trade with the EU.

So far we have identified a big cost because we are net importers of agriculture and manufacturing, and in the area where we are big net exporters, mainly services, there is no prospective benefit. But these 'costs' compare being inside the EU customs union with being outside under free trade. Some people then ask whether we could not still have some trade arrangement with the EU. But of course this is to miss the point of a customs union in which there is horse-trading between the producers of different countries, paid for by their consumers; if a country refuses to trade by penalising its consumers it has nothing to offer! Were the UK to be outside the EU and let its consumers pay world prices for products, continental EU countries would have no incentive to let UK producers have access to their markets at preferential customs union prices; this would amount to asking their own producers to transfer profits to UK firms with no quid pro quo. Thus it must be realised that ceasing to participate in EU customs union arrangements would be just that – free trade at world prices would be in its place, with no 'EU preferences'. From this, though, we would gain that 3 per cent of GDP.

Harmonisation
Employment rights

I come now to the fourth area, to which the draft constitution is particularly relevant – harmonisation. The constitution emphasises rights. The Charter of Fundamental Rights incorporated in it would take the UK back to the 1970s in terms of rights of collective bargaining and the unions. This may well be its most significant feature. There is also a great deal on workers' rights and social entitlements. One of the key things that the Conservative governments of 1979 onwards did was to destroy the ability of union power to hold back development in this country. All the evidence we have shows that this was probably the most significant factor in raising our productivity growth. The other thing they did was to make unemployment benefits highly conditional on the requirement to look for a job. So you would help people who cannot find a job but otherwise be tough on them. And all that is potentially rolled back by the constitution and the Charter of Fundamental Rights.

This would be harmonisation of a particularly damaging sort for the UK. The Liverpool Model of the economy has been used to cost the effect of such policy changes. If 'middle-of-the-road' changes were made, for example a minimum wage raised to 50 per cent of male median wages, union power restored to mid-1980s levels and social cost rises worth 20 per cent of current wages, the model predicts that they would raise unemployment by some 10 per cent – that is 3 million – and cost us around 10 per cent in reduced output. This would be a massive cost indeed – putting our losses from trade protectionism in the shade. Together these costs go well into double digits as a percentage of GDP. (In addition, the constitution appears to come close to mandating euro membership: in chapter II, article iii-69 it states that '… [the activities of the member states] shall include a single currency, the euro …', implying yet more damage to our interests.) These costs are now nearly double the cost of the NHS.

The EU pensions crisis

Finally, I come to the fifth area – the cost of potentially insolvent state pensions on the Continent. According to an OECD study completed in 1995, the projected deficits in state pension schemes in 2030, as a percentage of GDP, were 10 per cent in Germany and Italy and a little less in France. There have been some minor reforms in these countries which may have improved things slightly, but the impact of such reforms has almost certainly been offset by lower growth and higher unemployment than was projected. If we add up these deficits as a percentage of UK GDP, which is of similar size to that of each of these countries, it amounts to 30 per cent. If we were to pay a quarter of that cost because via some federal system we were asked to 'share the burden fairly', then the bill would be about 7 per cent of GDP, which as it happens is exactly the cost of the NHS!

I am not saying, of course, that this is necessarily going to happen, but federal structures have a way of enforcing burden-sharing (greatly emphasised in the draft constitution, which enjoins the bail-out of member economies 'in difficulties'); and this is certainly a burden we do not want to share or risk sharing, at even a modest level.

What should the UK do?

The economic cost of our current relationship with the EU is already high and carries the prospect that it might escalate alarmingly under the draft constitution, with its Charter of Fundamental Rights and its unleashing of powerful centralising processes; nor is there any prospect from the policy thrust in the draft constitution that the existing costs from protectionism will be alleviated. Briefly and brutally, this prospect amounts to little less than ruin for the UK– a return to the awful 1970s and yet worse again.

What is to be done? Plainly, to start with there must be debate on the constitution and a referendum on it. Assuming that the British people would reject this constitution, then the sequel must be a determined effort to reform the EU radically. Of course, were such an effort on our part to fail then the only possibility left would be to initiate a basic rene-gotiation of our relationship with the EU – such an 'associate' status could involve free trade together with cooperation in key areas and the keeping open of borders to people and capital as now. But it is hard to believe we are yet quite in such a drastic situation. Surely, since reform would not only benefit us but also our neighbours, rational policy solutions must intervene, even at this eleventh hour, to reverse the economic insanity currently dominating European Union policies?

So let us assume that reform is possible. How would we wish our relationship with European Union members to look in 50 years' time? In economic terms, the answer is obvious. We would like free trade both within and outside the European Union. This must be genuine free trade which accepts diversity of regulations, standards and product quality as part of the package of a genuine free market, as opposed to a regulated single market. Free trade must extend to services and agricultural products as well as manufactured goods.

We would like a European Union that limits its legislative powers only to areas where there is a genuine and overwhelming commonality of interest amongst its members. Areas such as labour market regulation, the regulation of corporate governance, solvency standards and so on fall firmly outside this remit. We would also like a European Union that was genuinely a force for free trade in the world.

In theory, this could be achieved within the EU as currently constituted, although probably not under the proposed constitution. The court, the parliament, the Council of Ministers and the Commission would have to put the freedom of movement of capital, labour, goods and services ahead of their quest for ever closer union – or uniformity. How close we can get to this utopia will depend on events outside Britain's control. Indeed, the implication of much of the analysis above is that, in practice, we may get closer to the relationship we would like with other members of the EU if we have a fundamentally different constitutional relationship with them.

We can be clear about the economic objectives that we wish to achieve. It is not possible to say whether, in the next 50 years, those objectives will be best achieved if the UK is outside the EU, has some kind of associate membership of the EU or is inside the EU.

9 REGULATING THE LABOUR MARKET

J. R. Shackleton

Increasing regulation

Since 1997, employment regulation has increased considerably in the UK. Some of the new regulation, such as the National Minimum Wage, has been domestically inspired, but a good deal (the Working Time Directive, the treatment of part-time and agency workers, legislation against discrimination on grounds of religion, sexual orientation and age) has come from the European Commission since we abandoned our opt-out and accepted a common EU social agenda in the Treaty of Amsterdam. Analysis suggests that about 40 per cent of recent regulation has its origins with the Commission (Better Regulation Task Force 2002; Ambler et al. 2004).

The distinction is not, however, completely watertight; 'gold plating' of European legislation can occur in response to domestic political pressures. Moreover it has been claimed that the UK enforces regulation more stringently than some other EU members. David Arculus, who chairs the Better Regulation Task Force, has suggested that domestic government guidance often goes beyond the original intention of European legislators and produces what he calls 'regulatory creep'.[1]

Whatever the origin of particular initiatives, UK employers are now faced with an increasingly complex web of obligations. There are over eighty areas of employment rights where breaches of the law can see an employer brought before an employment tribunal. Over 100,000 cases are started each year. The costs of these claims can be substantial

---

1 Press release, 14 January 2004.

Figure 9.1 **Business executive perceptions of labour regulation**
G7 comparison, 1996–2003

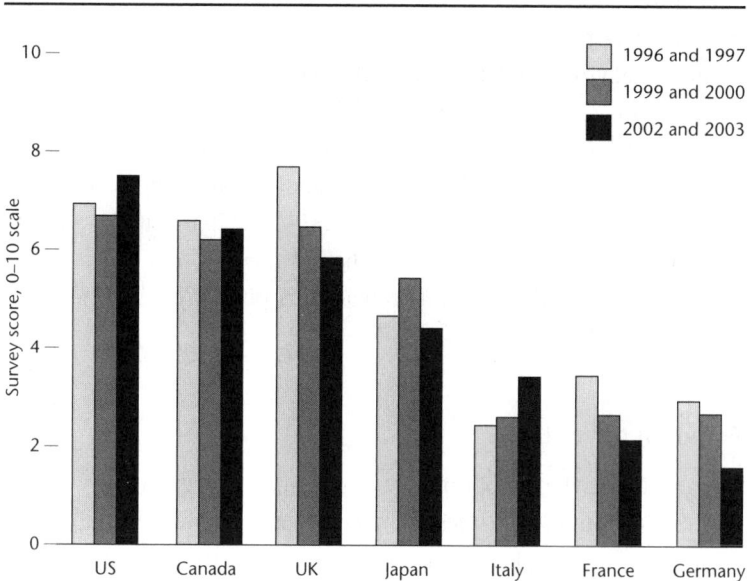

Source: International Institute for Management Development *World Competitiveness Yearbook*

(Shackleton, 2002). So too are the costs associated with avoiding claims. To take one example: the personnel function in firms has grown dramatically in recent years to cope with the expansion of regulation. The membership of the Institute of Personnel Management was 12,000 in 1979, and even as late as 1990 it was only 40,000. Today the grandly renamed Chartered Institute of Personnel and Development has around 120,000 members.

Although the UK is still seen as having a relatively favourable regulatory climate for business, its perceived comparative advantage in the employment area has diminished recently, as Figure 9.1 suggests.[2]

2 High values of the IIMD's index, used by the Department of Trade and Industry as one of its favourite indicators of competitiveness, suggest a favourable climate for business.

So far, however, increased employment regulation does not appear to have produced serious economic damage. This may be because there have been offsetting factors such as a favourable macro-economic environment (following the hand-over of monetary policy to the Bank of England), increased incentives to take employment through the New Deal and the various tax credit schemes for low-paid workers, positive effects on the labour market from increased immigration, and the relative ease with which it is still possible to start small businesses in the UK. Whether these factors will continue to provide a sufficient offset if regulation is pushed further, however, remains debatable.

Freedom of contract?

In considering the significance of labour market regulation, we need to start from first principles. Why are people employed in a market economy? Think of it in terms of the gains from trade: employers see opportunities for a gain – either directly (a family takes on a cleaner or a nanny), or indirectly (a firm employs a worker to help produce an output to be sold at a profit). Correspondingly, employees see a gain as they trade their time for money.

The employment relation, then, like other forms of trade, offers something to both parties. If people are free to form a wide variety of contracts, job opportunities are maximised and so, ultimately, is growth in national income and economic welfare. On this basis we could expect a predisposition amongst economists in favour of freedom of contract, just as we expect some prejudice in favour of unfettered international commerce.

Although there have been economists prepared unreservedly to defend the 'contract at will' (see Epstein, 1992), they have been few and far between. Many economists advocating regulation have invoked the concept of *market failure*, the textbook term which sees the allocative efficiency properties of markets being compromised by deviations from the assumptions of 'perfect' competition.[3] Let us consider some examples.

One apparently plausible case of market failure relates to *information imperfections and asymmetries*. Suppose an employer knows that a production process involves some danger to employees' health, but employees do not.[4] They take jobs that they would not have accepted given fuller knowledge. Wages will be below the level they would otherwise have been (dangerous jobs, other things being equal, carrying a wage premium). Some government intervention may be appropriate, perhaps to enforce information disclosure or regulate employment for minors who cannot yet take full responsibility for their choices.

Another argument points to *positive externalities* from some types of activity, for example, employer-provided training. This tempts firms to take a free ride, and as a consequence training may conceivably be under-provided if left to the market. A case is sometimes made for the mandatory provision of training by firms.[5]

Some economists point to *moral hazard* problems – the temptation to cheat – in private unemployment insurance markets. This can lead to *adverse selection* (i.e., only poor risks will take out such insurance). Insurance providers thus lose money and exit the market: the result is under-provision of private protection against unemployment. A *second-best* solution could involve compulsory, state-organised unemployment insurance.

Then there are *market power* issues, for example, those arising where a dominant employer in a region or sector can act as a *monopsonist* and keep wages and employment below competitive levels.

These arguments, however, are a very slender basis on which to erect today's huge structures of labour market regulation. Many alleged

---

3 There are other arguments for free markets which do not depend on mechanistic models of competition, notably those associated with the Austrian School.

4 Recent developments in information economics, however, suggest that the private provision of information through a variety of mechanisms is far more common than earlier writers believed (Klein, 2002).

5 Though see Shackleton (1992) for counter-arguments.

market failures seem relatively trivial, and have almost certainly diminished over time. For example, the increasing integration of labour markets must have reduced any monopsony powers possessed by employers: increased availability of information via the Internet and other media will surely have dispelled many information problems faced by workers and employers.

Moreover, those asserting the possibility of market failure often do not give equal weight to the danger of *government failure*, where inadequate information and incentive structures can lead to inefficiencies at least as great as those thrown up by private economic activity.

Of course, few politicians and voters work in the economist's allocative efficiency framework. They are more interested in 'fairness', often pursued with scant attention to cost–benefit analysis.[6] From Marx onward, many labour market analysts have alleged that workers are exploited by employers. There is an enduring belief that economic activity is a zero-sum game where profits are at the expense of workers, and where, conversely, governments can force firms to pay for employee benefits redressing market-generated 'unfairness'.[7] This unfairness can often be traced to poor original skill endowments and access to capital which could be tackled with redistribution through the tax and benefit system, but it is often asserted to be the result of employer greed and/or discrimination.

The range of perceived unfairness has extended as the workforce has become more diverse – with gender, race, sexual orientation, religion,

---

6   Although the UK government is now required to submit all new regulations to a 'Regulatory Impact Assessment', this is easily overridden. Published assessments show the recurrent costs of employment legislation introduced in 2002/03 at ten times the current benefits to business. Ministers simply certified that other non-quantified benefits justified the costs (Ambler et al., 2004: 12).

7   It should also be noted that in much of continental Europe, the tradition of Catholic social concern, together with a legal system based on civil law, produced a political consensus favouring detailed regulation of the workplace, generous social welfare provision and consequent high taxation. Notions of 'social partnership' between capital and labour were encouraged, leading in a number of countries to various forms of employee involvement in company decision-making (Botero et al., 2003).

age and disability now seen as generating unacceptable inequalities of outcome. These perceptions, rather than evidence of real market failure, have led to increasing restrictions on the abilities of firms and individuals to form employment contracts.

Regulation itself produces conflicts as measures to reduce one type of inequality exacerbate some other dimension – for example, reductions in the male–female pay gap increase inequality between families, because two-earner families are more common among the better paid than among the lower paid.

We should also remember that regulation can be pursued by interested parties as a way of undermining their rivals' competitiveness. Edward Lazear has described how the US Coal Mine Health and Safety Act, introduced in the 1970s, required the installation of expensive safety equipment. The act was promoted by western strip miners, for whom the costs were relatively low, at the expense of eastern underground mining companies which faced much higher costs from the legislation (Lazear, 1996: 116).

What does regulation do?

Employment regulation has sometimes been described as a form of 'stealth tax', an interesting description on two counts. First, it suggests one reason why regulation has been growing in a period when governments have been under pressure to keep overt taxation down: rather than the taxpayer funding a costly benefit to workers, the employer is obliged to do so instead.

The second point is that, as with indirect taxes (such as VAT), the apparent imposition is on employers, but the true impact lies elsewhere.[8] The cost of introducing mandated benefits – longer holidays, shorter working hours, paternal leave – does not ultimately reduce the

---

8   Although in the short run it damages particular employers, who may even be forced to quit the market.

profits of private business: it is instead passed on to workers in the form of cuts in wages and employment. A mandated benefit simultaneously improves employee working conditions and raises employers' costs. Thus the demand curve for labour shifts downward, leading to less demand at a given wage, and the supply curve of labour shifts downward to the right as more people now seek employment at any given wage rate. Consequently the equilibrium wage falls: if firms are obliged to pay increased non-wage costs, they offer less in wages, other things being equal.[9] Less obviously, equilibrium employment is also likely to fall if the average cost per worker of providing the benefit exceeds the average worker's valuation of that benefit. This is likely to be the case because firms often need to devote resources to ensuring compliance with legislation, as well as providing the actual benefit itself. The provision of parental leave, for example, involves detailed record keeping, formal application procedures and considerable amounts of training to ensure that line managers are fully aware of legislation. So much of the cost of the regulation is not translated into benefits provided to the workers.

There is another, more subtle, reason why the cost of a benefit is likely to be greater than the average worker's valuation of that benefit. In a market economy individuals can usually choose between many employers, some of whom offer different combinations of working conditions and wages. If workers value long holidays, say, more than it costs employers to provide them, some firms will offer such holidays to attract workers who value holidays more highly than income. But a worker who prefers to take shorter holidays and receive a higher income will not value a legally mandated holiday as much as the benefit costs

---

9   Defenders of regulation claim that improvements in working conditions may stimulate workers to higher productivity, offsetting the costs of the mandate and leaving wages unchanged. Many mandates, however, benefit only a small minority of employees (new parents, people with disabilities), whose own enhanced efforts would be unlikely to affect overall productivity.

the employer. Given the existence of this type of worker,[10] employment must fall, other things being equal.

If labour market regulation reduces employment, there are differential impacts on the workforce. Those already in jobs ('insiders') tend to keep them and are better off to the extent that they value the benefit. Some people, however, lose their jobs, and (quantitatively probably more significant) 'outsiders' – the unemployed and labour market entrants – find it difficult to get employment. This differential impact is heightened if employers try to reduce the impact of regulation by employing fewer of those likely to take advantage of a benefit. Thus a mandate giving parental leave tends to discourage employers from taking on workers who are, or seem likely to become, parents.

The impact on the economy as a whole

Evidence suggests that these microeconomic effects[11] can have a marked impact at the aggregate level. The overall extent of labour market regulation in an economy is difficult to quantify, but researchers have attempted to do so by compiling indices that weight various characteristics of a country's employment laws.

Despite differing approaches, there is a fair amount of agreement on the rankings of leading economies: the USA and the UK (even following the changes since 1997) typically come at the lightly regulated end of the spectrum, with Germany and countries in southern Europe at the more regulated end.

One indicator is the World Bank's Employment Law Index. This index, published on the World Bank's website, summarises regulations

---

10 Workers certainly differ in their taste for leisure depending on their circumstances. Blue-collar workers in France have protested against the compulsory 35-hour week, arguing that it prevents them working overtime and simply favours the middle class.

11 There are arguably also less tangible effects on the climate of the workplace as managerial suspicion on the one hand, and a 'victim culture' on the other, can begin to sour relations.

Figure 9.2 **Labour market regulation and employment**

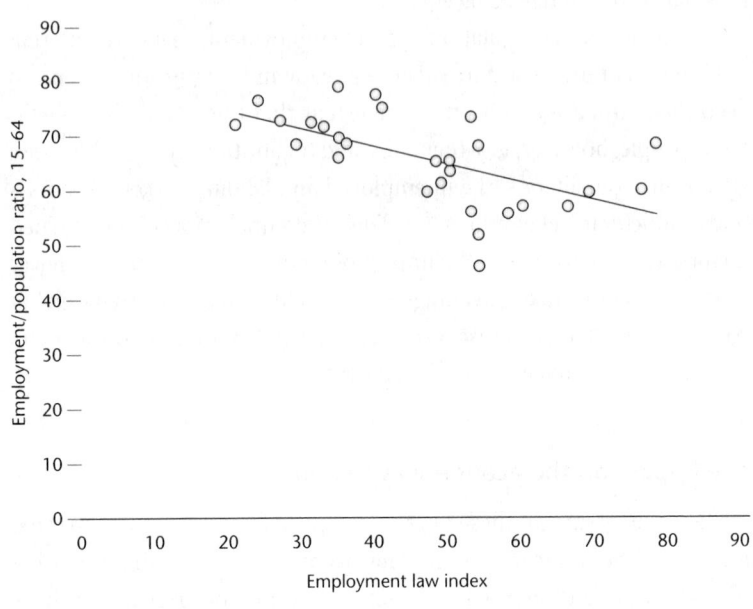

applying to a standardised individual – working time limitations, holiday regulations, minimum wage legislation, protection against dismissal, notice period, severance payments. An overall score of 0–100 is produced.

Figure 9.2 illustrates one impact which regulation may have on a country's labour market. The value of the World Bank Index for 28 major OECD countries is plotted against the percentage of the working-age population in employment. Generally speaking, the higher the index value (meaning the greater the extent of regulation), the lower the employment/population ratio. The suggestion is that tight regulation of employment reduces the availability of jobs.

For example, a study of 85 countries conducted for the US National Bureau of Economic Research, also using the World Bank Index, found heavier regulation of labour markets to be statistically associated with higher unemployment (particularly for young workers), lower labour force participation and a larger unofficial economy (Botero et al., 2003). The latter point is particularly interesting: one important effect of regulation appears to be that of driving activity out of the 'legitimate' economy. This is a particularly telling finding given that, following the recent Morecambe Bay tragedy, there has been a call for further regulation to stamp out the unofficial economy.

Employment regulation in the long term
The political reality

So employment regulation imposes costs, and these costs have been growing over time to such an extent that a large proportion of economists now recognise that a reversal of the trend is desirable.

One problem for the UK, unable since the Treaty of Amsterdam to follow its own policies, is that features of its labour market raise issues that do not arise to the same extent in most other EU countries. For example, temporary agency work – not a concern for much of continental Europe – has played an important role here. So has part-time employment, especially for women. The majority of EU countries are not seriously affected by increased regulation in these areas.

Much of Europe displays high levels of unemployment. While there is growing understanding that excessive regulation is a problem, the lessons are not yet fully absorbed and the current EU position seems contradictory. The Commission's draft Joint Employment Report, published in January 2004, recognises that the EU is failing to meet the intermediate targets of its European Employment Strategy (immodestly intended to make the EU 'the most competitive knowledge-based economy in the world' by 2010). The draft report draws attention to inadequate progress towards liberalising European labour markets. The Social Affairs Commissioner, however, has simultaneously continued to push vigorously for removal of the UK's Working Time Directive opt-out, and there seems no obvious sign that the regulatory spring is drying up.

Apart from these conflicting approaches within the Commission, the structural configuration of the EU's politics means that legislation tends to be one-way traffic, with deregulation very much an uphill struggle. The concept of the *acquis*, by which newcomers to the EU have to accept the whole body of earlier legislation, makes it difficult to reverse the process of regulation. Within countries, the dominance of 'insiders' (institutionalised by the EU's rhetoric of 'social partnership') constitutes a powerful coalition to resist deregulation – as, for example, the German and Italian governments have discovered.

The political status quo can be overcome

There are, however, forces that threaten the protected labour markets of the EU – and indeed of other parts of the developed world – and which may give a spur to deregulation in the longer term. Increasing immigration is one such factor, as it can be argued that tight regulation is likely to be undermined by a growing unofficial economy. Many existing EU member countries are trying to exclude even the new accession country workers from their labour markets, let alone migrants from outside the Union, but in the long run they seem unlikely to succeed given the relative openness of borders and political reluctance to adopt draconian policies towards individual illegal immigrants.

Globalisation more generally, and in particular the outsourcing of services as well as manufacturing, presents another challenge. In the USA (to a lesser extent in Europe), fear of job losses has produced the novel tactic of using the World Trade Organization to insist on 'improved labour standards' as a pre-condition for trade liberalisation. Imposing First World labour market regulation on Third World economies looks like an admirable gesture, but if it undercuts the competitive advantage of poorer economies it is likely to slow their development while raising costs to developed economies. This new form of protectionism has an obvious appeal to organised labour, but trade union power is continuing to diminish as unions find it difficult to attract young members. Business interests, on the other hand, forced by growing international competition to seek cheap labour where they can find it, are unlikely to support such policies indefinitely.

Although we may be stuck with something like the current level of labour market intervention for some time, intellectual fashions and the economic circumstances that shape them can change rapidly. Fifty years ago few people would have foreseen the immense liberalisation and expansion of world trade, the disappearance of huge nationalised industries and the decline of trade union power that we have experienced. Labour market regulation has a long history and is omnipresent today, but its continued expansion cannot be taken for granted.

At the moment it is a taken-for-granted assumption that government should fund and direct young people's education and prepare them for work, provide 'sheltered' routes into work via the New Deal or similar programmes if they have difficulty getting jobs, offer them a minimum wage, allow them to work only limited hours, in surroundings that meet a whole range of arbitrary criteria, require them to pay compulsory charges for their pensions and other benefits, alert them to a range of rights and persuade them to regard themselves as victimised if they do not earn as much as other people or get the jobs they want.

A new radicalism in labour market policy

A radical agenda should recognise that the nature of work is changing and that we need to embrace a much larger role for freedom of contract. As people develop more individual lifestyles, work at home or on a multitude of sites rather than in the employer's head office, set up their own businesses or adopt a portfolio of different jobs, make their own pension and financial arrangements, and so on, a constituency for change may begin to emerge as people seek greater variability in work arrangements. And as ambitions rise in our increasingly educated and open societies, we may hope that people will increasingly recognise that their own actions, rather than those of government, will determine where their future lies.

One problem is that opposition to government regulation to improve the employment conditions of workers is often confused with opposition to improving employment conditions. Nobody wants to be seen to be advocating sending little boys up chimneys again. We all want better lifestyles, and countries grow ever richer we naturally seek better jobs and more fulfilling employment, and increased flexibility. And most of us want others to share in our good fortune.

We should not forget that there is a business case for being a 'good' employer. Such employers gain staff loyalty, enjoy reduced labour turnover and absenteeism, and benefit from higher productivity. Many of our leading companies build their competitive advantage on this insight.

It does not, however, follow that there is an unequivocal gain if all employers are forced to meet the standards of the best. For one thing, we have noted that all employees are not seeking the same package of benefits, and a mandatory set of conditions reduces choice. Second, firms that are forced to come up to the employment standards of the leaders will fail to secure first-mover advantage and will face increased costs without accompanying benefits.

Regulation reduces the ways in which firms can compete. Excessive regulation reduces the incentives to innovation, entrenches the market dominance of existing firms, and ultimately slows the economic growth on which our prosperity depends. This is a hard idea to get over to the general public, which concentrates on the visible benefits to a sector of the workforce, while not being fully aware of the less overt costs – but it is the challenge for liberal economists.

It is difficult now to conceive of a developed economy totally free of employment legislation, and I am not going to attempt it. But it is surely possible to imagine a series of steps by which the UK labour market could be liberalised and could move towards greater freedom of contract. For one thing, a more radical approach to 'subsidiarity' within the EU could involve a redefinition of the boundaries of domestic and European legislative competence. A recognition of the benefits from regulatory competition, rather than a centralisation of regulatory power within the EU, could enable countries with poor employment records to experiment with more liberal regimes. If devolution of political power to the European regions also permitted some relaxation of employment regulation, we could imagine some interesting experimentation going on. Could Scotland, in time, be as attractive a country for employment as Ireland is for business location?

Some regions might relax rules for small and emerging enterprises, perhaps with a gradual phasing in of regulations as a firm matured. Others might experiment with different rules on working hours to meet the needs of particular types of production. Those with higher youth unemployment might raise the age at which minimum wages, employment protection or social security imposts were imposed. Even bolder experiments, such as 'free employment zones', modelled on tax-free ports, might permit some controlled areas to dispense with large swathes of regulation. Or individuals might be allowed to 'sell off' benefit entitlements to employers: for example, allowing them to commute their rights to employment protection for a lump-sum payment up front.

Defenders of the status quo argue that such regulatory competition would lead to a race to the bottom, with each country forced to the lowest possible level of regulation. This, however, seems unlikely: it hasn't happened in the analogous case of taxation. Barriers of distance and language, social and cultural ties limit the degree to which employees even in a globalised economy can be perfect substitutes. Different employees have different preferences for particular contractual terms and levels of employment security in different circumstances. Contractual and regulatory variety is much more likely than either uniformly high degrees of protection or uniformly low degrees of protection and non-pecuniary benefits.

Another method by which liberalisation might be encouraged is through ruthless insistence that all proposed regulatory measures, particularly those coming from the European Commission, be considered against alternative policies directly funded by the taxpayer. Instead of employers in effect funding mandated benefits, let the taxpayer pay the full price for these benefits – including dislocation and compliance costs. There could be a fixed proportion of GDP that can be allocated to the finance of such mandates, in the same way as there is currently a fixed tax rate which the EU can levy for its own expenditure.

A movement towards greater liberalisation also creates a need to educate the employees of the future so that they have a greater awareness of their own individual potentialities and are encouraged to acquire the skills and self-confidence that will enable them to exploit these potentialities to the full.

We need to reiterate that historically increases in employees' pay and improvements in other conditions of service have not come through government intervention, but as a result of economic growth resulting from entrepreneurial innovation and private investment by firms and individuals. Further improvements in working conditions and the continued generation of new job opportunities are more likely to continue if governments create a climate where such innovation and investment can occur. Such a climate surely places greater emphasis on allowing employers to reach voluntary agreements with their employees – and less on telling them exactly how to do so.

References

Addison, J. T. and W. S. Siebert (1993), *Social Engineering in the European Community: The Social Charter, Maastricht and Beyond*, London: Institute of Economic Affairs

Addison, J. T. and W. S. Siebert (1999) *Regulating European Labour Markets: More Costs than Benefits?*, Hobart Paper 138, London: Institute of Economic Affairs

Ambler, T., F. Chittenden and M. Obodovski (2004), *Are Regulators Raising Their Game? UK Regulatory Impact Assessments in 2002/3*, British Chambers of Commerce

Better Regulation Task Force (2002), *Employment Regulation: Striking a Balance*, London: Cabinet Office

Botero, J., S. Djankov, R. La Porta, F. Lopez-de-Silanes and A. Shliefer (2003), *The Regulation of Labor*, National Bureau of Economic Research Working Paper 9756

Epstein, R. A. (1992), *Forbidden Grounds: The Case against Employment Discrimination Laws*, Cambridge, MA: Harvard University Press

Klein, D. B. (2002), 'The Demand For and Supply of Assurance', in T. Cowen and E. Crampton (eds), *Market Failure or Success*, Cheltenham: Edward Elgar

Lazear, E. P. (1996), *Personnel Economics*, Cambridge, MA: MIT Press

Shackleton, J. R. (1992), *Training Too Much? A Sceptical Look at the Economics of Skill Provision in the UK*, Hobart Paper 118, London: Institute of Economic Affairs

Shackleton, J. R. (2002), *Employment Tribunals: Their Growth and the Case for Radical Reform*, Hobart Paper 145, London: Institute of Economic Affairs

10 FREE TRADE: THE NEXT 50 YEARS
Razeen Sally

It tells them of freedom, and how freedom was won, and what freedom has done for them, and it points the way to other paths of freedom which yet lie open before them.

John Bright (on the repeal of the Corn Laws)

To expect, indeed, that the freedom of trade should ever be entirely restored ... is as absurd as to expect that an Oceana or Utopia should ever be established ... Not only the prejudices of the publick, but what is much more unconquerable, the private interests of many individuals, irresistibly oppose it.

Adam Smith, Wealth of Nations

In the last half-century, expanding international trade and capital flows have progressively reintegrated the world economy in ever more complex ways. But protectionism lurks everywhere, always assuming new and potent forms. In the spirit of John Bright, one can fight for the freedom of trade in the next half-century; but, echoing Adam Smith, it would be utopian to expect outright victory. Protectionism will still be around in 2055, and the battle will continue to rage.

My task is to take stock of free trade today, in theory and in practice, and then to look ahead. What are the emerging facts on the ground in terms of global political and economic trends? And what of the case for free trade in the next 50 years?

Taking stock: the case for free trade, past and present

Meta-economic arguments for free trade date back at least two millennia.

An intellectual tradition from early Christian thought to Richard Cobden, Woodrow Wilson and Cordell Hull holds that open and flourishing international commerce brings about better understanding between peoples and buttresses peaceful, ever closer international relations.

The *economic* case for free trade emerged one and a half millennia later. Adam Smith's genius was to draw on pre-existing traditions of moral philosophy and economics to lay out a system of interrelating economic phenomena animated by laissez-faire, or what he called 'natural liberty'. This he extended to international trade.

Smith's system has been refined down the past two centuries. An international division of labour according to comparative advantage allocates resources more efficiently, resulting in the greater wealth of nations. It integrates hitherto separated national economies into a worldwide *co-operative* system that caters for reciprocal wants. There are all-round material gains, for rich and poor countries alike.

These are the short-term (or static) gains from trade. That is but the necessary preface to capital accumulation, economies of scale and other long-run (or dynamic) gains, such as the transfer of technology and skills, and the competitive spur that comes from exposure to world-class standards of practice. This feeds into productivity gains, increases in real incomes and economic growth. Indeed, it was the dynamic gains from trade which Smith and his contemporary David Hume emphasised. They strongly linked free trade (broadly defined to include cross-border flows of capital and people) to domestic institutions and growth, all on the canvas of the long-run progress of commercial society.

Adam Smith fortified his presumption in favour of free trade with an explicit political argument. Protectionism is driven by 'the clamorous importunity of partial interests' who capture government and prevent it from having 'an extensive view of the general good'. Free trade, in contrast, tilts the balance away from rent-seeking producer interests and towards the mass of consumers. It is part of a wider constitutional package to keep government limited, transparent and clean, enabling it to concentrate better on the public good.

As important to Smith and Hume was the *moral* case for free trade, centred on individual freedom. Individual choice is the engine of free trade, and of progressive commercial society more generally. It sparks what Hume called a 'spirit of industry'; it results in much better life chances, not just for the select few but for individuals in the broad mass of society who are able to lead more varied and interesting lives.

To sum up: free trade is of course associated with standard economic efficiency arguments. But the classical liberal case for free trade is more rounded, taking in the moral imperative of individual freedom and linking it to prosperity. Finally, free trade contributes to, though it does not guarantee, peaceful international relations. Freedom, prosperity, security: this trinity lies at the heart of the case for free trade.

Taking stock: free trade in practice

The historical record shows that countries that are more open to the world economy grow faster than those that remain closed. Post-1945, the gradual liberalisation of trade and capital flows in the OECD spurred western European reconstruction, recovery and catch-up growth. The outward orientation of Japan and other East Asian countries played an important role in their catch-up growth. The massive liberalisation of foreign trade and inward investment in China, in tandem with internal liberalisation, has contributed to spectacular and sustained growth since the 1980s.

Developing and transitional countries with progressively more liberal trade policies have growing ratios of trade and inward investment to national income, with rising shares of manufactures in total exports, and with sustained increases in real incomes per head. These are mostly middle-income countries bunched in East Asia, Latin America and eastern Europe, but now include low-income but fast-growing China and India. The bad news is that this leaves about 2 billion people in 75-plus countries with stagnating or declining aggregate growth. These are low-income and least-developed countries that have liberalised less, though they suffer too from other intractable problems such as poor climate and geography, rampant disease, civil war and chronically corrupt, predatory governments.

External liberalisation, it must be emphasised, is not a panacea. Questions as to how it is sequenced with other economic and political reforms, and whether it should proceed fast or slowly, will find different answers in different countries at different times. Furthermore, trade liberalisation on its own may not deliver much. But *in interaction with* improvements in domestic institutions there are abundant, long-term gains from trade liberalisation. External opening creates the spontaneous stimulus for institutional upgrading to better exploit trade and investment opportunities, for example, through better currency and banking practices, and the development of ports and inland communications. Reciprocally, better enforcement of property rights and contracts, cleaner, more efficient public administration, and more investment in infrastructure maximise the gains for importers, exporters and domestic and foreign investors. Openness, therefore, is a *handmaiden* of growth, not a quick fix.

What of the international political and policy framework to support a freer trading system? Right through the nineteenth century to 1914, *national governance*, in the context of a decentralised system of nation-states, coexisted with increasing international economic integration (what we now call globalisation). Has the globalisation-and-governance equation changed that much a hundred years on? Arguably it has not. It is national governments, not international organisations, multinational enterprises or NGOs, which fulfil the core functions of law and public policy. Not least, it is they who decide whether trade policies are more or less liberal.

This is not to deny the importance of international cooperation where national-level action is insufficient. Unfortunately, the record of most post-war international economic institutions has been one of ad hoc bureaucratic intervention in markets, often exacerbating misguided government intervention at home. The 'aid business' is a case in point. The General Agreement on Tariffs and Trade (GATT) was a notable exception: its non-discriminatory rules and reciprocal negotiations furthered the liberalisation of trade from the late 1940s onwards.

Looking ahead: world political-economic trends

What makes the crucial difference to globalisation today, and probably for the next half-century, is the dramatic opening of, first, China and then India. They are the world's second- and fourth-largest economies respectively (at purchasing power parity), and account for 40 per cent of humanity. With still-low levels of per capita income, they have the potential for stellar catch-up growth rates for decades ahead. Their integration into the world economy, still in its early stages, promises to be more momentous than that of Japan and the East Asian tigers, and perhaps on a par with the rise of the USA as a global economic power in the late nineteenth century.

These trends show that the classical argument for free trade is as relevant as ever. Trade and related economic reforms enable China and India to better exploit their comparative advantages in a more special-ised international division of labour. Market-based reforms also provide the stimulus for inward investment, the transfer of technology and skills, and a more competitive, entrepreneurial business environment. These replenishing gains boost growth, which in turn leads to poverty reduc-tion. China's breathtaking reforms have already delivered massive gains. India lags behind, but with glimpses of take-off on the back of acceler-ating reforms.

The rest of the world gains too. Consumers elsewhere can buy cheaper and more varied products. Developed-country firms cater to expanding Chinese and Indian demand for capital- and skill-intensive goods and services. By 'offshoring' manufacturing jobs to China and services jobs to India in low-value activities, they can scale up, improve productivity, and generate better-skilled, higher-paying jobs at home. Exporters in other developing countries also discover large new markets for oil and other commodities (witness China's voracious appetite for such imports).

Two other emerging global economic trends will likely move centre stage in years and decades to come: 1) the cross-border movement of labour; 2) South–South trade.

First, the freedom of people to move hither and yon in search of work was part of nineteenth-century free trade in practice. This was reversed in the twentieth century. Now, the relaxation of pervasive restrictions on cross-border labour movement promises huge gains for developing and developed countries. Opening borders to people can only be achieved gradually and piecemeal. It demands political patience and resourcefulness. Nevertheless, it should be at the heart of a twenty-first-century free trade agenda.

Second, inter-developing country trade – already 40 per cent of their overall trade – is throttled by the high barriers developing countries erect against each other. Significant developing-country liberalisation would not only improve their own productivity; it would also allow low-income and least-developed countries to better exploit their comparative advantages by exporting to the fast-growing markets of middle-income countries.

These trends, if not discouraged, will increase the wealth of nations. They will widen the horizons of individual freedom, especially for hundreds of millions in the developing world who have been cruelly deprived of it. Not least, commercial bonds across the North–South divide will make international relations more stable and secure. But none of this is pre-programmed – as we know from the eternal lesson of summer 1914. It depends crucially on the right political decisions, nationally and internationally.

Behind every free trade opportunity lurks protectionist danger. Four long-term threats come to mind.

First, organised interests benefiting from protectionism will continue to lobby against liberalisation, in both developed and developing countries. Second, the ideological opposition to free trade has changed form. It now unites anti-globalisation NGOs with more mainstream critics of globalisation who call for 'global governance' to redress global inequities. Concerted global action to provide aid, enforce 'corporate social responsibility' and harmonise labour, environmental and other standards seems to have a higher priority than market-based reforms in the developing world.

It is the alliance, witting or unwitting, between old-style rent-seeking interests and new-style ideological forces which will present a formidable political threat to free trade in decades to come.

Third, most developing countries are mired in wretched poverty, disease, crime and murderous internal strife. States are failing miserably or have collapsed. The old solutions of aid and policy driven by international organisations have not worked. But these countries are still ruled by venal and thuggish elites, and lack the history and institutions to sustain market-based reforms 'from below'. The dilemma is real; problems are likely to get worse; and they will spill over to luckier parts of the world in the form of refugees, illegal migrants and terrorism.

Fourth, the 'low politics' of trade and related economic policies cannot be divorced from the 'high politics' of international security (or the lack of it). There are new global security flashpoints post-cold war and post-11 September, chiefly Islamic fundamentalism and the international terror networks fanning out from the oil-rich Middle East. This poses an ever greater threat to the free movement of people, goods and services across land, sea and sky.

Looking ahead: making the case for free trade in the next 50 years

The core political and economic case for free trade, in the service of freedom, prosperity and security, will have equal force 50 years hence.

The point is to update it to keep up with ever changing realities. How must it adapt?

First, the post-1945 case for free trade has become too narrow and mechanical. Free trade should burst these chains and return to its classical liberal foundations in Smith and Hume.

The Bretton Woods and GATT settlements combined a *partial* restoration of nineteenth-century free trade with expanding government intervention at home. Post-war trade theory reflected such 'mixed-systems thinking' by decoupling free trade from laissez-faire. In addition, 'liberalism from above' has prevailed: trade liberalisation has relied on international organisations and inter-governmental negotiations. Both 'mixed-systems thinking' and 'liberalism from above' were politically expedient after World War II; but, over time, they have entrenched misguided conventional wisdoms. The first is that big-government infringements of private property rights at home will not flood across borders and overly damage international commerce. The second is that international institutions deliver trade liberalisation 'from outside', and only through 'concessions' to foreigners in a game of haggling.

'Mixed-systems thinking' forgets that free trade is part and parcel of free markets; it is but an element of a constitutional whole that includes limited government and laissez-faire at home. Of course, there can be no complete return to a mid-Victorian British social contract, especially in conditions of modern democratic politics. But free trade should be *recoupled* to (qualified, not unbounded) laissez-faire. It stands in contradiction to what Michael Oakeshott calls an 'enterprise association' in which government is an interfering 'estate manager', catering to a superabundance of rent-seeking interests. Rather it must fold back into a 'civic association' in which smallish (but not minimalist) government provides essential public goods.

Furthermore, twenty-first-century free trade should rely less on twentieth-century 'liberalism from above' and more on nineteenth-century 'liberalism from below'. With the latter method, the liberalisation impulse comes from national governments acting unilaterally (or autonomously), and spreads internationally by example (or competitive emulation). Unilateral free trade makes economic sense, since welfare gains come quicker from unconditional home import liberalisation than they do from protracted international negotiations. It makes political sense too. Governments have the flexibility to initiate policies and emulate better practice abroad in experimental, trial-and-error fashion, tailored to specific local conditions. The World Trade Organization (WTO) and bilateral/regional trade agreements can be helpful auxiliaries in advancing a liberalisation agenda, but they are poor substitutes for what David Landes calls 'initiation from below and diffusion by example'. Their importance should not be exaggerated.

Second, Western governments and intellectuals, on the right and the left, seem to prioritise democratisation in the Third World, partly in the belief that it will promote economic reforms. The evidence is mixed at best. In China and several other East Asian countries, market-based reforms, including trade and investment liberalisation, have occurred under authoritarian governments. In much of the rest of the developing world, *illiberal* democratisation has reinforced cartel-promoting and protectionist economic policies, and it has stunted the build-up of market-supporting institutions. Economic and related institutional reforms (such as internal and external liberalisation, and the enforcement of private property rights and contracts) should have top priority in China, Russia, Iraq, Afghanistan and elsewhere. This is what the West – particularly the USA – should be encouraging. Political democracy should be allowed to emerge gradually and organically in the wake of economic growth and institutional development, as it has done in South Korea and Taiwan.

Third, free trade must work with the grain of wider geo-political realities. There have been marked shifts in international politics since the end of the cold war, and more recently after 11 September. No serious challenge exists to US leadership abroad; Europe and Japan are internally sclerotic and externally pusillanimous; other powers are on the rise, notably China, India and Brazil; the transatlantic alliance is no longer the fulcrum of international relations; and politics and economics are moving inexorably in an Asia-Pacific direction, from the Indian Ocean to Tierra del Fuego.

The one constant in this shifting political template is US leadership. For the foreseeable future, the USA will remain the indispensable anchor for global security, prosperity and freedom – far more important than any international organisation or international treaty. It is vital that it leads from the front: in securing the global *pax* against systemic security threats; in helping to rescue and reconstruct failed states; in maintaining open and stable international financial markets; and, not least, in breaking down barriers to trade, investment and the movement of workers across the world. Above all, the USA must lead by example, setting the standard for liberal economic policies worldwide by what it does at home. This includes untying existing knots of domestic protectionism.

There will be times when the USA will have to resort to unilateral 'liberal imperialism' when international institutions dither and fail. Otherwise 'liberal internationalism' – the multilateral cooperation envisaged by Woodrow Wilson and Cordell Hull – should prevail. The GATT/WTO has been its foremost and most successful expression on the economic front. Robust US leadership is sine qua non to the future relevance and workability of a presently crippled WTO. The USA will need like-minded coalitions inside the WTO and outside it, however. In the future they will be found less across the Atlantic and more in Asia-Pacific, *especially* China. Not only must the USA lead by example at home: it must also display the enlightened sensibility to construct and maintain genuinely two-way 'coalitions of the willing' abroad. Free trade's future depends on it.

Conclusion

The power of ideas should not be underestimated. John Stuart Mill did say that 'a good cause seldom triumphs unless someone's interest is bound up with it'; but he also remarked that it is 'the word in season, which, at a critical moment, does much to decide the result'. It falls to free trade's friends to spread their word *in season with* global political currents, anti-protectionist interests (such as exporters, downstream users of imported inputs, multinational firms with global production networks) and (often unanticipated) events.

Historically, free trade has needed its commanding public champions. Cobden, Bright and Gladstone filled that role in Victorian Britain, as did Cordell Hull and Ludwig Erhard in the last century. There are precious few around today.

11 COMPETITION IN LAND USE PLANNING: AN AGENDA FOR THE TWENTY-FIRST CENTURY

Mark Pennington

Introduction

In *The Fatal Conceit*, F. A. Hayek argued that a vital challenge for the future of the market order was the development of more complex structures of property rights to cultivate market processes in areas such as environmental protection, where they had not previously been applied (Hayek, 1988). Nowhere is the need for an answer to Hayek's challenge more pressing than in the British system of land use planning, where evolutionary forces have been stultified since the nationalisation of developments rights in 1947. In a series of publications (Pennington, 1999, 2000, 2002), I have set out a detailed critique of the UK system of land use planning, which builds on Hayekian, public choice and Coasian ideas. In this short contribution to the volume published to mark the 50th anniversary of the Institute of Economic Affairs I extend these ideas by drawing on a variety of historical and contemporary evidence to outline a vision for a 'liberal utopia' in land use.

The case for markets in land use planning

One of Hayek's most profound insights was that competition should be seen as a discovery process that facilitates evolutionary learning (Hayek, 1948, 1978). A competitive market system is able to generate and test a greater number of production and consumption ideas than could ever be the case under a planned economy, *irrespective* of whether it is democratic or totalitarian in nature. Market processes allow contradictory ideas widely dispersed across individuals and firms to be simultaneously tested against one another without the need for majority approval. The most that the political process can do, by contrast, is to conduct consecutive experiments where there is only one or a very few sets of options being tried out at any time. Similarly, the most that politicians and interest groups that do not form part of the majority can do is to offer verbal critiques of current policy platforms. What they cannot do, however, is to actively supply alternative packages of goods. The range of plans that may be tested, therefore, and hence the scope for evolutionary learning, will necessarily be less than in a context of private exchange (see, for example, Wholgemuth, 1995, 1999).

In recognising the power of the market economy as a discovery procedure, it is crucial to recognise that the competition of which Hayek speaks refers not simply to competition between different goods and services, or even to competition between individuals and firms. On the contrary, in Hayek's view competition is a process that takes place (if it is allowed to do so) at multiple levels. It may include competition between different organisational forms (to discover at what point economies of scale are outweighed by the costs of centralisation, for example) and between different sets of rules for ordering social behaviour (to discover what sort of behaviour and manners promote harmonious coexistence, for example).

Consider the case of shopping malls. The proprietors of malls such as Bluewater in Kent or the Trafford Centre in Manchester do not allow a 'free for all' on their premises, but define a set of rules that govern the behaviour of retailers and shoppers alike, in order to benefit all who use the mall. Competition in such a context occurs on at least two different levels. On the one hand, the various retailers compete for customers *within* the boundaries of the mall. On the other hand, the proprietors of the mall compete for retailers and for consumers to patronise *their* mall rather than those owned by competitors. In the latter instance, it is the rules of conduct (such as regulations on shop frontages, smoking, animals and skateboarding) supplied by the proprietor, and the environmental characteristics of the mall (such as access to car parking, landscaping and architectural design), which are subject to competition from alternative proprietors who offer different arrangements.

The case for markets in land use control, therefore, is manifestly not based on the anarchic 'free for all' that critics of proposals for a more liberal planning regime frequently assert. Rather, it is based on an argument for competition between different types of control, or, to put the argument differently, for a 'market in regulation'. It is in precisely this context that the need for more complex structures of property rights to internalise environmental externalities and to subject these to a competitive test comes to the fore. In the case of urban land use, in many instances there is a need for institutions that can consciously plan the pattern of land development within a particular area in order to internalise potential third-party effects. What is at issue, however, is the existence of a mechanism that can subject such 'planning' to competition and a process that generates profit signals encouraging the spread of best practice and losses, which indicate poor practice, in serving people's preferences.

In one of his few published statements on land use planning, Hayek (1960: 351–2) put the issue very well:

> Most of what is valid in the argument for town planning is in effect
> an argument for making the planning unit for certain purposes
> larger than the size of individually owned property. Some of the
> aims of planning could be achieved by a division of the content
> of property rights in such a way that certain decisions could rest
> with the holder of the superior right … Estate development in
> which the developer retains some permanent control over the
> use of individual plots provides at least one such alternative to
> the exercise of control by political authority. There is also the
> advantage that the larger planning unit will be one of many
> and that it will be constrained in its powers by the necessity of
> competing with other similar units.

Supporters of the British land use planning system may argue that such processes are replicated by the variety of planning policies offered by different local governments. Government planning agencies, however, are *not* subject to competitive entry from rival organisational forms and are predicated on the suspension of competitive forces *from below*. It is, for example, far from clear that decisions over the location and design of new housing developments should be made by a county council, a district council, a parish council or even at the level of an individual street or neighbourhood. Moreover, in the final analysis the policies adopted by local government in Britain are subject to detailed approval at the national level by the Office of the Deputy Prime Minister, which is responsible for the planning system as a whole. District and county planning offices operate as little more than branch plants of one giant nationalised 'firm', which dwarfs *any* private corporation in terms of the power it wields over property owners and is entirely immune from competitive forces.

In order for a market in land use regulation to emerge, individuals and organisations must have the liberty to bundle and de-bundle different structures of property rights at their own risk. But for such a process to occur, development rights must reside with private agents and not with the state. Under private ownership, actors would have the freedom to experiment with different combinations of rights, divided between leaseholders and freeholders, for example, and with competition between organisational forms determining the most appropriate tier of decision-making to internalise externalities. Some freeholders may choose to provide services such as schools and leisure facilities directly as part of the package of goods they charge to leaseholders, in addition to land use and environmental controls. The bundling together of many such services and their delivery by large municipal governments is, however, largely reflective of the absence of competitive forces under the existing system. It seems more likely, therefore, that under a private system of planning, land management organisations would focus their activity on environmental controls and basic infrastructure provision such as roads. This would involve de-bundling many services currently supplied by local government with residents purchasing schooling and other goods outside the community concerned, or, alternatively, purchasing such goods directly from competing suppliers that set up in their own community subject to the controls laid down by the relevant freeholder.

Private land use planning: past, present and future

Historically, there is good evidence that private contractual arrangements based on the estate development model are able to internalise a wide range of external effects. Contractual approaches facilitate the creation of markets in amenity values as individuals choose between competing packages offering different bundles of contractual restrictions and their associated externalities. In the case of restrictive covenants, for example, developers specify in contracts the activities to be permitted with respect to a particular set of properties for sale. These terms are enforced by the developers, who retain title to the superior freehold rights or who hand over these rights to a home owners' association/board of residents.

Davies (2002) has shown that a large part of the urban infrastructure developed during and after the Industrial Revolution was the product of private planning and was responsible for what are now some of the most sought-after residential areas. Covenants and estate development provided for a wide range of 'public goods', such as street lighting, roads and sewerage facilities, as well as aesthetic controls, and successfully housed the vast majority of the middle and working classes in affordable accommodation.

According to Davies, a sophisticated market in property rights and amenity values was emerging prior to the advent of government land use planning, with a range of different amenities and pricing structures in competition with one another. These ranged from luxury resort developments such as Bath, Cheltenham, Eastbourne and Southport, with highly prescriptive aesthetic controls, to more basic environmental standards limiting only the most noxious land uses, as was the case in cities such as

Sheffield and Birmingham. Such devices were common across a variety of income brackets, with the unsanitary developments that are the stuff of Dickensian imagery the exception and not the rule. Even in the latter case, slum housing was gradually being eradicated by the general rise in wealth and could have been dealt with via policies aimed directly at alleviating poverty rather than the adoption of government land use planning. This is not to suggest that laissez-faire arrangements could not have been improved by judicious government action, such as appropriate refinements in property law, for example. What it does suggest, however, is that government action in the twentieth century would have been better had it worked with the grain of emerging market solutions, rather than directly thwarting them, as happened with the nationalisation of development rights in 1947.

More recently, the growth of innovations such as home owners' associations, condominium developments and private communities outside the UK illustrates the potential of market processes to evolve solutions to a variety of land use problems. In the USA, for example, the most recent data suggests that there are approaching a quarter of a million private contractual associations involving almost 50 million people deploying devices such as restrictive covenants (Nelson, 2002). These range from relatively small-scale associations of property owners working at the level of an individual neighbourhood or street to much larger developments where entire towns such as Reston, Virginia (population 50,000), have been developed on the basis of private contractual planning. Still more significant, however, is evidence from nominally communist China. According to Webster and Lai (2003: 62), in the city of Wuhan there are now two private neighbourhoods, built and managed by entrepreneurial firms that between them are investing in infrastructure to accommodate 500,000 residents. In total, 35 per cent of the municipality's 5 million inhabitants live in privately managed residential clubs.

The division of property rights between freeholders and leaseholders may raise the ire of those who view such arrangements as a quasi-feudal throwback where leaseholders are subject to the control of large estates. Fears that private planning would mark a return to the inequities of the eighteenth and nineteenth centuries, however, fail to recognise that many such inequities were due to the historical accident that saw the evolution of 'capitalism' in the UK take place in the context of a landed aristocracy. Far from involving feudal arrangements, a contemporary version of the estate development model would most likely be based on ownership of freehold rights by specialist land management companies funded from the capital market via institutional investors such as pension funds. These arrangements would subject freeholders to a vigorous process in which competing owners would offer alternative bundles of services and contractual restrictions in an attempt to attract residents, just as the proprietors of shopping malls are keen to offer environments that will attract both retailers and customers to their premises. Private planning would be noticeably *less* 'feudal' than the current British planning system, where property owners have virtually no rights other than to go on using their property for existing purposes and where even local authorities are subordinated to central government controls. Branded development communities such as those offered by Disney in the United States would probably form an important segment of such a market.[1] For those with 'cultural sensitivities' who are offended by such a notion, there is no reason why an equivalent of 'Duchy Originals' might not be an important competitor in the market for private planning,[2] which might in turn face competition from brands offering more 'modernist' conceptions of communal living.

Objections to this liberal vision of the future are most likely to arise from those with communitarian and egalitarian sensibilities. In the former instance it is frequently suggested that proposals to privatise

---

1   The Disney Corporation has built a number of privately planned residential communities in the USA, sometimes centred on a 'themed' concept. Probably the most famous of these is Celebration in Florida.

2   Prince Charles has already made forays into this market, most notably with his 'new community' at Poundbury.

planning functions and other local services such as street cleaning and security are incompatible with 'community values'. According to this view, only an active interventionist democracy can protect society from the degraded 'public sphere' that markets are alleged to bring in their wake (see, for example, Gray, 1993). Closely related to these claims are those of egalitarians who maintain that the privatisation of community planning would result in a deeply segregated society, where the rich escape to private enclaves with the poor left behind in degraded environments, predominantly in the inner cities. The arguments here have been manifested most clearly in the almost hysterical reaction to the emergence of 'gated communities', especially in the USA (see, for example, McKenzie, 1994).

Notwithstanding the frequency with which these arguments are heard, it is almost certain that they are misguided. With regard to the communitarian position, far from resulting in the decline of communal values and civic functions, private home owners' associations, condominiums and private communities in the USA have sprung up to rescue the 'public sphere' from the chronic deficiencies of the public sector. 'Community-enhancing' functions such as ensuring clean and safe streets, abysmally neglected by the political process, are performed by private contractual associations representing a market response to a government failure. There is no reason why, given the privatisation of development rights, similar forms of private community governance should not emerge widely in the UK. The great virtue of such market solutions is that they allow a variety of remedies compatible with a view of a free society not as one monolithic 'community' but as a 'community of communities' containing a diversity of cultural preferences and desired modes of living (Boaz, 2000; Kukathas, 2003).

Turning to the egalitarian objection, the principal reason why some inner cities have turned into ghettos, whether in terms of schools or the quality of residential environments, is not that the middle classes are able to escape bad services and leave the poor behind. On the contrary, it is because government agencies have precious few incentives to respond to such 'exit' decisions because they are *not* private, profit-making entities. If a local authority loses revenue because people and businesses leave, then it has few incentives to improve services and the quality of the environment for those left behind or to attract people and investment back. Indeed, more often than not 'failing local authorities' are likely to become eligible for additional subsidies available from central government. If a private firm loses customers to its rivals, by contrast, then it must improve services in an attempt to regain them, or face the threat of losses, bankruptcy or takeover. It is for this reason that the quality of service and the range of products provided by, for example, private supermarkets continue to rise steadily across *all* income brackets. There are, of course, Harvey Nichols-quality outlets that cater only to the well heeled, but the vast bulk of the supermarket sector caters to a broad range of income groups *within* the *same* stores. Tesco, Sainsbury, Wm Morrison, Asda, Marks & Spencer and the like aim to establish the widest possible market for their wares and do not segregate the shopping population into rich and poor ghettos.

In terms of a private system of land use and community planning one would expect to witness the same processes operating to improve environmental standards across the board. There will always be a market for 'deluxe' living in gated enclaves or equivalents, but a fully private system of land use control would also include mass-market developers catering to a broad range of incomes, as do private supermarkets. That such processes do not operate as effectively as they might in contemporary housing markets is largely a product of the fact that failing local governments cannot be driven out of business. Suburban private communities in the USA have had marked success in reducing crime, and given that lower crime rates are one of the most significant improvements in quality of life that urban residents seek, ways should be sought to establish private forms of community management in the poorest urban areas. A pre-condition of such a move would be the privatisation of development rights. In so far as there are residual concerns about income inequality, these would be better addressed via the tax system.

They do not, however, constitute an effective argument for government land use planning.

Conclusion: a liberal utopia

In a previous paper published by the IEA, I set out some practical proposals by which politically feasible steps towards the establishment of private land use planning in the UK might be made (Pennington, 2002). My purpose here, however, has not been to address political practicalities, but to set out a vision for the future of land use control that can act as an antidote to the belief that only a system of monopoly government planning can deliver the improvement in living environments that so many people desire. This vision of a liberal utopia could not be more different to the failed socialist utopia underlying the 1947 Town and Country Planning Act. At the heart of that philosophy was a view that the supposedly unique wisdom of government officials should be trusted to plan the lives of the people. By contrast, the liberal philosophy of planning seeks to create the conditions where evolutionary forces of trial-and-error competition allow voluntary communities the greatest possible scope to plan for themselves.

References

Boaz, D. (2000), 'The Benefits of Private Regulation', in C. Robinson and J. Blundell (eds), *Regulation without the State*, Readings 52, London: Institute of Economic Affairs

Davies, S. (2002), 'Laissez Faire Urban Planning', in D. Beito, P. Gordon and A. Tabarrok (eds), *The Voluntary City*, Ann Arbor: University of Michigan Press/Independent Institute

Gray, J. (1993), *Beyond the New Right: Markets, Government and the Common Environment*, London: Routledge

Hayek, F. A. (1948), 'The Meaning of Competition', in *Individualism and Economic Order*, Chicago, IL: Chicago University Press

Hayek, F. A. (1960), *The Constitution of Liberty*, London: Routledge

Hayek, F. A. (1978), 'Competition as a Discovery Procedure', in *New Studies in Politics, Economics and the History of Ideas*, London: Routledge

Hayek, F. A. (1988), *The Fatal Conceit*, London: Routledge

Kukathas, C. (2003), *The Liberal Archipelago*, Oxford: Oxford University Press

McKenzie, E. (1994), *Privatopia: Homeowner Associations and the Rise of Residential Private Government*, New Haven, CT: Yale University Press

Nelson, R. (2002), 'Privatising the Neighbourhood', in D. Beito, P. Gordon and A. Tabarrok (eds), *The Voluntary City*, Ann Arbor: University of Michigan Press/Independent Institute

Pennington, M. (1999), 'Free Market Environmentalism and the Limits of Land Use Planning', *Journal of Environmental Policy and Planning*, 1(1): 43–59

Pennington, M. (2000), *Planning and the Political Market: Public Choice and the Politics of Government Failure*, London and New Brunswick, NJ: Athlone Press

Pennington, M. (2002), *Liberating the Land: The Case for Private Land Use Planning*, Hobart Paper 143, London: Institute of Economic Affairs

Webster, C. and L. Lai (2003), *Property Rights, Planning and Markets*, Cheltenham: Edward Elgar

Wholgemuth, M. (1995), 'Economic and Political Competition in Neo-classical and Evolutionary Perspective', *Constitutional Political Economy*, 6(1): 71–96

Wholgemuth, M. (1999), 'Entry Barriers in Politics, or: Why Politics, Like Natural Monopoly, Is Not Organised as an On-going Market Process', *Review of Austrian Economics*, 12(3): 175–200

12 BEYOND KYOTO: REAL SOLUTIONS TO GREENHOUSE EMISSIONS FROM DEVELOPING COUNTRIES

Roger Bate and David Montgomery

Introduction

With the Kyoto Protocol all but dead and antagonism between Europe and America over climate change at an all-time high, now is a good time to assess the real world and think about the long-term future of climate policy. One of the main reasons why the USA refused to ratify the Kyoto Protocol was that it addressed only the emissions of the wealthy countries (members of the OECD). While the protocol seems fair on one level (developed countries have benefited from our massive use of energy and should pay the price of any harm caused), it ignores the fact that most of the forecast emissions will come from the developing parts of the world.

Developing countries seem unwilling to be drawn into a new, updated Kyoto-style process of targets and timetables since they refuse to limit their energy requirements. These countries rightly see increased energy use as a prerequisite for the economic development so badly needed to combat the major problems they face today, including disease, famine and violent conflict.[1]

---

1   The Copenhagen Consensus Project, founded by 'skeptical environmentalist' Bjorn Lomborg and run by some of the world's best-known economists, recently considered GHG-emission reductions a 'bad' policy investment (especially when compared with combating disease, lowering trade barriers and dealing with chronic water problems). This study is available at www.copenhagenconsensus.com. The World Summit on Sustainable Development (WSSD) reaffirms the need to have balanced economic development, social development and environmental protection. In addition, it reaffirms poverty eradication and preservation of the environment as the over-arching objectives of sustainable development (United Nations, 2002).

The result of thinking about the needs of developing countries, rather than the desires of Western greens, leads to certain questions: given that developing countries will need to use energy to develop economically, can their energy use, and hence greenhouse gas (GHG) emissions, be lowered through improved technologies while not endangering wealth creation? Can this shift in technology be achieved by policies that also advance the economic development of developing countries? These are important long-term questions of principle, the sort of questions that the IEA has always addressed.

Economics, energy and emissions

Production requires energy, and countries with a low income per capita use little energy per capita. On average, developed countries together produce about 10.8 tonnes of carbon dioxide per person per year. The figure for developing countries is 1.9 tonnes.

Proponents of the approach to climate change laid out in the Kyoto Protocol claim that we should base policy on reducing Western per capita emissions (IPCC, 2000). But consensus is missing on the desire to follow a Kyoto-style approach in the face of its high costs using currently available technologies. The result is that no openly democratic and informed political system can coerce its citizens to reduce energy use in the near term without much better evidence that climate change will be harmful; few countries have been able to persuade their citizens of the importance of such action.

Similarly, no democratic system can hold developing countries back from economic progress and using whatever energy they require. We must take a different approach to policy.

We need to make a realistic engagement with the needs of developing countries because it is impossible to address the risks of climate change without making substantial changes in how developing countries use energy. Although developing countries have low per capita emissions, they have huge populations. The rapid growth of this already large population leads to the paradox that developing countries will contribute the bulk of GHG emissions over the next century.

The question, then, is how this engagement can be accomplished. Developing countries clearly and rightly place the highest priority on addressing current problems that pose real risks to life and health – disease, food, and sanitation – which can be alleviated only by rapid economic growth. Engagement on climate will be possible only if the route to bringing down projected GHG emissions simultaneously contributes to economic growth. To begin to develop answers, we start with a review of how developing countries use energy in comparison with developed countries, and how changing energy usage is connected to economic growth. We then review the current understanding of some of the key requirements for economic growth and ask whether there are policies that can simultaneously advance economic growth and reduce energy usage significantly.

Energy use and economic growth in developing countries

Two key facts about energy use and carbon emissions in developing countries emerge clearly from historical statistics: energy use per dollar of output (energy intensity) and GHG emissions per dollar of output (emissions intensity) are far higher in developing countries than in developed countries.[2] Both energy intensity and emissions intensity are improving in developing countries, but even the modernising sector of developing countries still has intensities far higher than seen in developed countries.[3]

---

2 If purchasing power parity exchange rates are used instead of market exchange rates, then the differences in intensities will change, and will be closer together. The convention established by the IPCC and other agencies, however, is to use market exchange rates, and hence this is done in this paper.

3 The energy intensity differences could also result from differences between the structure of developed and developing countries' economies.

The theory of economic growth based on embodied technical progress, originated by Solow (1956, 1957) and Swan (1956), helps determine the extent to which key developing countries continue to lag behind industrial countries in their energy and emissions intensity. Solow and Swan introduced the key notion of 'embodied technical change', postulating that the level of productivity is 'built in' to capital equipment, and that new technologies can be brought into play only through new investment. The subsequent growth literature suggests that technical change is a key component of growth. The theory reinforces the empirically demonstrable idea that new technologies, which are embedded in new equipment, improve labour productivity, improve energy efficiency and hence reduce carbon emissions. To achieve these improvements, it is necessary to retire old and build new equipment embodied with better technology.

Bernstein et al. (2004) used this approach to examine the historical record for economic growth and emissions reduction and found a clear lag in the impact of new technology, even that accompanying new investment. They combine these growth rates with information on the level of investment and estimates of the life of capital equipment and some other macroeconomic indicators. They estimate the energy/GDP ratio associated with new investment. What they find is not encouraging. The results for China, and similar calculations for India, the USA and Japan, are summarised in Figure 12.1. China is rapidly improving its energy/GDP ratio, but its new investment is still characterised by much higher energy use per dollar of output supported by that investment than the USA or other OECD countries.

Figure 12.1 shows that in 2001 emissions intensity associated with the installed base substantially exceeded emissions intensity associated with new investment in China and India. China produced on average about 0.7 million tons of carbon emissions for every billion dollars of GDP (measured in constant US dollars at market exchange rates), and about 0.4 million tons of carbon emissions for every billion dollars of GDP produced from new capital equipment. India produced about 0.5

Figure 12.1 **Greenhouse gas emissions per dollar of output**

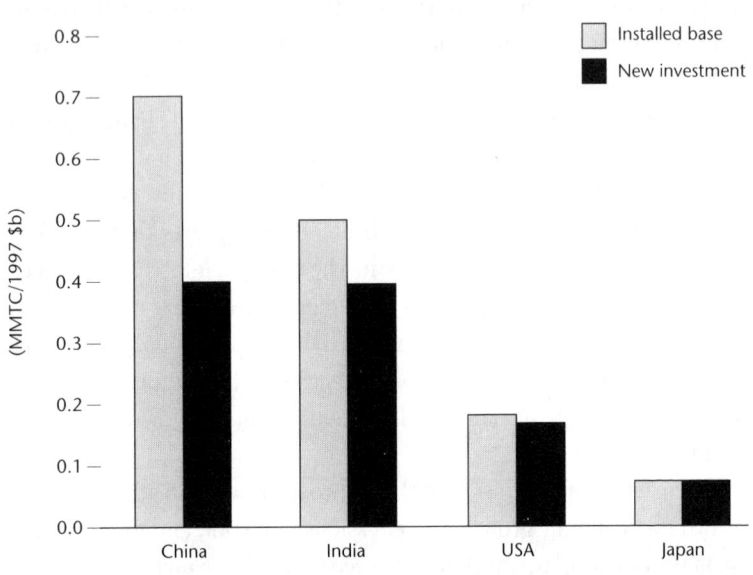

million tons on average from the installed base, and also 0.4 million tons per billion dollars of GDP from new capital. In contrast, the USA produced under 0.2 million tons per billion dollars of output and Japan under 0.1 million tons. Even new equipment in China and India had an emissions intensity more than twice that of new equipment in the USA.

These findings suggest that there is significant potential for reducing emissions from developing countries by increasing the rate of investment to speed the process of modernisation and capital turnover that is even now reducing emissions intensity and improving the technology used in new investment to a level comparable to that in developed countries. Although China has continuously improved its energy efficiency, historical evidence shows that the embodied technology in new investment in China and India has not caught up with that in the West. Our finding that even new investment in developing countries embodies far lower energy efficiency than new investment in developed countries suggests that an efficient way to reduce global emissions is to stimulate additional investment in developing countries, to replace their existing energy-inefficient technologies with more energy-efficient ones. These countries could achieve higher energy efficiency if there were rapid technology transfers.[4] There are immediate benefits from making this transition.

Bernstein et al. (2003) estimate that if just China and India were able to adopt the technology now in use in the USA in their new investment and were to accelerate the replacement of their existing capital stock with its high emissions, the resulting savings in carbon emissions by 2012 or 2017 would be comparable with the emission reductions that could be achieved by the Kyoto Protocol over the same period, *if all Annexe B parties met their original commitments.* In the real world, in which Kyoto commitments are likely to be met by relatively few countries, the emission reductions available through improving technology in developing countries dwarf those achievable in the developed countries. The question is whether this potential can be achieved and in a fashion consistent with the development goals of developing countries. The key to answering this question is found in another question: are lack of economic freedom and remediable market imperfections in developing countries responsible for the observed differences in technology?

Choice of technology in developing countries

Can developing countries make more cost-effective energy technology choices, or do they suffer from market imperfections that hinder such choices? If the latter is true, policy changes that benefit economic development and reduce GHG emissions are possible.

---

4   Z. Zhang (2003) points out that the shift in the structure of economies from energy intensive to less energy intensive caused real energy intensity to decline over the past two decades. Fisher-Vandan et al. (2003) suggest that the main reasons for improvement in energy use in China are increasing energy prices, research and development expenditures, reform in the ownership structure of the enterprise, and structural shifts at the industrial level.

As Figure 12.1 shows, new investment in China and other developing countries clearly does not incorporate world-class technology. What is responsible for these differences in technology? One theory is that optimal allocations (including energy technologies) will have occurred given supplies of labour, capital, energy and other factor endowments. Under this theory, in order to slow emissions growth in developing countries it is necessary to undertake costly measures to restrict energy use or deploy expensive renewable energy technologies to replace fossil fuels. If these countries are already using energy optimally, given their resource endowments, then any change will entail a cost, just as it does in advanced, free market economies. These changes in patterns of energy use will occur only if forced by a policy regime that limits or penalises GHG emissions. This is the fundamental idea behind the notion that the way forward under the Kyoto Protocol (and beyond) is for developing countries to agree to emission limits and participation in the international emission-trading system.

Participating in international emission trading is seen as a means of providing compensation to developing countries for the additional costs they would have to incur. The inducement would be to make those emission limits sufficiently higher than projected emissions growth, so that developing countries could sell their excess permits and use the proceeds to cover the cost of emission reductions. This is the same concession that Russia negotiated for the first commitment period, with an emission cap considerably greater than its actual emissions. Russia can profit from selling the excess permits, which have come to be referred to as 'hot air', to other countries – the European Union, Japan and Canada in particular – which need the permits because they cannot meet agreed emission limits on their own without great economic cost.

To some extent, this approach shifts the burden of paying for emission reductions in developing countries to the developed countries that will buy the permits. But the cost remains, and developing countries doubt that adequate compensation for restraint on growth will be provided. They also rightly perceive that this system will systematically slow their industrial development and put their future well-being at the mercy of the developed countries' willingness to continue these transfers.

Fortunately, existing market failures in developing countries strongly suggest that it is possible to involve these countries in a process of improving their well-being while simultaneously reducing their GHG emissions. First, it is far from clear that energy is currently used optimally in developing countries. Second, there is also strong evidence from a variety of sources that developing-country markets do not function as freely and effectively as those in the developed countries of the world, and that lack of economic freedom is a very strong reason why they remain poor and underdeveloped. Third, there is very strong evidence that market imperfections in developing countries explain why their energy use and carbon emissions per dollar of output are so high. If this is the case, then cooperative efforts to remove these market imperfections and improve economic freedom can therefore also be highly effective in reducing GHG emissions. To develop evidence on the extent and importance of market imperfections, we examined some of the recent comprehensive studies of economic freedom and market institutions throughout the world.

Economic freedom, market imperfections and greenhouse gas emissions
Freedom and wealth

Ever since Adam Smith asserted in 1776 that freedom from government intervention is essential for economic growth and thus the wealth of a nation, economists have attempted to gauge the relative importance of various determinants of growth. These variables include economic factors such as private and government spending, flexibility of tax regimes and investment in the form of domestic or foreign capital, as well as broader, societal parameters. Those in the latter category include key social, legal and political institutions; rule of law; property rights; and enforcement of contracts.

Clearly, then, there are numerous variables and indicators that can be linked to economic development. In assessing any nation's economic health, various research studies argue for the importance of judicial independence (Berkowitz et al., 2000); the impartiality and integrity of the court systems (Sen, 2001); the level of overall governance (Kaufmann et al., 2003; Kaufmann and Kraay, 2003); the adequacy of business and economic laws and regulations (World Bank, 2002); the protection of investment and recognition of ownership of intellectual property rights (Maskus, 2000); an increase in openness to internal markets (Antweiler et al., 2001); the development of an enabling investment climate, policies and institutions (Moran, 1998); and political freedom (Friedman, 1962; North, 1990). Dawson (1998) provides strong empirical evidence demonstrating the relationship between institutional visibility and economic growth, as well as the causal effect of economic freedom on both political and civil liberties.

To gain a better understanding of the connection between economic freedom and economic welfare, various groups of researchers have compiled detailed data on over 120 countries into indices of economic freedom. For our purposes, it is also important that the indices identify many of the market imperfections and distortions that prevent developing countries from accessing and adopting the technologies that produce low emissions per dollar of output in the West.

We used data from the Economic Freedom of the World (EFW) index developed by the Fraser Institute[5] in order to investigate whether economic freedom has a strong influence on the energy technology used in a country.[6] The index correlates positively with measures of income per capita, economic growth, the UN Human Development Index and longevity. It correlates negatively with indices of corruption and poverty.

---

5   The authors would like to thank Neil Emerick for providing electronic versions of the Economic Freedom Index.

6   The Economic Freedom Index contains 38 variables, including eighteen survey-based variables obtained from survey data published in the *International Country Risk Guide* and the *Global Competitiveness Report*, which cover a variety of aspects of economic freedom and are weighted into an overall index for each country.

Table 12.1 **Energy and carbon per GDP and economic freedom for five countries (2001)**

Country	Energy per GDP (Btu per 1995 $)	Carbon per GDP (MMTC per 1995 $b)	GDP per capita (000s of 1995 $)	Freedom Index
China	36,578	0.77	0.9	5.49
India	27,053	0.54	0.5	6.12
Indonesia	20,376	0.37	1.0	5.57
Russia	75,546	1.15	2.5	5.04
South Africa	25,568	0.58	4.0	6.77

Source: Energy Information administration, International Energy Annual

The analysis in the literature demonstrates that the correlation is most likely causal and the direction is certain – overall freedom drives development. This conclusion has also become one of the central lessons of modern development economics.

We do, in fact, find that there is an equally striking connection between levels of economic freedom and key indicators of how efficiently energy is used in developing countries. Countries with low scores on economic freedom have above-average energy use, and vice versa. Table 12.1 illustrates this relationship with data for five economies – four developing countries and one economy in a transition country (Russia).[7]

Based on statistical analysis of the two data series, we find that the Economic Freedom Index explains over 36 per cent of the variation in energy use per dollar of GDP across countries.[8] We also examined the relationship between the Economic Freedom Index and greenhouse gas (carbon) emissions per capita, and found an association nearly as strong. Moreover, we separated the developing countries and examined the relationship between the Freedom Index and energy and emissions intensity and found that the Economic Freedom Index has similar power in explaining differences in energy and emissions intensity among developing countries. That is, the overall relationships between economic freedom and energy or emissions per dollar of GDP are not based solely

7   Energy per GDP, carbon per GDP and Freedom Index for the USA are 31,695, 0.17 and 7.8 respectively (source: EIA).

8   This is a very high percentage for cross-sectional data of this type.

on differences between developed and developing countries. Even within developing countries, a country with a higher freedom index is likely to have significantly lower energy use and emissions per dollar of GDP.

There are several causal routes through which greater economic freedom could lead to lower energy use and emission per dollar of output. One is by improving economic well-being per se. Other researchers have addressed the question of wealth and GHG emissions by analysing the relationship between per capita income and GHG emissions per dollar of output. Schmalensee et al. (1998) find that there is a relationship and that emissions per dollar of output increase until a middle level of per capita income is reached, and then begin to decline. The 'inverted U' pattern, often referred to as the environmental Kuznets curve, is based on Simon Kuznets' studies of how demand for various goods changes as income increases. Schmalensee and his colleagues find evidence of the environmental Kuznets curve with a within-sample peak between carbon dioxide emissions per capita and per capita income. Developing countries with low levels of income tend to see accelerating growth of emissions, while for the developed countries this growth trend is relatively flat or may even be decreasing. None of these studies included indicators of economic freedom as explanatory variables. Based on the relationship identified by Schmalensee et al., it is likely that increasing per capita income is associated with economic changes that increase energy and emissions intensity in the short run for developing countries, and thus is working in the opposite direction to the relationship we found between economic freedom and energy or emissions intensity.

The adoption of technology is also a specific process of supply and demand. Countries that are successful in growing rapidly also benefit from the diffusion of technology throughout their economy and the establishment of modern business and production techniques that displace traditional practices and outdated equipment. All countries start with a legacy of plant, equipment and infrastructure from pre-market, pre-industrial or centrally planned eras. More rapid investment speeds the process of replacing this legacy of less efficient capital equipment. Economic freedom promotes all these processes. Market imperfections that hinder investment – particularly foreign direct investment – discourage outside investors from transferring their best technologies. Imperfections that protect domestic industries from competition will frustrate the economic changes that lead to lower energy use and carbon emissions.

Evidence shows that technology used in developed countries is not being adopted in developing countries, even in their new investment. Acquiring new technology requires replacing old capital with new capital through higher rates of investment. New investment could be domestic or foreign. For most developing countries, foreign direct investment (FDI) has been the engine for more rapid technological progress. The technology from the developed countries diffuses to developing countries largely through the process of FDI or aid from individual countries and multilateral institutions (official development assistance, or ODA), though FDI dwarfs ODA in magnitude. But there are several barriers standing in the way of that investment and technology. If there are obstacles to the inflow of foreign investment or disincentives for use of technology that is cost-effective in developed countries, then there will be less transfer of technology to developing countries. Similarly, if there are policies in developing countries that distort factor prices, such as subsidies for energy use or protection of domestic industries, the adoption and diffusion of technology will be hampered. The Economic Freedom Index also includes data on these types of obstacles to FDI and domestic market imperfections relevant to the choice of energy technology.

Since economic freedom increases per capita income and also reduces GHG emissions per dollar of output, it is indeed difficult to disentangle the effects of greater economic freedom that work through increased income from those that work through removal of market imperfections hindering technology transfer. We made one simple test, which was to include per capita income as an explanatory variable for emissions per dollar of GDP. Although not as sophisticated as Schmalensee et al., this test reveals that economic freedom, as measured by the Economic

Freedom Index, continues to have a significant effect on emissions over and above that of per capita income.

Energy technology and market imperfections

So, economic growth, which improves income per capita, is stimulated by economic freedom. Economic freedom is also associated with much lower energy use per dollar of output, and lower energy use per dollar of output translates into lower emissions of greenhouse gases per dollar of output.

Understanding this effect requires a closer look at how energy is used in developing countries and how those patterns of use are caused by lack of economic freedom. Doing this requires looking more closely at the components of economic freedom that have the most influence on energy choices.

The same set of market imperfections that slow progress of economic and overall social well-being are connected with high carbon emissions per dollar of GDP.

The following list provides some of the components of the Economic Freedom Index that can directly influence the energy technology used in a country: pricing distortions that remove the incentive to adopt cost-effective technologies, including distorted internal pricing mechanisms; a lack of markets, and subsidies administered through state-run enterprises; internal policies that make markets inhospitable to foreign investment with world-class technology owing to the lack of contract law, protection of property rights, protection of intellectual property, protection of inefficient industries, restriction on free flow of funds into and out of a country; and the lack of infrastructure, education and skills to handle technology.

We expect, in principle, that certain of these market imperfections will slow investment and retard technology transfer, thus impeding the development of the energy sector. They will also prevent more efficient technologies from competing effectively with the protected and subsidised status quo. These elements of economic freedom are important because the process of investment and technology transfer can be frustrated by barriers to foreign investment, pricing systems that make technologies with lower energy use less economically viable, and protection of domestic industries with their legacy capital and lack of access to world-class technology for new investment. Barriers to foreign investment include explicit barriers, such as prohibition of foreign ownership in specific industries or regions; these are endemic in the developing world. Lack of both strong contract law and protection of property rights, as well as excessive currency controls, clearly discourage foreign investment, since they introduce risks that expected returns will not be earned or that invested capital will be lost or that owners will not be allowed to repatriate capital. Lack of protection for intellectual property discourages multinational companies from using their best technology for fear it will be illegally copied. Protection of inefficient industries implies that even if FDI is successful in bringing in new technology, that technology will be confined to the industries in 'foreign enterprise zones' where multinational companies can compete but will not diffuse technology to the rest of the economy.

How market prices are formed, and whether they reflect true economic conditions and world prices or are distorted by internal regulations and subsidies, is critical to the success of the transfer and diffusion of new technologies. Most developing countries have some form of subsidised or regulated pricing of energy, with little competition. In many cases dominant state-run enterprises administer prices far removed from economic reality through cross-subsidisation of inter- and intra-industry processes, which benefit selected vested interests.

The Economic Freedom Index also includes variables that reflect infrastructure investment and access to education. Case studies of developing countries make it clear that wasteful energy use is caused by lack of gas and electricity transmission capacity. This reduces the availability of the most efficient fuels and interferes both with the economic dispatch of electricity generation and with competition between efficient large-scale units and inefficient local generators. Diffusion of technology can also be hindered by a lack of skills in the labour force which is often remedied directly through FDI in which global enterprises provide training as well as financial resources and technology.

To perform an empirical test of the theory that market imperfections are significant contributors to excessive energy use and emissions, we therefore examined each of these components of the Economic Freedom Index. We discovered that there is a highly significant relationship between energy intensity and the specific market imperfections that could be expected to prevent increased investment and technology transfer through FDI. Government transfers and subsidies and hidden import barriers were particularly important variables. The combination of variables explains energy use and emissions even more effectively than the Economic Freedom Index as a whole.

In understanding the causes of economic growth, the statistical maxim that 'correlation is not causation but it's a pretty strong hint' is particularly useful. There are strong theoretical reasons for believing that the processes that lead to lower energy use per dollar of output are frustrated by market imperfections of particular types (Bernstein et al., 2004). This theoretical connection is supported by the strong statistical association between economic freedom as a whole and energy use and the even stronger association between specific market imperfections that frustrate investment and technology transfer and energy use.

In addition, we examined other explanations of energy intensity and GHG emissions per dollar of output, and none is as strong as the link to economic freedom. One idea is that increasing income itself produces a preference for environmental benefits and leads directly to lower emissions. This is likely to be true for such pressing environmental needs as clear air, clean water and efficient sanitary systems, but we find a relatively weaker relationship between per capita income and GHG emissions per dollar of output. We have also partially controlled for the type of goods produced in different countries, and this does not alter the relationship between GHG emissions and GDP.

Impediments to efficient energy use in particular countries

To provide context for the statistical studies, it is worth summarising some of the impediments to efficient energy use in developing countries.

China's low score on economic freedom indicates pervasive market distortions. The large state sector is insensitive to market pressures to improve efficiency. Subsidised energy prices remove incentives for energy efficiency and promote coal use. Regulation, institutional bias (Blackman and Wu, 1998) and lack of protection for real and intellectual property discourage multinational companies from using their best world-scale technologies, and the prevalent restriction of FDI to specific enterprise zones producing export goods does not provide for technology diffusion through the domestic economy. The European Union's refusal to recognise China as a market economy is indicative of the extent of market imperfections in China.[9]

In India large state enterprises are insulated from the market forces that promote efficiency. Many domestic industries are protected and offered favoured financing that allows them to continue using inefficient technology and practices without losing out to international competition. There are also restrictions on technology imports, designed to protect domestic industries, and restrictions on FDI that prevent technology transfer. Energy price regulations encourage inefficient energy use, and lack of infrastructure limits the available skills for using new technology.

Indonesia combines four of the most damaging market imperfections: pervasive government enterprises indifferent to efficiency, price regulations that discourage energy efficiency, severe restrictions on FDI, and a legal and political regime that puts all investments at risk and discourages the kinds of projects that bring in new technology.

---

9   The *Financial Times* (28 June 2004) reported that the European Union will refuse 'market economy' status to China. The European Commission believes that China has a long way to go, and the report identifies four major challenges: reduce government influence on the economy; implement transparent and non-discriminatory company law; implement effective and transparent property rights laws; and build an independent and market-driven financial sector.

South Africa's policies are improving, but regulated prices that reduce market incentives for efficient energy use and political instability that discourages foreign investment are problems. South Africa is an interesting case, in that it also uses cheap and dirty domestic coal for power production and has an economy highly geared to energy-intensive activities such as gold and platinum mining and aluminium smelting. The modest score on economic freedom might be a reason why South Africa does not attract investment creating greater value-added in mining and minerals that would reduce energy intensity. South Africa's energy and carbon intensity may require a combination of policies addressing market imperfections and research and development to find new processes and forms of energy with lower emissions.

Russia has a long list of severe market imperfections, encompassing most of the examples listed above for other countries. This explains how such a powerful economy still lags so far behind in energy technology and GHG emissions.

Policy implications

Policy towards the environment in the last few years has developed from grand conferences attended by politicians and bureaucrats who wish to impose further regulations on the world economy. This is not a viable long-term approach. Instead we should think about the long-term policy framework that, if adopted across developing and developed nations alike, will lead to more efficient energy use and greater economic growth. That policy framework should include the following elements.

- With good institutions (property rights and contracts protected, and freedom of capital flows), energy technology will become available from overseas and it will be viable in developing countries' domestic markets if subsidies are removed and protection of state-run enterprises reduced. Inefficient technologies will be replaced faster as investment increases.

- Traditional 'sustainable development' projects sponsored by USAID and the Clean Development Mechanism (CDM) under the Kyoto Protocol will not be successful unless these market imperfections are remedied. An approach of building one project at a time with heavy subsidies in a hostile economic environment will produce no diffusion of technology – even if the project itself succeeds.
- One size does not fit all. Different countries have very different types of market imperfections, and in some countries emissions intensity follows logically from resource endowments. Finding the right mix of policy changes requires dialogue between individual countries, most likely starting with a diagnosis of what market imperfections exist and how they can be addressed.
- While technological advances improve ratios of GDP to carbon dioxide output, this says nothing about overall emissions. If improvements in economic freedom are achieved so that countries grow rapidly, their ratios of overall emissions to GDP will improve – but they may produce more emissions in the short run. If that occurs, more attention will need to be paid to research and development so that the emissions intensity of new investment can be brought below levels that are now cost effective in developed countries. The good news is that by improving economic freedom there is a good chance that new technologies will actually be used once they are developed.
- A successful policy would reconcile desire for development with reduction of carbon intensity. To achieve this, policy-makers could focus international programmes to change the fundamental economic conditions in developing countries that simultaneously inhibit economic progress and keep GHG emissions high.
- Improving economic freedom is necessary for the functioning of traditional aid programmes that support investment in cleaner energy technologies. Otherwise, these projects are fighting a losing battle against an inhospitable economic and regulatory environment, and will, as they have in the past, remain white

elephants that exist only while they are paid for by donor countries.

Raising the level of economic freedom will be sufficient for most desirable outcomes as the clear association between economic freedom and energy efficiency suggests. A necessary condition is to have in place the right institutions to allow for the inflow of FDI and the diffusion of new technology. Until that happens, developed countries should provide the necessary financial support only on the condition of demonstrated market reform. Such policies can ensure that growth is fostered and that the environment is not harmed by inefficient and government-distorted practices.

References

Antweiler, W., B. Copeland and S. Taylor (2001), 'Is Free Trade Good for the Environment?', *American Economic Review*, 91(4): 877–908

Berkowitz, D., K. Pistor and J. Richard (2000), *Economic Development, Legality and the Transplant Effect*, CID Working Paper, Center for International Development, Harvard University

Bernstein, P., W. D. Montgomery and S. D. Tuladhar (2003), *Potential for Reducing Carbon Emissions from Non-annex B Countries through Changes in Technology*, Charles River Associates Inc.

Bernstein, P., W. D. Montgomery and S. D. Tuladhar (2004), *Market Imperfections, Foreign Direct Investment, and Technology Transfer*, Charles River Associates Inc. (draft)

Blackman, A. and X. Wu (1998), 'Foreign Direct Investment in China's Power Sector: Trends, Benefits, and Barriers. Resources for the Future', Discussion paper

Cameron, L. J., H. L. Foster and W. D. Montgomery (1997), 'The Economics of Energy Conservation Strategies to Reduce Greenhouse Gas Emissions', *Energy Studies Review*, November

Dawson, J. W. (1998), 'Institutions, Investment, and Growth: New Cross-country and Panel Data Evidence', *Economic Inquiry*, 36: 603–19

Fankel, J. A. and A. K. Rose (2002), 'Is Trade Good or Bad for the Environment? Sorting Out the Causality', NBER Working Paper 9201, National Bureau of Economic Research

Fisher-Vanden, K., G. H. Jefferson, M. Jingkui and X. Jianyi (2003), *Technology Innovation and Diffusion in Transition Economies: The Case of China*, forthcoming

Friedman, M. (1962), *Capitalism and Freedom*, Chicago, IL: University of Chicago Press

IPCC (Intergovernmental Panel on Climate Change) (2000), *Summary for Policy Makers: Emission Scenarios*, Special report of IPCC Working Group III

Kaufmann, D. and A. Kraay (2003), 'Governance and Growth: Causality Which Way? – Evidence for the World', Ms

Kaufmann, D., A. Kraay and M. Mastruzzi (2003), *Governance Matters III: Governance Indicators for 1996–2002*, World Bank Policy Research Working Paper 3106

Jacoby, H. D. (1998), *The Uses and Misuses of Technology Development as a Component of Climate Policy*, MIT Joint Program on the Science and Policy of Global Change, Report 43

Maskus, K. E. (2000), *Intellectual Property Rights and Foreign Direct Investment*, Centre for International Economic Studies, Policy Discussion no. 22, Adelaide: University of Adelaide

Moran, T. (1998), *Foreign Direct Investment and Development: The New Policy Agenda for Developing Countries and Economies in Transition*, Washington, DC: Institute of International Economics

North, D. (1990), *Institutions, Institutional Change, and Economic Performance*, New York: Cambridge University Press

Schmalensee, R., T. M. Stoker and R. A. Judson (1998), 'World Carbon Dioxide Emissions: 1950–2050', *Review of Economics and Statistics*, 80: 15–27

Sen, A. (2001), *What Is the Role of the Legal and Judicial Reform in the Development Process?*, World Bank Conference on Legal and Judicial Development

Solow, R. M. (1956), 'A Contribution to the Theory of Economic Growth', *Quarterly Journal of Economics*, 70: 65–94

Solow, R. M. (1957), 'Technical Change and the Aggregate Production Function', *Review of Economics and Statistics*, 34: 214–31

Swan, T.W. (1956), 'Economic Growth and Capital Accumulation', *Economic Record*, 32(2): 334–61

United Nations (2002), Draft Resolution, World Summit on Sustainable Development

World Bank (2002), *World Development Report 2002. Building Insitutions for Markets*, Washington, DC

Zhang, Z. (2003), 'Why Did the Energy Intensity Fall in China's Industrial Sector in the 1990s? The Relative Importance of Structural Change and Intensity Change', East–West Center Working Paper

13 THE ENVIRONMENT IN 2055
Julian Morris

Introduction

London, 2055. Fifty years ago, I wrote an essay in which I imagined what the environment would be like today. So I thought I would take this opportunity to review the changes that have actually occurred in the past half-century.

Looking back to 2005, one thing that immediately struck me was the level of concern among Europeans about issues such as climate change, biodiversity loss and the use of synthetic chemicals, which to us seem prosaic. With hindsight, we can see that the level of regulatory intervention used to deal with these supposed problems was massively excessive – and probably contributed to the relative economic decline of countries such as Germany and Sweden over the past half-century. But at the time there was little resistance to such measures, with most big businesses believing that they could adapt to – and possibly even benefit from – the regulations. Meanwhile, the concerns of small businesses and the population at large went largely unheard.

Benefits, risks and trade-offs

Without labouring the point – and bearing in mind that this essay is intended mostly as an overview of the current environmental situation – it is nevertheless instructive to look at the mistakes of the past. Understanding what went wrong may help us avoid a similar situation in the future. A case in point is the current debate about the alleged impact of the widely used Beckermonium-based polymers. Some claim that these

B-polys (used as an inert coating on nano-tools, especially in medical applications) are responsible for the recent rise in Kong's disease.

Kong's disease is a fatal brain disorder that exclusively affects people over the age of 110. Until recently, fewer than one in twenty of us could expect to live beyond 110. In fact it is only the recent increase in the availability of nano-medicine which has given us the expectation of such long lives. And without B-polys that would not have been possible. So, if it turns out that B-polys do increase the risk of Kong's disease, the question is: would you rather have a 50 per cent chance of living to 120 without any mental problems, or a 95 per cent chance of dying of Alzheimer's, cardiovascular disease or cancer before the age of 110? As with most new technologies, B-polys pose the problem of trade-offs.

Today, all decisions relating to such trade-offs – where the risks and benefits predominantly fall on the individual making the decision – are made by individuals, not by the government. As a result, those people who believe that the benefits of using a technology outweigh the risks are able to choose to use that technology. Those who believe the risks outweigh the benefits may choose not to use it.

At the turn of the century, similar problems were posed by the development of biotechnology and other gene-based products, from stem cell research to herbicide-tolerant maize. The difference is that back then decisions concerning the utilisation of new technologies were largely in the hands of politicians, who were prey to the pressures of powerful interest groups claiming to represent 'the environment', 'consumers' and 'the poor', not to mention the power of vested interests such as the purveyors of 'organic' food (a label briefly popular among middle-class consumers who had been made fearful of conventional food technologies by a series of real and imaginary problems).

The turning point in the development of gene-based technologies came around 2020. For a decade, investments in these technologies had been shifting to East Asia, where the regulatory environment was more relaxed and intellectual property (IP) protection had improved dramatically (previously, poor IP protection had discouraged investment in much of Asia, but this shifted after Singapore enacted strong laws and set the scene for the region). Then, as part of the legislation associated with Britain's exit from the European Union, product and environmental regulation ceased to be a function of government and was instead left to the private sector. Statutory regulations were replaced by a combination of product certification, contracts and civil liability.

Private regulation: So Safe and Bright Future

We have by now become used to brands such as So Safe and Bright Future, and few of us probably think about why they exist or what came before them. Their origin actually pre-dates the removal of state regulation. By 2010, people had become so disillusioned with the failure of the state adequately to inform them of the quality of the products they were buying that several entrepreneurs started their own quality assurance programmes. Building on the experience of well-established quality assurance schemes such as those run by Underwriter's Laboratory and Good Housekeeping in the USA, the British Standard Institute's 'kite' mark and the Woolmark, So Safe and Bright Future sought to provide the same quality assurance for a broad range of products.

As you know, So Safe focuses primarily on the safety of food, ensuring that retailers have in place adequate supply-chain management systems, thereby limiting the possibilities for food to be contaminated between the farm and the fork. Retailers pay a fixed fee for each food item branded 'So Safe'. A portion of this fee goes into an insurance fund, which pays out if a consumer is injured by a product bearing the So Safe label.

By contrast, Bright Future was established as a niche scheme aimed at satisfying the demand for products that support certain kinds of environmental objectives. Unlike earlier schemes, which often made ridiculous claims such as 'this product is environmentally friendlier', Bright Future merely certifies the environmental claims made by manufacturers (general 'environment friendlier' claims are not allowed because they cannot be verified and may even be counter-productive – points I made in a monograph for the IEA way back in 1997). As a result, consumers are able to choose to support those environmental concerns they prefer.

One of the early products to obtain a Bright Future label was maize containing a gene that made it resistant to heat, drought and salt. The label stated that by reducing the need for water and by enabling production on land that had been subjected to over-cultivation, the maize reduced pressure on wild lands and thereby helped conserve biodiversity. The maize proved popular, not only because it had a Bright Future mark but also because it was naturally slightly salty and was cheaper than most other brands.

Those of us getting on in years also perhaps remember some of the other schemes that were devised by enterprising souls. Although some were briefly popular – even rivalling So Safe – most failed within a few years. Some failed because of poor marketing, others because of a lack of consumer interest. But several temporarily successful ones failed because of a lack of adequate control processes – leading to several poisonings and at least one death. This last – which concerned a mark originally devised by the British government but subsequently privatised – led to one of the largest personal breach-of-contract suits in legal history. In each case, the failure of the control processes quickly became public knowledge and consumers soon became disenchanted with the marks. In spite of pleas from the major shareholders and several consumer groups (who claimed that the marks deserved subsidies in order to promote competition!), the government resisted proposals to bail out the marks and they went to the wall.

Ironically, some people have complained that the existing assurance schemes are too conservative, leading to a two-tier world in which the rich can afford to buy certified products and the poor are left with the dregs. The reality, however, is quite different. There are few independent certifiers because most goods are packaged and branded by private companies that have no need for independent certification – the brands themselves are the greatest security that can be offered to the consumer.

Admittedly, not all the brand owners guarantee to pay out in the event that someone is harmed by the product, but they don't need to – they have established their reputation over a long period and know that if there is a failure in their control processes and hence a negative hit to their reputation, the financial consequences in terms of lost business would be dramatic.

While concerns over consumer safety have to a very great degree been resolved by the increased dominance of brand goods and the emergence of private sector quality assurance schemes, Bright Future and other similar programmes have played only a relatively minor role in environmental protection. Far more important has been the shift away from centralised government ownership, management and regulation of air, land and water.

Over-fishing and individual transferable quotas

One of the precipitating events that led to this widespread privatisation was the crisis that affected the world's major fisheries at the turn of the century. After years of failing to solve the problem of over-fishing through ever stricter regulations, governments eventually accepted that something radical was necessary. So, in 2017, 87 nations signed the Global Agreement on Privatisation of the Oceans (GOPA). The model for GOPA was the successful privatised fisheries management systems in New Zealand and Iceland. From the 1980s onward, both countries had begun to decentralise their management of fish stocks, introducing 'individual transferable quotas' (ITQs) – which essentially created a long-lasting right to a share of the total catch of fish.

Before the introduction of ITQs, fisheries organisations would lobby government to increase catch levels and fund 'decommissioning' of boats, while individual fishermen resisted measures to ensure that they stuck to their own annual quotas, for example by landing catches at night and refusing to allow the introduction of external monitoring. After the introduction of ITQs, the owners actually called for lower catch levels – because they realised that by reducing catch levels temporarily they could increase catch levels and hence the value of their ITQs in the future. Owners also called for the introduction of satellite-based monitoring – in order to stop their fellow fishermen from cheating.

During the initial phase of ocean privatisation, ITQs were seen as the ideal solution. They rapidly proved effective in increasing stock levels and enhancing the wealth of the fishermen to whom they had been granted. The result, dramatically observed in Iceland, New Zealand and subsequently Spain, the UK, the USA, Russia, Japan and other major fishing nations that took up ITQs, was that they enabled catch levels to be reduced without requiring the state to intervene by purchasing boats or paying welfare to fishermen.

Over time, however, the management companies established to run ITQ programmes gradually invested in the development of hatcheries and spawning grounds (including working with the owners of large offshore structures such as oil rigs, to convert these into artificial reefs). As a result, they found that they were able to increase the available catch of fish. In order to protect their investment, the management companies negotiated greater levels of control over the seabed and the column of water above it – effectively privatising large areas of the ocean within the various countries' Exclusive Economic Zones (EEZs – the areas of the ocean deemed to be under the control of the individual nation-states).

Once the EEZs were effectively privatised, wild fisheries gradually gave way to open-water aquaculture – giant oceanic farms able to produce vast quantities of fish of every kind at far lower cost than wild fisheries. Although oceanic fish farms had emerged before the privatisation of the EEZs, they did so on a relatively small scale and mostly inside specially designated areas that could not be fished by commercial trawlers. The reason is the lack of secure ownership. Few entrepreneurs would be willing to risk investing in an activity, on land or at sea, where they might simply have the fruits of their labour stolen with no recourse.

Just as privatisation of EEZs was the stimulus for larger-scale ocean aquaculture, so GOPA extended this to the high seas and all countries that had not yet privatised their EEZ. Under GOPA, the area within a country's EEZ was automatically partitioned and either 'grandfathered' to existing ocean resource users or auctioned off. Where there were competing users, special private arbitration bodies were established to decide who should have what rights. Often different users would be entitled to different rights in the same area, just as in parts of England the general right to a moor has often been separated from the right to the grouse living on that moor, for example. Areas outside the EEZ were subject to homesteading, so that the first user to invest in the protection of a specific volume of water could claim it, so long as they had the backing of the state in which they were registered. Again, where there were pre-existing users, private arbitration bodies were established to resolve disputes.

By shifting pressure away from wild fisheries, these fish farms also aided in the recovery of stocks. Nowadays, the seas are once again teeming with fish, and those who hanker after wild fish are once again able to fish them relatively unhindered on the open seas (those areas deemed uneconomic to fence). But more than that, ocean aquaculture has reduced pressure on land-based agriculture. As most readers will know, ocean aquaculture now accounts for approximately 30 per cent of all the protein we consume.

Privatisation and conservation

Privatisation was also important in the management of other species. In Sub-Saharan Africa, conservation suffered throughout the twentieth century. Both colonial governments and their despotic and corrupt replacements ran roughshod over the interests of the locals, preventing them from owning the wildlife and discouraging investments in conservation. The situation was not improved by the governments of rich countries supplying 'aid' to the governments of these poor countries. But in the past 30 years, African governments, led by Botswana and Senegal and closely followed by Mozambique, Uganda and Zimbabwe, have largely shaken the aid habit and have decentralised their governmental structures, giving power back to the people.

As a result, many communities have invested in conservation programmes, seeking to reap what they can out of an unwieldy landscape through hunting, eco-tourism and mixed game farming. Others have chosen to convert their land for other purposes and many have done extremely well. But what is interesting about the situation not only in Africa but also in Asia and South America is that intensive farming and a shift to industry and services have taken pressure off the wild land. Poaching is rarely a problem these days and populations of charismatic species such as elephant, rhino, lion, cheetah, leopard, tiger and even panda are higher than at any period since 1900. At the same time, people in all these countries have become massively wealthier (average per capita incomes in Papua New Guinea, Bangladesh and the Congo are now higher than average incomes in the USA in 2004). Moreover, people everywhere are using modern technologies. As a result, people no longer die from what were called the 'diseases of poverty', and average lifespans in the poorest ten countries are 89 for men and 93 for women.

The decline of natural disasters

One of the sharpest declines has been seen in deaths from 'natural disasters'. The readers of 2055 may wonder why I even mention this: natural disasters rarely make the news these days. Fifty years ago, however, the newspapers were full of reports that 'climate change' would result in a huge increase in deaths from flooding, heat, drought, and so on. Indeed, one British science adviser famously claimed that by 2100 the only places on the planet that would be inhabitable would be the poles. Even at the time I thought that this was obviously arrant nonsense and that the official should have been sacked on the spot for making such a daft proclamation. But amazingly his assertions were widely repeated in the national press, helping promote the government's claim that drastic action was needed to halt dangerous climate change.

Well, 50 years later the world is again going through a warm patch, but this time we know it is mostly caused by natural changes – the cooling from 2018 to 2034 finally put paid to the global-warming doomsayers. Moreover, we know that with modern technology and wealth, nobody will suffer unduly. Indeed, some are calling for policies to increase warming – noting that at the height of the last warm period yields of crops were considerably higher, as growing seasons had been extended.

The last 50 years

But I digress! I had wanted to explain how our green and pleasant land has improved over the past half-century. First, though, some background on the situation as it was in 2005. Until the twentieth century, Britain's landowners had for hundreds of years invested in the improvement and conservation of land largely as they saw fit. Diverse competing experiments in land management led to new discoveries, the best of which were copied, with the result that management gradually improved. During the twentieth century, however, investments were distorted by a series of subsidies, land use planning restrictions and other interventions, first from Westminster, then from Brussels. Combined with the rapid technological innovation that occurred over the period, these distortions caused a dramatic shift in the structure of land use.

The problem was not, as many conservative groups claimed, that there was too much building on the land. Indeed, to the extent that there was a problem relating to the construction of buildings it was that there wasn't enough and that there was too much aesthetic control by government. As a result, a large proportion of the citizens of towns such as London and Manchester were condemned to live in small, ugly Victorian and Edwardian houses, many of them poorly subdivided into apartments. Others commuted from sleeper towns located outside the 'green belts'. These towns had once constituted thriving communities, but by 2005 the high price of property in cities – caused mostly by government restrictions on alterations to and construction of buildings – had forced people farther and farther out of town. Commuters bought up properties in satellite towns, using them as little more than dormitories.

The green belts, rings of mostly barren pasture deemed inviolate by town planners, had originally been justified on the grounds that suburbs should not be allowed to continue indefinitely into the countryside. The idea was that the countryside and the communities that lived there needed 'protection' from development. How ironic that this legislation ended up destroying the very communities it sought to protect!

During the first two decades of this century, the state land use planning system was gradually replaced by private measures, such as easements and covenants. As a result, individuals and groups are now able to protect what they really value without imposing unnecessarily bureaucratic constraints on alterations and new building. The beginning of the end came with the Labour administration that came to power in 1997. Realising that rising property prices were harming the poor, Labour made the planning system simpler and more flexible.

The next step came when Britain's farmers were forced to accept the end of subsidies (as part of Britain's exit from the EU) and in turn lobbied hard for the removal of land use planning restrictions – so that they could finally realise the development value of their land. Predictably, preservationist groups such as the Commission for the Preservation of Little England lobbied against changes to the planning system. But the farmers made their point by staging a massive and convincing rally at Westminster. The result was the removal of nearly all restrictions on building on farm land (the only exceptions were for listed buildings – all other planning designations were removed).

Contrary to the predictions of those who favoured state planning, the removal of restrictions on building in the countryside did not lead to the paving-over of the British landscape. Quite the contrary – with no government restrictions on plot size, people were able to have relatively large gardens. Moreover, with no aesthetic restrictions, people invested in architects, who were once again free to experiment with designs and materials without fearing a costly redesign courtesy of a bureaucrat in the local planning department taking against the new, the old or simply the different. The British idyll of a beautiful house and garden for the first time came within the reach of the masses.

With state planning more or less eliminated in the countryside, the battle moved to the towns and cities. There, environmentalists actually came out in favour of a relaxation of the rules – in order to reduce building in the countryside! In place of planning, they argued that the owners of buildings should make agreements with one another, enforceable in courts of law, that limited changes being made voluntarily. They were opposed by some of the big building firms, which tended to benefit from the restrictive rules and claimed that the easements and covenants proposed by the environmentalists would be excessively difficult to overcome. The environmentalists won.

Although many old buildings were torn down and replaced with modern houses and apartment blocks, historians have often expressed surprise at the number of beautiful squares and even whole streets that have been kept intact. One wonders how horrendous the housing situation might have been if the rules had not been changed. Given the record of government building during the latter part of the twentieth century, one also wonders how much damage might have been done to the places that were subsequently preserved if councils still had the right to requisition buildings and convert them for their own purposes.

While easements and covenants have proved to be an extremely effective mechanism for conserving buildings and land, alone they would not have been sufficient. Crucial, also, has been the application of tort law – from nuisance to riparian rights. Nuisance law enables property owners to protect themselves from harms such as noise and air pollution. The basic principle of nuisance law is *'sic utere tuo ut in alienum non laedas'* (so use your own as not to harm another's), which has been applied more or less strictly over the course of the past 500 years. As with many aspects of private law, nuisance was weakened during the twentieth century, with judges accepting a wide interpretation of the defence of 'statutory authority' (for example, allowing that a statute which provided a particular company with a right to operate overrode the local people's right to clean air) and also allowing a shift in the interpretation in the law so that plaintiffs had increasingly to show negligence on the part of defendants.

In order to enhance the extent to which individuals were able to protect the environment – partly in response to fears created by environmentalists as Britain pulled out of the EU and repealed all EU-associated environmental legislation – the British government passed legislation that had the effect of removing statutory authority as a defence except in extreme cases (for example, where an act expressly permits a specific harm), and even then compensation is payable. Meanwhile, following a series of law review articles critical of the shift to a negligence standard, the British Supreme Court ruled that nuisance cases should once again be governed by the *sic utere* rule.

In addition to the changes in the rules, which significantly increased legal certainty, the government instituted changes in legal procedures, making it much easier to settle a disagreement through arbitration. This reduced costs and enabled many more people to bring actions. As a result, property owners found that they were in a much better position regarding the perpetrators of nuisance. Contrary to the apocalyptic predictions of some businesses, this did not have a negative impact on business. Rather, it ensured that people who were harmed were able to obtain compensation. Many plaintiffs actually entered into long-term contracts with the creators of nuisances, which permitted the nuisances to continue – for a price.

The past 50 years have also seen a burgeoning of the use of private riparian rights to protect the quality of streams and rivers. The right to 'an undiminished flow of water of undiminished quality' had been established in the late nineteenth century and enabled riparian owners to sue those who caused all manner of interferences, from polluters to companies abstracting water. As with nuisance law, the situation was improved through the repeal of statutory authority. Also, the conversion of statutory rights to abstract water into fully tradable property rights also helped considerably. And, as with nuisance law, many riparian owners have made bargains with polluters, water companies and others who had interfered with their rights.

Conclusion

Over the course of the past 50 years, the environment in Britain and around the world has improved dramatically to the benefit of all. In addition, people are wealthier than ever before and have access to superior technologies, enabling them to cope better with the environment in which they live. These improvements have come about as a result of the private actions of individuals and companies operating within the institutions of the free society – property rights (bound by effective remedies in tort), contract law, markets, the rule of law and limited government. In countries that took longer to adopt these institutions, improvements were slower and people are poorer.

14 CAPITALISM
David Henderson and Geoffrey Owen

Capitalism yesterday and today[1]
The survival of the market economy

Viewed in the perspective of the past 60 years, the first point to be made about capitalism today, in the world as a whole, is that it has survived. At the close of World War II such an outcome could by no means be taken for granted. The war and events leading out of it brought a vast extension, in both Europe and Asia, of the area in which communist regimes held sway. Before long, the break-up of the former empires of leading capitalist countries led to the establishment of a host of newly independent states; and in virtually all of these, governments were committed to socialism. In the leading capitalist countries themselves, where in the past the system had clearly made possible substantial economic advances, it was widely questioned, rejected or condemned. Alongside older criticisms, it was now blamed for the chronic instability of the inter-war period and the calamitous Great Depression of the 1930s: it was seen as no longer able to deliver. Even those who took a favourable view of capitalism's past achievements and future potential, despite the setbacks of the 1930s, did not necessarily expect it to survive. A leading instance was Joseph Schumpeter, in his great book *Capitalism, Socialism and Democracy*, first published in 1942. He argued that '... a socialist form of society will inevitably emerge from an equally inevitable decomposition of

---

1 This opening section, and some of the later argument, draws on the final chapter of Henderson (2004).

capitalist society', and foresaw 'a conquest of private industry and trade by the state'.[2]

Six decades further on, it is obvious that confident predictions of this kind have not been borne out. Capitalism has not disappeared from the scene, and few people now expect it to do so. Aside from a few fringe cases, such as Cuba, Libya and North Korea, there is probably no country in the world where, over the whole course of these six decades, private industry and trade have been 'conquered' by the state. Why is it that, contrary to what so many expected, capitalism has emerged at the end of this period more generally accepted and more securely established than at the beginning?

Both positive and negative influences have been at work. The main positive factor has been the remarkable and unforeseen record of economic progress across much of the world over the second half of the twentieth century. During this period the world economy as a whole, and many countries within it, have grown at rates that were substantially higher than past history would have suggested as likely or even possible. Every member of the group of capitalist countries that were already relatively rich in 1950 has shared in this increased prosperity. But the record of economic progress over the period goes well beyond this group, in ways that no one foresaw or even imagined, and which mark a decisive break with the past. In the course of this past half-century, an increasing number of previously poor countries achieved sustained rates of growth in material standards of living which were either rare or wholly unprecedented anywhere in earlier history.

How far this record of widespread (though not universal) economic success can be attributed to 'capitalism' as such is debatable. But almost all the countries concerned had economies that were market-based rather than centrally planned, while in some cases, with China since 1978 as the leading example, high growth rates were achieved as a direct

---

2   Schumpeter (1942). The first quotation is from the preface to the first edition, and the second from the final chapter of the fourth edition.

result of policies that greatly widened the scope for private business initiative. Even though capitalism was not necessarily given credit for the successes, rising prosperity weakened the case for making radical changes in the system within which it was occurring. Economic progress has brought acceptance of the market economy, though not necessarily enthusiasm for it.

Gaining ground

On the negative side, capitalism has gained, perhaps decisively, from the revealed weaknesses of its rival. Exposed to the test of results during this half-century, the socialist alternative has disappointed both hopes and expectations. The most conspicuous evidence of its failure, and the most momentous in its consequences, has of course been the collapse of communism. Less dramatically, and outside the former communist countries, disillusionment with the performance of public enterprises has been the main single factor in generating, and lending impetus to, the process of privatisation which has been taken a long way in a substantial and growing number of countries. Across the world, the trend towards public ownership of enterprises has been reversed.

As a result of these recent developments, capitalism is no longer so closely linked to the countries where it first developed and is still in place: its hold has extended. Several interrelated factors have been at work here. One is the collapse of communism, which has opened the way for private business in most of the former communist countries of central and eastern Europe. Second is the still-continuing trend towards closer international economic integration in the world, and with it the extraordinary growth in cross-border trade and investment flows: 'globalisation' has enlarged the scope and improved the functioning of markets. A third factor has been privatisation in a growing number of developing countries. Last but not least has been the notably high growth of output in a number of these latter countries where economic policies have become more market-oriented, with China and India as the outstanding cases. Capitalism is now big business outside its former strongholds.

Continuity and change

Although capitalism has thus made gains across the world in recent decades, this is not because its character or its rationale have changed. Today as in the past, the main justification for capitalism is the decisive contribution that it makes to furthering economic progress. The main direct impulse to such progress comes from the profit-related activities and initiatives of business enterprises: from an economy-wide viewpoint, as distinct from that of the individual firm, this is the primary role of business. Recent developments in the world economy, including 'globalisation', have served to confirm and reinforce that role.

The business contribution to the general welfare does not depend on a commitment by enterprises to furthering 'social' objectives. It results from the combination of entrepreneurial opportunities and competitive pressures that only a market economy provides: it is these twin influences which give rise to the unceasing process, described by Schumpeter as one of 'creative destruction', that is the hallmark of such an economy.

That process can bring significant changes within the world of business itself. A recent instance is the trend, first apparent in the 1980s and still running strongly, towards the 'de-integration' of the large, vertically integrated corporations that once dominated many of the world's industries. Because of technological change, pressure from the financial markets and more intense global competition, companies such as General Motors and IBM have abandoned their old attachment to doing everything in-house and now rely to a much greater extent on market-based relations with outside suppliers. By the 1990s 'the large corporation that had looked inevitable and invincible in the 1950s and 1960s had become an organisation increasingly misaligned with economic realities' (Langlois, 2003).

Another manifestation of change within the business world is that the rate of turnover among the world's largest companies has accelerated. Many of those giant corporations (which according to some widely believed 1960s predictions were about to take over the world) have either disappeared from the scene or are greatly reduced in size; new firms in new industries have come to the fore. It is arguable that economies of scale and scope – chronicled by Alfred Chandler in his studies of American capitalism – are less relevant today (see Chandler, 1990). The world may be moving towards a more entrepreneurial economy, in which competitive success depends on speed and flexibility rather than size.

Such far-reaching changes, however, are not only consistent with capitalism but part of it. They exemplify the combination of market-originating opportunities and pressures that make the system a force for innovation and progress.

Continuing opposition

It is now widely argued, or simply assumed, that capitalism, and with it the market economy, has finally triumphed; but this is far from being the case. In spite of its survival, the ground that it has gained, and the discrediting of many traditional socialist arguments and claims, the future of capitalism cannot be taken for granted. In all but a few countries today, hostility to the market economy and to private business is widespread. In no country in the world is there a government, or even a political movement with strong support, that takes as a guiding principle the case for greater economic freedom. The future of capitalism has still to be assessed against a background of suspicion, questioning and distrust, which recent corporate failures and scandals have served to reinforce. In this respect also, and notwithstanding the collapse of communism, the world has not greatly changed.

Capitalism tomorrow
Challenges to the market economy

For the time being, and perhaps for the indefinite future, capitalism as such appears secure, in that state socialism no longer presents a serious challenge. But the competitive market economy is less secure: everywhere there are forces and influences at work to restrict rather than enlarge its scope. It is possible to imagine a capitalism of the future that would become on balance increasingly collectivised and denatured, even without a restoration of either central planning or public ownership of enterprises. The main challenges to the market economy now come, not from full-blooded socialism, but from a range of interventionist measures, trends and possibilities. The effect of these is to constrain market opportunities and competitive pressures.

As in the past, the sources of interventionism are numerous and often mutually reinforcing. In part, they result from the limits to what a market economy can accomplish. Such an economy acts as a vehicle for material progress, through an unceasing process of change; and the argument in its favour refers to the general welfare only, without regard for who may gain or lose from the working of competitive markets or an extension of their scope. But governments and their voters do not necessarily favour change as such, and they are deeply concerned with issues of distribution, fairness, equality and security. These concerns open the way to a range of actions to restrict the scope of markets or regulate their working.[3]

Such actions can often be justified, or at any rate defended, as giving expression to the general interest. But the readiness of governments to move in this direction, and the pressures on them to do so, can arise in more questionable ways, most of which are not new. First and arguably foremost are the unceasing pressures from interest groups of many

---

3   Of course, government involvement may be called for, even in a well-functioning market economy, to deal with 'externalities' and to provide adequately for 'public goods'. Such actions, however, are largely undertaken with the aim of promoting the general material welfare.

kinds, including business lobbies, to protect established positions or to obtain new favours and concessions from governments. Alongside these pressures, and often reinforcing them, are firmly held anti-business and anti-market attitudes, beliefs and assumptions. These include the age-old hostility to the profit motive; the conviction that good outcomes can be realised only from motives that go beyond self-interest; and the perception of markets as anarchic as well as amoral. More recent variations on the anti-market theme include the beliefs, first, that profit-directed economic activities are putting the planet under threat, and second, that globalisation together with privatisation has conferred on businesses undue benefits and dangerously extended powers.

Such influences and pressures can be translated into policy along several lines of action. One is through increasing the scope or extent of public transfers, in ways that further loosen the connection between rewards and economic activity. A second is by raising barriers to international flows of trade and foreign investment. A third is through what might be termed 'demarketisation' – that is, extending the sphere in which goods and services are provided free or almost free of charge. Last (and as we believe the most serious single threat to the competitive market economy today and in the future) is a trend towards increasingly strict and intrusive regulation – for example, in environmental and 'social' codes; through taking farther the already well-established trend towards the erosion of freedom of contract; and in the international domain, through pressures to establish common norms and standards even though local circumstances are widely different.

Taming capitalism: the 'stakeholder model' and 'CSR'

Some forms of intervention, current and prospective, are designed to affect the governance and conduct of businesses. One of these, well established, is the 'stakeholder model' of capitalism, while a more recent development is the doctrine of 'Corporate Social Responsibility' (CSR).

One of the characteristics of the stakeholder model, of which

Germany is the prime exemplar, is an attenuated role for financial markets in influencing the way industries and firms are organised. Companies, including those listed on the stock exchange, are held to be accountable, not just to shareholders, but to a range of other stakeholders, including employees, customers, suppliers and local communities. There is a consensual element in the governance of large corporations, reflected in the presence of employees and trade union officials on supervisory boards. These arrangements, coupled with the absence of an active market for corporate control, tend to promote stability, continuity and a sluggish response to external shocks. In the USA, by contrast, shareholder value is the chief measure of a company's performance. Financial markets play a larger role, putting continuous pressure on businesses to run their affairs efficiently and providing the means by which new firms can challenge incumbents. It is a system that facilitates the rapid shift of resources from low-growth to high-growth sectors of the economy.

In recent years, because of the closer integration of world financial markets (largely driven from the USA), the shareholder model has been gaining ground. At the same time, however, there has developed a potentially countervailing movement of opinion to reform capitalism everywhere, including the USA. According to this view, businesses everywhere should now redefine their role and objectives, and change their ways of operating, in the name of CSR. They should embrace the notion of 'corporate citizenship', and run their affairs, through 'multiple stakeholder engagement', so as to pursue the goal of 'sustainable development'. Only by acting in this way (it is said) can businesses respond to what are now 'society's expectations' and earn their 'licence to operate'. In so doing lies the key to long-run commercial success, since profits today depend largely on reputation, which in turn depends on being seen to act in a socially responsible way.

One of several objections to the doctrine of CSR is that it typically presumes, mistakenly, that globalisation, together with privatisation, has had the effect of transferring power from governments to businesses.

It thus rests on a view of the world that is false. More important, its probable consequences appear as damaging. In particular, in so far as its adoption becomes legally or effectively binding, whether as a result of strong social pressures or through legislation, the effect will be to narrow market opportunities and reduce competitive pressures, and hence to weaken the performance of business in its primary role.[4]

Extending and strengthening the market economy

Both stakeholder theory and (still more) the doctrine of CSR presume that the world will be a better place, and capitalism more benign, if businesses consciously aim to further the public good. But as we have noted, economic progress does not depend on a commitment by enterprises to bring it about. Now as in the past, the business contribution to the general welfare arises from the combination of opportunities and pressures that a competitive market economy generates; and the opportunities are widened, and the competitive pressures increased, in so far as economies become freer and the scope of markets is extended. This depends, not on enterprises, but on governments. Hence it is not through redefining enterprise motives, goals and ways of operating – for example, along the lines of CSR – that business performance of its primary role can be effectively improved: this requires official actions that fall outside the competence of even the largest corporations. Such actions by governments come under the heading of economic *liberalisation*. This is the route to extending and reinforcing the market economy.

To be sure, liberalisation is not the be-all and end-all of economic policy. In all too many economies today, especially though not only in Africa, the future of capitalism chiefly depends on the secure establishment of public order, property rights and an effectively functioning legal system. In every country, now as always, the extent to which

---

4   A critique of CSR is to be found in Henderson (2001), and the argument is taken farther in Henderson (2004).

liberalisation matters, and should be pursued, is a matter of debate. But there is obvious scope, in virtually every economy today, for enlarging the domain of competitive markets in ways that would make capitalism function better as a vehicle for economic progress.

What liberalisation chiefly comprises is easily stated, though the agenda must depend on each country's situation. It has both an internal and an external dimension. Internally, it has three main heads of action. First comes further *privatisation* of public enterprises, in ways that will give full opportunity to new entrants into the markets concerned. Second is *marketisation*, that is, replacing free or heavily subsidised public provision of goods and services by user charges or earmarked taxes, so as to open up possibilities of wider choice and competitive supply. Third is *deregulation*, and the relaxation of regulations and controls that are over-strict, under a wide variety of headings. The regulations in question include those that limit the scope for new enterprises to be set up or for new entrants to compete in specific markets.

The international dimension

Now as ever, liberalisation has an important external aspect. The effective functioning of market economies depends to a large extent on their openness to cross-border flows of trade and foreign direct investment, which create market opportunities and competitive pressures. Hence the future of capitalism, and the degree to which it takes competitive rather than collectivised forms, will be strongly affected by the external economic policies of governments. The story of economic progress since the end of World War II has been in large part one of external liberalisation – of the opening up of national economies to new possibilities for competition, innovation and change. Broadly speaking, this trend towards closer international economic integration is still proceeding. Even now, however, protectionist policies of various kinds retain their hold in virtually every country; and as a result, integration still has a long way to go. Given the resulting possibilities for external liberalisation, and the potential for the growth of cross-border transactions that now arises from the communications revolution, the freeing of former communist economies and the rapid growth of a number of poor economies among which both China and India are included, the scope for extending and diffusing the world market economy is vast. It remains to be seen how far governments will permit or encourage this scope to be realised. In particular, much depends on whether the USA and the EU will further open their markets for imports from developing and transition econo- mies, rather than maintaining their long-established restrictions on agri- cultural imports, continuing to resort to anti-liberal defensive responses such as safeguard and anti-dumping actions, and pursuing demands for 'acceptable' environmental and labour standards in poor exporting countries.

Economic progress and individual freedom

For the foreseeable future, capitalism as such appears secure. But the future of the market economy is by no means clear or assured. As in the past, economic policies across the world are likely to contain both liberalising and interventionist elements, and the balance between the two is not pre-determined. A reasonable prediction is that capitalism will become more widely diffused than now, while broadly retaining its powers of 'creative destruction', but that everywhere, with many local variants, it will to continue to bear collectivist aspects and features. The balance will be decided by the extent of liberalisation.

Contrary to what is often asserted or assumed, liberalisation is not, in either intention or effect, a means to furthering business interests. Its aim is not to placate or enrich businesses – which in fact are often opposed to it, with good reason, as contrary to their interests – nor to increase the power of corporations which it has no tendency to do. Its twin related purposes are, first, to further the material welfare of people in general, and second, to enlarge the domain of economic freedom for people and enterprises alike.

The latter aspect is especially to be stressed. The argument for capitalism, and for policies that will make it less collectivised than it is today, does not rest only on the ways in which they will further material welfare, but also on the other gains that go with economic freedom. Well-functioning market economies, and forms of liberalisation that will serve to extend and improve them, are a source of opportunity for rich and poor alike. They enable people to act in ways that will make their lives more complete, as well as materially richer.

References

Chandler, A. D. (1990), *Scale and Scope: The Dynamics of Industrial Capitalism*, Cambridge, MA: Harvard University Press

Henderson, D. (2001), *Misguided Virtue: False Notions of Corporate Social Responsibility*, London: Institute of Economic Affairs

Henderson, D. (2004), *The Role of Business in the Modern World: Progress, Pressures, and Prospects for the Market Economy*, London: Institute of Economic Affairs

Langlois, R. N. (2003), 'The Vanishing Hand: the Changing Dynamics of Industrial Capitalism', *Industrial and Corporate Change*, 12(2)

Schumpeter, J. A. (1942), *Capitalism, Socialism and Democracy*, London: Allen and Unwin

15 A CONSTITUTION FOR LIBERTY
John Meadowcroft

This chapter sets out a liberal constitutional and institutional structure towards which Britain should aim over the next 50 years. To lay out such an 'ideal' constitutional structure may at first sight appear at odds with the fundamental principles of classical liberalism: classical liberals reject the idea that there is a blueprint for an ideal society that can be imposed on a population and are extremely sceptical as to the possibility of deliberately constructing social or political institutions that are superior to those institutions that have evolved spontaneously. Rather, in the words of Czech President Václav Klaus – who oversaw the Czech transition from communism to liberal democracy as prime minister – successful institutions must be 'a delicate mixture of intentions and spontaneity' (Klaus, 1994). That is, they must set foundational rules that provide a framework within which society can flourish as a spontaneous order, developing in unforeseen and unpredictable ways (see also Hayek, 1973).

The task of a liberal constitution, then, is not to impose a preconceived structure upon society, but to provide a background structure within which a spontaneous social order can develop and thrive. Such an evolutionary process can take place only where government provides little more than a basic framework of law and private property rights and individual citizens have the greatest possible sphere of personal freedom.

Accordingly, the constitution for liberty proposed in this chapter sets out a framework for minimal government. The proposed constitution combines modest constructivism and evolution. It argues for the creation of a written and codified – though extremely limited – constitution to impose formal limits on governmental power, and for the further development of the UK's tradition of local and regional government to facilitate inter-jurisdictional competition. Beyond these changes, however, no great acts of constructivism are proposed. Rather, it is argued that all other political institutions should be largely left intact to operate within the new constraints that will be imposed by the written constitution and the devolution of power to largely autonomous devolved authorities.

A written, codified constitution

The United Kingdom is almost unique among contemporary liberal democracies in not having a written, codified constitution.[1] The absence of a written constitution need not imply weak or unstable political institutions, however. On the contrary, Britain, with its entrenched and enduring political institutions which have evolved in the absence of a written constitution, may be contrasted with those nations that carefully crafted constitutions to guarantee freedom and democracy but nevertheless descended into authoritarianism or totalitarianism. The collapse of the German Weimar Republic after 1933 is the most powerful and salient example of the absolute failure of a constitution that supposedly enshrined liberal democratic principles.

While it is true that the UK's unwritten and uncodified constitution has served the country well over many centuries, allowing, in particular, for a gradual evolution of political institutions, it is also true that, as Gladstone famously suggested, the UK constitution 'presumes more boldly than any other the good sense and good faith of those who work it'. The fundamental principle of the UK's unwritten constitution is parliamentary sovereignty; that Parliament can pass any law and no parliament may bind its successors. Because it is impossible for Parliament to act *ultra vires* within UK law, the only possible avenue for

---

1 The other liberal democracies without a written, codified constitution are Israel – which has recently moved to adopt one – and New Zealand.

appeal against parliamentary legislation is to supra-national authority, for example the European Court of Human Rights. While this institution may safeguard the basic human rights of UK citizens, it does not offer protection against the more prosaic but still harmful pathologies of majoritarian democracy, which in the UK have included the abolition of minority pursuits such as fox-hunting, successful rent-seeking by public sector trade unions and the imposition of pecuniary externalities in the form of excessive regulation and taxation.[2] Gladstone's presumption of good sense and good faith now appears to have indeed been presumptuous.

A written, codified constitution is necessary to safeguard the liberties of individuals against the danger of majoritarian tyranny inherent in any democratic polity. A constitution must have special legal authority – it must be a higher law than statutory legislation passed by Parliament – but to survive indefinitely it must also be open to change and evolution. It is proposed, then, that a written, codified constitution be created that has authority over Parliament. A constitutional court – which will be the highest court in the land – will be created to rule when Parliament or government has acted *ultra vires*. Amendments to the constitution may be considered by a constitutional convention that can be convened by a two-thirds majority in both Houses of Parliament. To take effect, all amendments to the constitution proposed by the convention must be approved individually by a two-thirds majority of the population (not of those actually voting) in a referendum.

Constitutional limits on government

The most important task of a constitution for liberty is to set constitutional limits on the ability of government to create legislation; all the institutional arrangements that will be described below are secondary to these basic restrictions on what government can do. Liberty can be

---

2   On externalities and government, see Meadowcroft (2004).

guaranteed by three relatively simple and straightforward restrictions on the power of government.

First, legislation may not discriminate against particular groups or categories of people. Legislation that discriminates on the basis of sex, race, age or religion, or on the basis of occupation, income or wealth, will be dismissed as unconstitutional. By making all taxes other than a flat rate income tax or sales tax unconstitutional, and outlawing the allocation of special government privileges to particular occupations, this measure will prevent the exploitation of particular groups or categories of people via the political process.[3]

Second, all legislation will automatically expire five years after it becomes law; for legislation to remain on the statute book it must be re-enacted by Parliament. This will ensure that all legislation has popular consent and is not assumed to have consent because it was approved by Parliament decades or centuries earlier. It will also ensure that the inherent conservatism of tight constraints on the legislature does not create a situation of stasis where the size and scope of government cannot be reduced from its present level. This measure will also mean that politicians will be fully occupied re-enacting expired legislation and therefore will not constantly devise new laws and legislation to fill parliamentary time.

Third, all new taxes and increases in the rates of existing taxes must be approved by a two-thirds majority of the population (not just of those who actually vote) in a referendum. This will help to ensure that increases in public spending have the consent of those who will be required to pay for them.

---

3   The idea of genuinely non-discriminatory legislation was proposed by Frédéric Bastiat (1850 [2001]) in the nineteenth century and is central to the constitutional political economy of Nobel laureate James Buchanan (for example: Buchanan, 1996).

Inter-jurisdictional competition: national, regional and local government

Competition between different jurisdictions must be central to a set of institutional arrangements that protect and maximise individual liberty and facilitate the evolution of a spontaneous social order. Inter-jurisdictional competition provides a framework for the provision of public goods that allows citizens the greatest opportunity to exit from those transactions in which they do not wish to participate in. Tiebout (1956) famously showed that the existence of competing jurisdictions of public goods provision can create an exit option comparable to that which exists in private markets; if public goods provision is devolved to a series of local municipalities, then it will be possible for consumers to move to those localities where the public goods provision most closely matches their preferences. Local authorities will also have an incentive to create regimes of taxation and service provision that will attract residents.

Inter-jurisdictional competition requires that public goods are provided at the 'lowest' possible level of government – that is, wherever possible by local government – and that each level of government raises all (or at the very least the great majority of) the money that it spends. It is proposed, then, that the great majority of public goods will be provided by a single tier of small, unitary local authorities (though in practice it is expected that most public goods will actually be provided by the private sector and provision be merely overseen by local authorities). Those services that are deemed to span multiple local authorities, such as certain aspects of policing, will fall under the remit of a system of regional government similar in size and scope to the present Welsh Assembly. The process of inter-jurisdictional competition will determine which public goods are provided by which local authorities and exactly how those public goods are provided. The national parliament will be left with principal responsibility only for national defence and foreign policy. This institutional structure will be constitutionally protected so that it cannot be arbitrarily amended by Parliament.

Separation of powers and a constitutional court

One of the principal idiosyncrasies of the British political system is the absence of a clear separation of powers between the executive, legislative and judicial branches of government. At present, the three branches are intertwined, as the executive is drawn from the legislature and the highest court in the land (the House of Lords) is part of the legislature. Consequently, checks and balances are limited: the executive is able to dominate the legislature to the point that the latter is unable to perform an effective scrutinising role, and the lines between law-making and law-interpretation have become blurred because the senior judiciary participate in the passing of legislation.

The lack of a clear separation of powers between the executive and the legislature is not easily remedied in a parliamentary, as opposed to a presidential, system of government. The constitutional limits on the powers of Parliament to make law described above, however, will provide a satisfactory check on the power of the government without the necessity of a complete separation of executive and legislative powers.

The introduction of a written constitution, and the concomitant creation of a constitutional court as the highest court in the land, will, however, create a complete separation of powers between the judiciary and the other branches of government. The constitutional court will be a separate, independent entity, composed of seven senior judges. Appointments to the constitutional court would be proposed by the Prime Minister, but must be ratified by a two-thirds majority of both Houses of Parliament.

A constitutional monarchy

As described at the outset, successful political institutions must be, to a large extent, path-dependent, reflecting the traditions of the country that they govern. Those constitutions that have failed have tended to neglect the importance of traditions and customs. The UK's political institutions must therefore reflect the fact that the UK is a constitutional monarchy with a long history of absolute monarchy before that. While there is a case for ending the special privilege enjoyed by one particular family by fortune of birth, in reality a constitutional monarchy does not pose a threat to individual freedom, whereas its abolition would have a destabilising effect by undermining respect for the hereditary principle in private property on the one hand and galvanising monarchist sentiments on the other.

The monarch should remain the ceremonial head of state, though he or she will be subject to the constitution and the law in the same way as any other citizen. The continuation of this ceremonial role would also ensure that the head of state remains outside the realm of party politics, thus providing a further limit to the power of elected politicians. In addition to the ceremonial role, the monarch would also be able to use his or her power as head of state to dissolve Parliament and would continue to give royal assent to legislation.

The Houses of Parliament

Within the context of the constitution described above, Parliament will be a much less powerful and less important body than at present; its law-making powers will have been constrained by the constitution and most of its present responsibilities will have been transferred to a largely self-financing and self-managing system of regional and local government. Nevertheless, Parliament will still be the principal legislative body in the land and it will have ultimate responsibility for national defence and foreign policy. Its composition, therefore, will still be a matter of some importance.

It is proposed that Parliament should remain a bicameral legislature, in accordance with the traditions of UK politics, but that a less powerful Parliament should be a smaller body. No major changes are proposed to the composition of the House of Commons. While the present first-past-the-post electoral system is far from perfect, it does reflect the political culture and traditions of the UK. The dangers of majoritarian tyranny inherent in the 'winner's bonus' that the electoral system usually gives to the party that wins the most votes will be curtailed by the constitutional limits on its powers described above. The first-past-the-post system also has the advantage that electorates can easily remove governments that abuse their powers or become corrupt.

Reform of the second chamber, and in particular reform of its composition, has bedevilled successive governments during the past century; in 1911, 1968, 1999 and again in 2003 radical reform of the Lords appeared to be imminent only to be abandoned on each occasion. Lords reform has proved so problematic because the transaction costs of change are likely to be high. If the Lords were to become 'more democratic' than the Commons, for example, if the second chamber were elected by proportional representation, then the relationship between the two chambers would change, perhaps making the Lords the senior partner. Alternatively, if the Lords were composed of prime ministerial appointees, this might prove unpalatable to the public, thus reducing the popular legitimacy of Parliament and increasing the power of the executive relative to the legislature.

The second chamber should continue its role as a reviewing and revising chamber, secondary to the Commons. Because the two chambers perform different functions it is logical that they should be constituted differently. In order to reduce the size of Parliament, it is proposed that the second chamber be limited to 500 members. The creation of an independent constitutional court will end the role of the House of Lords as the highest court in the land and the necessity for members of the judiciary to sit in the Lords. The removal of the final 92 hereditary peers from the Lords would further reduce the membership of the second chamber and be a logical next step in an ongoing process of change that has seen the hereditary element gradually removed from Parliament. It is proposed that an independent Appointments Commission be established to appoint 500 new members of the second chamber. The Appointments Commission would be charged with making appointments from across the party political spectrum, from outside the world of politics – in particular, members should be sought from the world of business and finance – and with as broad experience as possible. It should strive to maintain the tradition of the non-partisan cross-benchers within the second chamber. Current members of the Lords would be eligible for consideration by the Appointments Commission. Such an arrangement will probably not be considered ideal by many, but it would maintain an independent second chamber able to perform a specific revising and reviewing function, as well as being congruent with the historical traditions of the UK Parliament.

Conclusion

This chapter has set out a constitution for liberty for the UK. This involves a written, codified constitution that sets clear limits on what government can do and the creation of inter-jurisdictional competition between regional and local authorities within a highly devolved system of government. Within this new framework it is proposed that the principal institutions of UK central government should remain largely unchanged. The UK should remain a constitutional monarchy with a prime ministerial system of government. It is proposed that the second chamber of Parliament should no longer be the highest court in the land – this role is to be assumed by a new constitutional court – and that it should be composed of members appointed by an independent Appointments Commission. It is important to emphasise that the most important and radical aspects of these constitutional proposals are the limits on government's powers of action. The other proposals help provide the supporting framework. The framework without the specific limits on the powers of government will not be effective in promoting liberty and restraining the power of government.

Even if such a constitutional and institutional framework were created, however, liberty could still be threatened by a supra-national institution with claims to legal sovereignty over the UK. Indeed, many would argue that the European Union presently poses such a threat. The proper role of supra-national institutions, such as the United Nations and the European Union, is to provide a framework to ensure the international rule of law and facilitate free trade between nations. As such, while beyond the immediate scope of this chapter, supra-national institutions such as these would form part of an ideal global liberal economic order if they were committed to ensuring the international rule of law and global free trade: these issues are covered in the chapter by Minford and, to some extent, the chapter by Sally in this volume.

The adoption of the ideal liberal constitutional and institutional structure outlined in this chapter may seem politically impossible at present, but it is no more far fetched than the privatisation of the principal utilities, the abolition of exchange controls or the introduction of some form of road pricing in central London appeared when the Institute of Economic Affairs was first established 50 years ago. Hence, it might not actually be too unrealistic to believe that such a constitution might be in place when the IEA celebrates its centennial anniversary.

References

Bastiat, F. (1850 [2001]), *The Law*, London: Institute of Economic Affairs

Buchanan, J. M. (1996), 'Distributional Politics and Constitutional Design', in V. A. Muscatelli (ed.), *Economic and Political Institutions in Economic Policy*, Manchester: Manchester University Press

Hayek, F. A. (1973), *Law, Legislation and Liberty, Volume 1: Rules and Order*, London: Routledge

Klaus, V. (1994), 'Systemic Change: The Delicate Mixture of Intentions and Spontaneity', *Cato Journal*, 14(2): 171–7

Meadowcroft, J. (2004), 'Externalities and the Proper Role of Government', *Economic Affairs*, 24(3): 77

Tiebout, C. (1956), 'A Pure Theory of Local Expenditures', *Journal of Political Economy*, 64: 416–24

16 THE HAYEKIAN FUTURE OF ECONOMIC METHODOLOGY
Paul Ormerod

Introduction

Hayek as an economic theorist was 50 years ahead of his time. At the frontiers of thought, contemporary economics is gradually embracing the Hayekian vision. As the twenty-first century unfolds, economic theory will correspond more and more to Hayek's thinking about how the social and economic world works.

This essay is different from most of the others in the volume, because it deals in the main with theory rather than with practice. Of course, it is impossible to predict developments in economic methodology 50 years hence, or even to say what discoveries would be desirable. But abstract theory can have profound political implications. So this paper looks at recent developments in economic thinking that are likely to have a significant impact over the next 50 years.

Empirical evidence that market-oriented systems work better than centrally planned ones is overwhelming. Yet it is always open to the would-be planner to argue that previous designs were flawed, whereas his or her current scheme is bound to work well. Indeed, belief in the inherent efficiency of planning still permeates much economic and social policy-making in the West.

Hayek's achievement was to show that *theoretically* market-based economies are inherently superior to planned ones. Paradoxically, conventional free market economic theory cannot demonstrate this result. Hayek demonstrated that desirable social and economic outcomes arise not merely from the actions of isolated individuals, which is the postulate of orthodox economics. Rather, they are the *joint* product of both individual actions and the institutional framework in which individuals operate. Individuals and institutions arrive at efficient outcomes by a process of evolution and competition. Rigid, centralised planning operating under a fixed institutional structure is the very antithesis of what is required.

In this short essay, I first of all discuss the key achievement of conventional economic theory in the twentieth century. Second, I describe the limitations of this approach, and the intellectual impasse that it reached. I then contrast Hayek's approach with the orthodox one and show why his was so powerful and original. I go on to give examples of how the most exciting developments in economics in the past couple of decades are taking the discipline in the direction of the Hayekian vision.

The Hayekian challenge to twentieth-century economics

Over two hundred years ago, Adam Smith gave examples of particular industries – the canonical butcher, baker and brewer are perhaps the most famous – in which the self-interested actions of producers responding to incentives lead to benefits for everyone. Economic theory in the twentieth century was able to show that this could lead to a desirable outcome not just in a few but in *all* markets at the same time. Supply and demand would balance everywhere, and there would be no unused resources. An efficient, overall outcome would prevail. In the jargon of economics, this is the model of 'general equilibrium'.

General equilibrium theory is often seen as the crowning achievement of economics in demonstrating the superiority of free markets over planning. But, as Hayek realised, the *theoretical* implications of general equilibrium are that a centrally planned economy can be at least as efficient as a free market one, and may even be superior.

An important problem for conventional economic theory, both in this immediate context and more generally, is that in order to demonstrate the efficiency of markets, it requires its actors to be very clever.[1] They must be able to gather and process enormous amounts of information.

According to this theoretical view, efficient outcomes arise for the system as a whole because of the amazing cognitive powers of its component parts, the individuals and firms that comprise the system. Individual agents are able to decide not merely a good strategy to follow, but one which is *the* best – the optimal, a word used a great deal in economic theory. In situations where there is a 'best' strategy for an agent, the agent must be in possession of *all* relevant information. And to compute the optimal strategy with this information, a great deal of processing power may be needed.

The cognitive demands placed upon agents in the model of general equilibrium are so strong that, in principle, a central planner in a socialist state might well be able to satisfy them more readily than a more decentralised, market-based decision-making framework. During the 1940s and 1950s, the concept of planning was very fashionable in the West. It was also during these decades that the first really powerful mathematical results on general equilibrium emerged.[2] A number of academic articles at the time demonstrated that an omniscient socialist planner, by using the price mechanism as a way of deciding how resources should be allocated, could achieve results identical to those of an equally idealised free market economy, but with a more egalitarian distribution of income and wealth.

In other words, in the world of general equilibrium, the great theo-

---

1 Or, to be more precise, to act 'as if' – a favourite phrase in economics – they are very clever. In other words, they may not actually be very clever, but as long as they act as if they are, everything is fine.

2 The research programme on general equilibrium was finalised by the mid-1970s. But the definitive results are not good news for the theory. Radner in 1968 demonstrated that in order to be able to prove the existence of general equilibrium, all agents have to have access to literally an infinite amount of computing power. In the early and mid-1970s, Sonnenschein, Debreu, Mantel and Bliss showed that there is no theoretical presumption in general equilibrium either that market demand curves slope downward, or that market supply curves slope upward. For some reason, which is open to speculation, these central results of high economic theory are taught to very few students.

retical achievement of conventional economics in the twentieth century, socialism could be better than capitalism. Socialist planning in theory could be just as efficient as free enterprise, and at the same time more equitable.

It was Hayek's genius to offer a completely different, and much more realistic, view of how economies operate. In a Hayekian world, decentralised decision-making by individual agents is *unequivocally* superior to central planning. Indeed, a central plan may well be the worst possible institutional framework an economy could have.

Hayek anticipated by many years the modern theory of complexity, which is now being applied in both the social and natural sciences. In complex systems, the individual components of the system interact with each other directly to produce order and regularity at the aggregate, system-wide level. Their patterns of behaviour are not fixed, but may change as they observe the behaviour of their neighbours. Often, the system-wide patterns that emerge are unexpected and cannot be deduced from the rules of behaviour followed by the individual components. The whole is *different* from the simple sum of the parts.

In contrast, in general equilibrium the individual components interact only *in*directly via the price mechanism. Their rules of behaviour are fixed. And in principle the behaviour of the system as a whole can be deduced from the individual parts.[3]

The two visions of the world are fundamentally different. Conventional theory describes a highly structured *mechanical* system. Both the economy and society are in essence gigantic machines, whose behaviour can be controlled and predicted. Hayek's view is much more rooted in biology. Individual behaviour is not fixed, as a screw or a cog in a machine is, but evolves in response to the behaviour of others. Control and prediction of the system as a whole is simply not possible.

---

3   The increasingly narrow confines of modern orthodox theory reduce this to absurdity with the postulate that the workings of the economy as a whole can be understood from those of a *single*, 'representative' agent.

Hayek, complexity and knowledge

Interestingly – and how unlike most modern-day economists! – Hayek understood and admired the achievements of other intellectual disciplines. Anthropology attracted his particular attention, and of all the social sciences he regarded this as the one that produced people who thought in a sensible way about the development of society. For Hayek, an economist who is only an economist could not be a good economist.

The complex interactions between individuals give rise to *inherent* limits to knowledge of how systems behave at the aggregate level. No matter how smart the planner, no matter how much information he or she gathers, there are inescapable limits to how much can be known about the system.

An echo of this is found in the public choice literature. Public choice economics (for example, Tullock, 1976; Buchanan, 1978) tells us that planners can be as imperfect as the market. They are chosen by imperfect processes that can no more be perfected than market processes can be perfected to look like the textbook models of 'perfect' competition.

Vernon Smith (2003) gives a practical illustration of the limits to knowledge in his brilliant Nobel lecture. Airline route deregulation in the United States has led to the emergence of the so-called hub-and-spoke system. There are few direct flights between cities, and most journeys involve a change at one of the small number of 'hub' airports. Smith describes this as an 'ecologically rational' response. Significantly, as he points out, *no one* predicted in advance that this institutional structure would evolve. This is not because airlines were stupid. It is because customers did not know themselves in advance that this was the system they preferred. They were not cogs in a machine following fixed rules of behaviour. They had to learn which system they actually preferred through a process of market experimentation. Following deregulation, different types of route structure were tried, but the hub-and-spoke evolved as the most efficient. This institutional structure was discovered through a process of evolution and competition.

The world of economic forecasting gives another illustration of the inherent limits to knowledge in complex systems. The short-term fore-casting record of, say, GDP growth or changes in inflation is known to be very poor. This is the case not just in the UK, but across the West. In general, the forecasting record exhibits a certain degree of accuracy in that the average error over time is smaller than the size of the variable being predicted. But the error is still large compared to the actual data, and most of the accurate forecasts are made when economic conditions are relatively stable. Exactly when they are most needed, at turning points in the economy, forecasts are at their least accurate.

Very considerable high-powered resources are devoted, in treasuries and central banks across the world, to trying to make accurate forecasts. They are essential for successful control of the economy. If we are very unsure about where the economy might be in a year's time, we are of necessity unclear about what policy changes we should be making now. Yet the forecasting record shows no sign of getting better over time, despite the incentives for policy-makers to get it right.

A branch of modern mathematics enables us to show that the poor forecasting record is inherent in the nature of the economy. The precise details need not concern us here, but essentially the technique decomposes data or information into two separate parts. One is the bit that contains true information, and the other can be thought of as noise, or interference. The latter contains no information at all, as if it arose purely at random. Economic series such as GDP growth or the change in inflation can be shown to contain very little true information (see, for example: Ormerod and Mounfield, 2000). So systematically accurate prediction over time is impossible. The Hayekian interactions of the millions of individuals and firms that make up the economy as a whole lead to the unpredictability of the system as a whole.

Bounded rationality and imperfect information: the real world of markets

All the main developments in economics since 1970 can be thought of as moving the subject in the direction of Hayek's view of the world. There are two main ways in which this is being done. First, advances in theory have involved the gradual relaxing of the cognitive powers that are attributed to agents – to the individual firms and people in an economy. In Hayek's world, individuals do not need to have exceptional cognitive powers. Efficient outcomes arise not by design, but by the process of evolution through the complex interactions between individuals. Second, by acknowledging the fact that people's tastes and preferences are not fixed. They are influenced by the behaviour of others.

An important step took place in the 1970s, when economists such as George Akerlof and Joseph Stiglitz (2001 Nobel laureates) introduced the concept of 'bounded' rationality. Some, and possibly all, agents in any given context may lack access to full information. So their ability to gather information is restricted. They still follow the rules of maximising behaviour, however, and try to find the optimal strategy given the set of information they have.

The concept of bounded rationality has undoubtedly extended the power of conventional economics to understand the world. There are many situations in which it is more reasonable to assume that some or all of the relevant agents have access to partial rather than full information.

But bounded rationality can be used as an excuse to let the central planner in by the back door. Agents are still postulated to have the capacity to maximise, to find the best possible solution by processing information efficiently. All they lack is the means to gather all the relevant information. So here is a potential role for the planner, as a uniquely capable gatherer and provider of information, who thereby overcomes the deficiencies of the market.

It is only in the past ten to fifteen years that economics has made the decisive break, and has begun to embrace the Hayekian view of the world. Individuals and firms may not only lack complete information, but it may be impossible for them to work out the 'best' strategy to follow. The game of chess gives a simple example of this latter point.

Here, in fact, the rules are transparent and known. But the possible number of permutations of moves is so huge that no one knows the answer to the simple question: what is the best move for White to play when starting the game?

The problem is compounded when individuals can change their rules of behaviour depending upon what other people do – imagine playing chess if the rules that governed the moves changed unpredictably during the course of the game!

In the 1980s, Brian Arthur provided a realistic model of behaviour in such circumstances,[4] which has many practical illustrations. Like any theoretical model, it is only an approximation to reality, and needs to have customised bits added, as it were, when any particular application is being considered. But the general approach is powerful.

Arthur was interested in new technology markets, where very often one company or brand comes to dominate the market, even though from a purely technical point of view it may not be quite as good as its erstwhile rivals. Obviously, each product needs to satisfy a certain minimum level of quality, but it is not clear that the best product always wins out. Video recorders are a commonly cited example, and many people believe the same to be true of Microsoft and its suite of products (see Liebowitz and Margolis, 1999).

If consumers – or the central planner! – have perfect knowledge, such an outcome is impossible. The best will always win. But the key to Arthur's model, as with Smith's airport route example, is that consumers do not know themselves in advance what their preferences are. They have to learn them when the products become available. Lacking information, it makes sense to observe what others do and follow their example. If a friend or neighbour buys a VHS video recorder, say, and is satisfied, you are more likely to do the same. Once this process gets under way, the lead in market share which VHS obtains encourages retailers, for example, to stock tapes for these machines rather than for its rival Betamax, which

---

4   His original article (Arthur, Ermoliev and Kaniovksi, 1983) is highly mathematical.

in turn gives an incentive for new purchasers to choose a VHS machine, so that a virtuous circle comes into existence for VHS, which becomes a vicious one for Betamax. This is the key to Arthur's theoretical model, though the actual mathematics are pretty hair-raising.

The implications are very Hayekian. There is structure and order at the overall level, in the sense that we know that one product is likely to secure a dominant market position. The qualitative structure of the market that will emerge is known, but it is impossible to predict in advance which product will be the dominant one.

There are a growing number of models such as this. Their precise subtleties vary from context to context, but they each provide a better account of reality than conventional economics. Examples include explaining the volatility of financial markets, accounting for why the successes and failures of Hollywood films are inexplicable, understanding why dramatic changes in crime can take place, and the distribution of honesty ratings among sellers on websites such as eBay (see: Kirman, 1995; De Vany and Wallis, 1996; Glaeser et al., 1996; Ormerod et al., 2003; Laureti et al., 2002).

Even financial markets, the domain par excellence of free market theory, are not immune to this approach. For example, a recent model (Farmer et al., 2003) analyses the mechanics of price formation and the accumulation of stored supply and demand under the simple assumption that people place orders to trade at random. The model makes excellent predictions for transaction costs, price diffusion rates and a quantity closely related to supply and demand, using actual data from the London Stock Exchange. In other words, it appears that the price formation mechanism strongly constrains the market, playing a more important role than the strategic behaviour of agents.[5]

---

5   For a general discussion of the importance of low cognition among agents, see P. Ormerod, 'What Can Agents Learn?', opening plenary address to the Australian Economic Society conference, September 2003, at www.paulormerod.com.

Hayek, Vernon Smith and the future of 21st-century economics

The brilliant work of Vernon Smith has been at the forefront of this development, and is taking it in even more exciting directions. His Nobel lecture, referred to above, is an intellectual tour de force that helps to define the Hayekian research agenda for the twenty-first century. The challenge is not only to understand better how individuals behave, but to show how, through their interactions, institutions themselves evolve. Economic efficiency, we have finally realised, does not arise solely through the behaviour of individuals. It is a joint product of their behaviours *and* the rules of the institutional structure under which they operate. Hayek knew this all along. His giant figure looms at the threshold of twenty-first century economics.

References

Arthur, B., Y. Ermoliev and Y. Kaniovski (1983), 'A Generalised Urn Problem and Its Applications', *Kibernetica*, 19: 61–71

Buchanan, J. (1978), 'From Private Preferences to Public Philosophy: The Development of Public Choice', in *The Economics of Politics*, Readings 18, London: Institute of Economic Affairs

De Vany, A. and R. Wallis (1996), 'Bose-Einstein Dynamics and Adaptive Contracting in the Motion Picture Industry', *Economic Journal*, 106: 1,493–514

Farmer, J. D., P. Patelli and I. I.Zovko (2003), 'The Predictive Power of Zero Intelligence in Financial Markets', Los Alamos National Laboratory Condensed Matter Archive 0309233

Glaeser, E. L., B. Sacerdote and J. A. Scheinkman (1996), 'Crime and social interactions', *Quarterly Journal of Economics*, CXI(2): 507–48

Kirman, A. (1995), 'The Behaviour of the Foreign Exchange Market', *Bank of England Quarterly Bulletin*, August

Laureti, P., F. Salnina, Y.-K. Yu and Y.-C. Zhang (2002), 'Buyer Feedback as a Filtering Mechanism for Reputable Sellers', *Physica A*, 316: 413–29

Liebowitz, S. and S. Margolis (1999), *Winners, Losers and Microsoft*, New York: Independent Institute

Ormerod, P. and C. Mounfield (2000), 'Random Matrix Theory and the Failure of Macro-economic Forecasting', *Physica A*, 280: 497–504

Ormerod, P., C. Mounfield and L. Smith (2003), 'Non-linear Modelling of Burglary and Violent Crime in the UK', in *Modelling Crime and Offending*, Home Office Occasional Paper no. 80, London: Home Office

Smith, V. L. (2003), 'Constructivist and Ecological Rationality in Economics', *American Economic Review*, 93: 465–508

Tullock, G. (1976), *The Vote Motive*, Hobart Paperback 9, London: Institute of Economic Affairs

Part 2
Times past

17 AN INDEPENDENT STATION
Ralph Harris

Fifty years ago the outlook for the newly formed IEA was hardly promising. The post-war Labour government under Attlee had been followed by the Conservatives under Churchill, followed briefly by Eden and then Macmillan. Between them, the political stage was already being set for the long-running drama of the 'mixed economy', with the mixture, like Scotch on the rocks, becoming less and less Scotch and more and more rocks. The prospectus was never clearly set out. Policy was improvised on the remnants of wartime planning and high taxation, on to which Labour had grafted an ill-prepared programme of extensive nationalisation. Both parties broadly accepted the proposals for a comprehensive welfare state set out in the Beveridge Report to the wartime coalition government.

It did not take long to discern the emerging pattern of inflation, balance-of-payments crises and recession that were the beginnings of the boom-and-bust cycle that was to plague the British economy with widening swings for more than three decades. The first of Labour's two post-war devaluations occurred in 1949. Before his resignation as Chancellor, following a careless budget leak, Hugh Dalton, formerly a lecturer at the London School of Economics, had coined the description of inflation as 'too much money chasing too few goods'. Commentators began talking of an 'over-loaded economy' and looked for cuts in public spending. In 1950 the new Chancellor, Sir Stafford Cripps, reluctantly felt driven to impose charges for NHS prescriptions, thereby provoking a political crisis and the resignation of Aneurin Bevan.

By 1958 continuing anxieties about inflation had prompted the Treasury, now under the Tories, to propose a similar token cut in budget spending. The patrician Harold Macmillan rejected the proposals, thereby provoking the resignation of Peter Thorneycroft and his complete Exchequer team, including Enoch Powell. That 'little local difficulty', as Macmillan described it, can be seen in retrospect to have been the last stand of the old orthodoxy. The next two decades saw the era of Butskellism (named after the Conservative and Labour Chancellors, respectively Rab Butler and Hugh Gaitskell). What I came to call the 'Keynesian collectivist consensus' allowed little scope for fundamental change in economic policy right up until the Callaghan government was reluctantly forced to accept the inevitability of change in 1976.

Against such entrenched all-party opposition, the prospect for the fledgling IEA seemed hardly stronger than that for the British economy. Although our founder, Antony Fisher, had first voiced his dream of a kind of independent 'anti-Fabian' society to raise the banner of a free society ten years earlier,[1] building-up his Buxted Chicken enterprise necessarily took first priority. It was not until 1955 that he felt able to register the IEA as an educational charity, and a further two years before he took the plunge with my appointment as part-time general director in January 1957.

Looking back, it may seem that we embarked on our great adventure with no 'road map', nor even a business plan. We simply had start-up capital of about £1,000 and ran our budget on a monthly cash-flow basis, holding back printing bills to pay my retainer of £50 a month and the £3 a week rent for a tiny shared office in the City. If we were ever to find authors to write for us, it would certainly not be for the money.

Once Arthur Seldon joined me as editorial director, becoming full time in July 1961, we found that in reality we had a sheaf of road maps. These took the form of the luminous writings of the great classical liberal economists going back to Adam Smith and David Hume, enriched by Mill, Marshall, Cannan, Robbins and the neglected Austrian school

---

1   The full story of the creation of the IEA is well recounted in *Antony Fisher: Champion of Liberty* by Gerald Frost, Profile Books, 2002; see also John Blundell, *Waging the War of Ideas* (2nd edn), IEA Occasional Paper 131.

of Bohm-Bawerk and Mises. Miraculously, both Arthur Seldon and I, having proceeded to university from state grammar schools, had enjoyed a powerful inoculation against fashionable collectivism: he from the LSE, home of Hayek and Lionel Robbins, and I from the Cambridge of Dennis Robertson and Stanley Dennison before the Keynesian curtain descended on independent scholarship. Furthermore we had both had our fill of party politics: he with the shadowy remnants of the Liberal Party under Clement Davies, and I with the Conservative Party under Churchill's call to 'set the people free'. At last, in our first basement office together at Hobart Place, we had what Fisher, himself a disillusioned Conservative, liked to call, quoting Aristotle, 'an independent station'. If I showed the slightest political backsliding, Arthur Seldon was at my side to warn me, like a freed prisoner, to 'keep going straight'.

That he issued such a warning was just as well since the IEA was a charitable trust and therefore forbidden from conducting anything approaching political propaganda. We also came to see independence as expedient as we learned that party politicians were more or less impotent to reverse policies in the face of the hostile climate of opinion that confronted those sharing our classical liberal conception of the free society in the post-war years.

In the wake of Keynes – and Hayek

So, with slender resources, how could we hope to spread a better public understanding of the true contribution that a study of economics might make to public affairs? The answer, surprisingly, was first provided by Keynes. In the last paragraph of *The General Theory of Employment, Interest and Money*, he explained why he anticipated that his revolutionary doctrine would pass into general acceptance:

> ... the ideas of economists and political philosophers, both when they are right and when they are wrong, are more powerful than is commonly understood. Indeed the world is ruled by little else. Practical men, who believe themselves to be quite exempt from

any intellectual influences, are usually the slaves of some defunct economist ... the power of vested interests is vastly exaggerated compared with the gradual encroachment of ideas ... soon or late, it is ideas, not vested interests, which are dangerous for good or evil.[2]

With equal confidence in the eventual acceptance of our own very different ideas, we had this passage framed and displayed prominently on our board-room wall.

This confidence was mightily reinforced by Hayek's more penetrating elaboration of the same thesis in his impressive 1949 essay *The Intellectuals and Socialism*, in which he wrote: 'It is no exaggeration to say that once the more active part of the intellectuals has been converted to a set of beliefs, the process by which these become generally accepted is almost automatic and irresistible.'[3]

Hayek explained that intellectuals are not generally original thinkers and may not even be particularly intelligent. In fact, he lumped together teachers, journalists, broadcasters, priests, commentators and other communicators as 'professional second-hand dealers in ideas'. There is a further passage in this essay which inspired us at the IEA in difficult times:

> We must make the building of a free society once more an intellectual adventure, a deed of courage ... Unless we can make the philosophic foundations of a free society once more a living intellectual issue, and its implementation a task which challenges the ingenuity and imagination of our liveliest minds, the prospects of freedom are indeed dark ...[4]

---

2   J. M. Keynes, *The General Theory of Employment, Interest and Interest*, Macmillan, London, 1936, p. 383.
3   *University of Chicago Law Review*, spring 1949; reprinted by the IEA Health and Welfare Unit in 1998, p. 13.
4   Ibid., p. 26.

Harris and Seldon begin the fight back

We had an early opportunity to put to the test both the relevance of our shared liberal heritage for contemporary policy, and also our personal compatibility in working together on practical projects. As we settled into our first shared office in 7 Hobart Place, an ideal challenge presented itself. The new post-war experience of progressive inflation was prompting the press, as always, to search for scapegoats. Public debate dwelt on two related developments that emerged in the wake of the pent-up post-war demand for popular motoring and domestic consumer durables such as television sets, washing machines and refrigerators. Both these early manifestations of popular prosperity naturally expanded the two largely novel secondary markets of television advertising and instalment credit. The 'great and the good', from Lady Bonham Carter (Liberal), Quintin Hogg (Tory, later Lord Hailsham) to the Archbishop of Canterbury, joined other highbrow commentators in denouncing hire purchase ('never, never') and 'high-pressured salesmanship' for inciting the common man to live beyond his means and so push up prices. The more or less simultaneous appearance in 1958 of Galbraith's *The Affluent Society* enabled critics to link the advertising industry in this highbrow campaign against free markets.

Arthur Seldon and I found ourselves in spontaneous agreement that both these activities were closely related to neglected aspects of competitive marketing, and merited independent economic analysis. The only recent academic work on advertising had been by Nicholas Kaldor, a leading champion of the Keynesian collectivist consensus, who had myopically concentrated on the apparently high cost of advertising, without any attempt to analyse its effectiveness in building sales and reducing unit costs of production. Since we knew of no academics equipped to supply an alternative view, we decided to set about performing the analysis and writing a study ourselves. Accordingly, much of our first two years together was devoted to conducting original research into these two fascinating aspects of marketing: the first the supply of finance for domestic durables and the second the promoting of consumer demand for the changing goods and services on offer in the marketplace. This led to the publication by the IEA of *Hire Purchase in a Free Society* in January 1958 and *Advertising in a Free Society* in February 1959.

We practised a rough division of labour. My primary responsibility was what might be called the leg-work of extensive interviews and reading to assemble the facts about the origins, development, conduct, statistics, costs, effects and regulation of these two lively commercial activities. Arthur Seldon's primary role was to set these findings into a broad analytical framework showing their contribution to a free and rapidly developing economy resting on consumer demand and competitive supply.

Both books were widely reviewed and welcomed in the trade and financial press as up-to-date texts of value to practitioners no less than to students. Despite our specific criticisms of the practice of hire purchase, as of advertising, we had no doubts about their valuable contribution to a modern, progressive economy based on the primacy of consumer sovereignty. We found that controls over instalment credit through varying deposits and periods of repayment were seriously disruptive of production and irrelevant to the prevention of inflation caused by the government's monetary laxity. On advertising, we were critical equally of practitioners being paid by uniform commissions from the media as of Galbraith's scorn, even contempt, for consumer choice. Despite his air of authority, he also failed completely to understand that commercial promotion was but a small part of the ubiquitous 'salesmanship' and competing for attention conducted ceaselessly by politicians, clergymen, journalists, broadcasters and writers – including authors of campaigning books such as *The Affluent Society*.

This work together, which we had embarked upon almost on a whim to challenge what we regarded as superficial anti-capitalist stereotypes, had a number of unforeseen benefits. First, we made a good profit for the IEA on both books, which went into further editions. Almost as pleasing was the suggestion by Professor Paish at the LSE that we both deserved

PhDs for more useful contributions to knowledge than many tortuous, unpublishable academic theses. Second, we attracted donations to our funds from entrepreneurs in both advertising and hire purchase who were impressed by the practical value of our economic analysis. Third, and above all, the new editorial director and I had established a way of working together which was to bear fruit in many future Harris and Seldon joint products, and in a dozen less visible ways up until his delayed retirement a little ahead of me some 30 years later.

The genius of Arthur Seldon

It was Arthur Seldon's genius to build up over 30 years an extensive library of publications which, with hindsight, can be seen to follow the single insight of Keynes, elaborated by his arch academic adversary, Hayek, on the crucial role of intellectuals in opening minds to radical changes in public and business policy.

With our slender resources, there was no question of the IEA launching into a large market with hefty tomes for national distribution. Nor could we contemplate fat fees to commission authors ambitious to conduct new research at someone else's expense. As so often, poverty was the spur to invention. We settled for a modest niche market, specialising in short, scholarly texts aimed principally at teachers and students of economics, but accessible to interested laymen, journalists and the minority of politicians with a taste for serious reading. Each paper would appeal to intellectuals by rigorously applying standard market analysis to a contemporary issue of public or business policy that was of wide interest – or to neglected topics we judged worthy of public discussion. We were in effect entering the market for student texts once largely monopolised by the Fabian Society, but without its enfeebling constraint of having to conform to a party political agenda. We were therefore enormously encouraged when, within a decade, a Fabian Tract with the explicit title *The New Right: A Critique* was published in 1968 (Fabian Tract 387). The author was David Collard, who later joined our list of authors, and the tract devoted itself mainly to an earnest, respectful discussion of IEA publications as the 'most coherently expressed' samples of that genre. The author expressed his worry that the left was being successfully outflanked by the New Right.

Many authors will still remember, some ruefully, their first encounter with Seldon as what might be called a 'hands-on' editor. In addition to circulating guidance notes on length of manuscripts, house style, layout with side headings and the all-important question of timing, he required discussion of the literature, including alternative views, and forthright conclusions for policy without the least deference to what was conventionally regarded as 'politically possible' or even 'administratively feasible' – on neither of which could economists claim special authority. As an incomparable wordsmith, he would often pepper first drafts with suggestions in the margin on content, language and punctuation, and frequent one-word questions: 'source?' or 'evidence?'. He also had an ear for music and the rhythm of good prose which led him occasionally, when words failed him, to scribble in the margin: 'ugh'. When printer's proofs arrived, he would eagerly seize them from our colleague, Mike Solly, who worked with us from the early days as production manager, hand me a copy and invite comments. But I never forgot his early, emphatic warning that he worked best 'on a loose rein'.

His skill was not only in identifying topics but in matching them with authors who could draw on their existing work to produce a 10,000-word text for a Hobart Paper within a few months. He scoured the universities and journals to discover authors, not excluding civilised left-wingers, who understood the power of standard market analysis and could apply it to their special subjects. As members of the Mont Pèlerin Society, we were able to extend our search for authors to America, Europe, Australia and Hong Kong, among the distinguished fellow members of Hayek's informal international academy, formed in 1947 explicitly to bring scattered but like-minded scholars into regular communion every year or two at week-long conferences on almost every continent.

Our authors were attracted less by the modest fee, which in the early days might be 50 or 100 guineas for 10,000–12,000 words. More important was getting their distinctive views into print promptly and the growing evidence that publication by the IEA impressed more scholarly colleagues and was certainly no barrier to academic promotion.

Recruiting among the awkward squad

Nevertheless, in the early years we found some more established academics understandably reluctant to become too closely associated with a new, untried institute which our enemies regularly sought to dismiss as outdated, 'right wing' or worse. In retrospect it is easier to forgive those university teachers who privately shared our doubts on the ruling collectivist consensus but chose to keep their heads below the parapet out of anxiety about how talk of market forces would go down in the common room or among radical students, confused by the Keynesians or bemused by the Galbraithians. All the more credit is due to those early, mostly junior, academics whom our lively early patron, Graham Hutton, taught us to value as fellow members of the 'awkward squad' who positively relished acting as early path-finders for our educational mission. From them Arthur Seldon coaxed a stream of challenging studies on an almost bewildering range of topics such as the role of trade unions (Ben Roberts of LSE), the incurable flaws of the NHS (Dennis Lees of Nottingham), the case against farm subsidies (Eric Nash and Richard Howarth of Aberystwyth), the abolition of resale price maintenance (B. S. Yamey of LSE), the folly of rent control (Norman Macrae of *The Economist*), the potency of monetary policy (Alan Walters of LSE and Victor Morgan of Swansea), the case for education vouchers (Alan Peacock and Jack Wiseman of York), paying for parking and self-financing roads (Gabriel Roth, who had studied this subject while researching at the University of Cambridge), liberalising road transport (Gilbert Ponsonby of the LSE and John Hibbs of Birmingham), and the inevitable decline of British coal (Colin Robinson of Surrey). Arthur Seldon and I were both proud of having won places from grammar schools to leading universities and therefore took satisfaction in the fact that the majority of our most robust authors came from similarly unprivileged backgrounds. So far from enjoying 'gap years', quite a few of us had an enforced spell as wage-earners before moving into higher education.

Many more senior academics were to follow, including internationally famous names such as Hayek, Friedman, Buchanan, Stigler, Meade and Hicks, all of whom were to be crowned Nobel laureates,[5] and the legendary Harry Johnson (of LSE and Chicago), whose untimely death deprived him of the chance to achieve that distinction.

But it was no use publishing lively studies unless we could get them distributed and read. In the absence of salesmen to travel round bookshops, we depended on getting our papers reviewed by journalists in the right quarters or indeed in any quarters. We started with a number of allies, mostly among old-style City editors – before the days when every newspaper had at least one 'economic correspondent'. The allies included such heavyweights as Harold Wincott (*Financial Times*), Oscar Hobson (*News Chronicle*), William Clarke (*The Times*), Richard Fry (*Manchester Guardian*), Paul Bareau (*Statist*) and Andrew Alexander (*Yorkshire Post* and later the *Daily Mail*). The *Daily Telegraph* rarely missed welcoming the latest publication from the IEA, by many outstanding writers, such as Colin Welch, Maurice Green, John O'Sullivan, Peter Utley and later the powerful former Fabian, Patrick Hutber. Our deepest disappointment was the invariable neglect of IEA publications by *The Economist*, which we had expected to give special attention to our revival of classical liberalism, but which, in the early days of the IEA, adopted a conventional Keynesian viewpoint.

Within the office, which moved from 66a Eaton Square to 2 Lord North Street in 1969, the ceaseless flow of publications, meetings, monthly Hobart lunches[6] and special events came to rely on the total

---

5   Douglass North later wrote for the IEA and Coase, Becker and Vernon Smith all contributed to our mission in other ways.

6   Hobart lunches were named after Hobart Square, one of the IEA's early homes. This was to make clear the essential detachment from the day-to-day deliberations conducted across the road from our current home in the Houses of Parliament.

dedication and unquestioning loyalty of a compact staff headed by Joan Culverwell as my secretary, personal assistant and protector, as well as office manager, from 1959 to 1986. Further office stability was provided by the unswerving commitment of Mike Solly, also dependable and in proud charge of the printing and production of our handsome papers since the earliest days in the Hobart Place basement back in 1959; by the energetic Ken Smith, who joined us as librarian in 1968, but cheerfully found himself covering all the office chores that fell between the rest of us; and finally, as accountant, the ever patient George Laxaton, who kept our growing, though still hazardous, finances in perfect order before the days of spread-sheets. Marketing was greatly enlivened when John Raybould returned from Canada in 1975 to devote his experience and rare enthusiasm to extending sales and subscriptions for our dozen or so new titles each year. Our dozen-strong staff was completed by the gentle Sheila Shah working on subscriptions, and three all-purpose secretaries and copy typist/telephonists, forever 'bashing out' second and third drafts of much-amended letters and manuscripts in the days before the joys of word processing and photo-copying machines.

In 1969, pressure on Arthur Seldon and me was eased when John Wood joined us from Associated Electrical Industries (and earlier Lazards) as deputy director, to help with fund-raising, industrial contacts and general office oversight, as well as writing or contributing to half a dozen seminal studies, on subjects including the distribution of wealth, the measurement of unemployment and the evils of exchange control. I had first met John at Cambridge in 1945, when we were both supervised in economics by Stanley Dennison of Caius College, and so saved from the fashionable statism of Joan Robinson. Professor Dennison thought himself amply rewarded by becoming a dedicated trustee of the IEA in the 1970s and 1980s.

And the world said ...

In the early days, it was little comfort to identify other intellectual allies if they felt inhibited from proclaiming the missionary truths we shared with most of our authors. Indeed, their failure to speak out lent credence to critics who were more easily able to mock the brave minority who did as a remnant of outdated, fringe cranks intent on returning to a vanished past. The superficial plausibility of such early dismissals prompts me to conclude this first chapter with a selection from the growing flood of tributes which gave us all the more satisfaction for being often from unexpected sources.

> These new radicals are Jacobin inegalitarians, the sea-green incorruptibles of the Institute of Economic Affairs, who combine irreverence and power of analysis with a certain political naivety
>
> Brian Walden, Labour MP, 1969

> Ten years ago the IEA with its devotion to Adam Smith, free market economics and guidance of the economy by the money supply ... was still regarded as a bit of a joke. Today, helped by the pressures of real life, it has shifted some of the best known economic writers in its direction ... the analysis of Hayek and Friedman has taken on a new relevance to Chancellors and shadow Chancellors
>
> Ronald Butt, *The Times*, 1976

> The IEA for many years has been dismissed as a crank outfit ... its ideas now have much wider currency. In large parts of the Press they are the new orthodoxy and the Labour Government is by no means immune from them
>
> *Labour Weekly*, 1976

> Most of the axioms of economic Thatcherism are still intact. Consider some of them: the need to liberate the economy; the need to reduce central control and planning; the assertion that incomes cannot be regulated by laws; the belief in efficiency and competitiveness as absolute priorities; the contention that public spending must be paid for by productive output; and the sacred incantation that there is indeed no such thing as a free lunch
>
> Hugo Young, *Guardian*, 1985

The long uphill struggle of the IEA, which I stupidly wrote off as an amusing collection of cranks only 15 or so years ago, will surely come to constitute a vital part of any serious history of late-20th century Britain

Joe Rogaly, *Financial Times*, 1988

18 PLAYING THE FOOL WITH INFLATION
Ralph Harris

The post-war battle over economic policy can be seen as an unequal tug-of-war between two contrasting conceptions of the ability of party politicians to advance economic welfare. The dominant, collectivist view, bolstered by the apparent success of wartime planning,[1] assumed large scope for governments to improve economic progress by restricting the freedom of individuals as producers, traders and consumers. Almost unheard was the broad classical liberal alternative which rested on an essential but limited role for government to enforce a framework of laws within which the interplay of competitive enterprise and consumer choice could promote prosperity by allowing wider freedom for individual effort, innovation and judgement. The extensive and intellectually distinguished literature of economic freedom had by 1945 been swamped by the sub-Marxist assertions of collectivists, cunningly allied to the posthumous perversion of the teachings of John Maynard Keynes by the highly partisan 'Keynesians' after his premature death in 1946.[2]

Although dressed up in abstruse theorising, the vulgar lesson spread by the Keynesians was that market forces were defunct and that Labour's post-war aim of full employment without inflation required a combination of high public spending and low interest rates ('cheap money') buttressed by incomes policy. At Cambridge, the intellectual home of

---

1 Professors John Jewkes, Ely Devons and Stanley Dennison were among the academics who drew on direct experience with the Economic Secretariat of the war cabinet to reveal the shortcomings of wartime planning.

2 A devastating exposure of the ideological anti-capitalism of Joan Robinson, Kahn, Kaldor and other self-appointed 'Keynesians' will be found in 'Cambridge in the 1950s' by Harry Johnson: *Encounter*, January 1974.

Keynes, a spirited rearguard action from a scholarly liberal perch was conducted by Professor (later Sir) Dennis Robertson. There can be no doubt who were the targets of his urbane 1949 presidential lecture to the Royal Economic Society, significantly entitled *On Sticking to One's Last*: '... if the economist is in too much of a hurry to pose as the complete man – too anxious to show that he is duly sensitive to "the changed temper of the age" and has taken full account of what is "politically and psychologically possible" – he will be in danger of betraying his calling ...'

Such strictures did not deter the militant Keynesians from vying with one another in displaying their cleverness by constructing abstract mathematical macro-models of how economies were supposed to work. It was their remoteness from the real world which prompted Robertson to brand them in private conversation as 'clever sillies'. Their barren theorising explains how it came about that of the several hundred authors Arthur Seldon was to commission for IEA Papers over 30 years from perhaps 50 universities, I can recall only three from my own university of Cambridge – the robust Donald Denman, Professor of Land Economy, a lively New Zealander named Malcolm Fisher, who was at home with econometrics, and a Keynesian deliberately chosen to write on living with inflation. In contrast, Arthur's LSE supplied more than a dozen authors, including Lionel Robbins, Sydney Caine, Frank Paish, Ben Roberts, Alan Walters, Jack Wiseman, Alan Peacock and Brian Hindley.

Full employment at any price

The post-war stage was set by the 1945 Labour government's glib promise of 'full employment without inflation' in place of the more cautious 'high and stable employment' proposed by the wartime coalition government. The Labour government's simplistic logic was that if high pre-war unemployment was due entirely to a Keynesian deficiency of demand, then the remedy was clearly to raise demand until the entire labour force had jobs. The flaw was in treating 'unemployment' as an undifferentiated macro-total, which ignored the margins necessary to accommodate the real world with its immobility of labour, regional imbalances, shortages of particular skills, the impact of technical change and, not least, fluctuations in foreign trade. The obvious danger was that if total demand increased faster than the supply of output, then beyond a certain level the beneficial employment effect would be swamped by the baneful inflationary effect.

It was this search for a safe balance between full employment and inflation which ushered in the post-war era of 'macroeconomic fine tuning'. That proved a fancy name for the 'stop-go' policy, which might better be rechristened 'go-stop', since it was the overriding urge to raise employment which caused the need to check the resulting inflation. By 1957, when the IEA came on the scene, inflation rising towards 5 per cent had begun to trouble Harold Macmillan's Conservative government, as it had its predecessor. Yet it was when the Chancellor proposed a modest cut in public spending that the Prime Minister preferred to claim 'we've never had it so good' and accepted his resignation.

Before quitting office, Thorneycroft had set up a Committee on the Working of the Monetary System under a distinguished judge, Lord Radcliffe, with the usual quota of 'the great and good', including two professors of economics (Cairncross and Sayers). Their unanimous report in August 1959, with its vague talk of 'general liquidity', was widely interpreted as a complacent Keynesian dismissal of the use of monetary policy for the control of inflation. At the IEA we were not impressed. Within a month, Arthur Seldon had assembled half a dozen economists and leading financial journalists (Peter Thorneycroft, Professor Victor Morgan, R. F. Henderson, Professor F. W. Paish, Wilfred King and Sir Oscar Hobson) for a symposium to which I gave the challenging title *Not Unanimous*, with the cheeky subtitle 'A rival verdict to Radcliffe's on money' (IEA, 1960). It was a devastating critique which stands today as a damning indictment of the sloppy, fashionable thinking of a now vanished era when Robertson's 'clever sillies' ruled the roost. In little over one hundred pages, it concentrated a combination of scholarly analysis, historical reflection and seasoned judgement on the practicalities of banking and monetary policy.

Our authors boldly favoured control of the money supply by varying interest rates and traditional debt management as the most effective way of keeping down inflation. Indeed, Sir Oscar Hobson, the doyen of old-style City editors and an early member of the IEA's Academic Advisory Council, proved himself decades ahead of politicians, whom he shrewdly saw would always err in favour of full employment rather than stable money. He boldly proposed that the Bank of England be given 'a status in the sphere of monetary policy as autonomous as the status of the judiciary or the Comptroller and Auditor General in their respective spheres'. It amounted to privatising the Bank of England, which Labour had exultantly nationalised after the 1945 election. His aim was to remove from politicians control over money, which they would always exploit for crude electoral purposes. Most reviewers did not think the suggestion worth mentioning.

It was almost forty years later, immediately after their electoral victory in May 1997, that 'new Labour' broadly implemented this reform by the appointment of the Monetary Policy Committee and the granting of independence to the Bank of England. It has proved the bedrock of Gordon Brown's single major achievement, that of establishing a national framework of monetary stability. It helped to break the inflationary expectations that had dogged Britain ever since Keynesianism was unleashed after 1939. In the intervening half-century, the politicians and their academic claque band had reduced the value of the 1945 pound to less than four new pence, with incalculable damage to family and national fortunes.

Earlier monetary instruction

Throughout the 1960s and 1970s, instead of deploying monetary policy to check the root cause of inflation, Labour and Tory governments concentrated on the symptom of inflation: rising wages. Inflation, they argued, was due to the 'cost-push' of trade unions rather than monetary excess. There followed a succession of incomes policies, at first voluntary, by what the irreverent Bernard Levin used to mock as 'Solomon Binding' agreements, with 'plateaus', 'norms', 'pauses' and 'social contracts'; and, when exhortation predictably failed to stem wage demands, policy moved on to full-blown statutory controls over wages, profits and prices. It is hardly too harsh to say that, until 1979, politicians can be seen to have been playing the fool with inflation.

Here was a splendid opportunity for the IEA to demonstrate its independent station by challenging the consensus which party men took almost as a test of patriotism. In the wake of *Not Unanimous*, Arthur Seldon proceeded to commission a series of uncompromising critiques. The case for dissent was powerfully reinforced by the mild, whimsical Professor Frank Paish of the LSE, first in 1964 with *Policy for Incomes?* (Hobart Paper 29, with a separate contribution by Jossleyn Hennessy), followed in 1969 by *Rise and Fall of Incomes Policy* (Hobart Paper 47). His central analysis led to the unpalatable, and therefore generally unheeded, conclusion that inflation resulted from aiming at too high a level of 'full employment', leading to excess demand which, even in constrained labour markets, exerted irresistible upward pressure on money wages and other costs.

The lesson was further reinforced by Professor Victor Morgan, whose *Monetary Policy for Stable Growth* (Hobart Paper 27), published in 1964, stubbornly instructed readers on the standard theory and practice of financial policy. If interest rates were used more flexibly against inflation, he concluded, monetary stability would enable average long-term interest rates to be lower, which would both 'ease the tax burden [of the national debt] and give a direct stimulus to growth'. Then in came a powerful academic polemic from Professor Alan Walters, then little known outside the profession but later to become famous as Margaret Thatcher's private guru. His *Money in Boom and Slump* (Hobart Paper 44), published in 1969, concluded with a lesson that the author put in italics for emphasis: 'One of the main conclusions is that the government should stabilise the quantity of money'.

In his editorial preface, Arthur Seldon took the opportunity to pay tribute to: '… a small body of economists who refused to be stampeded by the over-simplifications drawn by over-zealous acolytes from Keynes's supposed destruction of the classical system of economic thought' (p. 6).

Our independent station was already drawing more academics and journalists into its camp, and there were yet more to come.

Friedman enters the fray

In 1970, a decisive chapter was opened by inviting our fellow Mont Pèlerin Society member, the sparkling, gnomish, intellectual wizard Milton Friedman of the University of Chicago, to deliver the first annual lecture established by the Harold Wincott Foundation to commemorate the *Financial Times* columnist whose premature death in 1969 robbed us of an outstanding ally. When Friedman outlined with gusto the essence of monetarism to a select British audience of academics and journalists, with a sprinkling of politicians, Arthur Seldon at once recognised the text as a classic restatement of Fisher's 'quantity theory', which he immediately published in our Occasional Paper series under the title *The Counter-revolution in Monetary Theory* (Occasional Paper 33) in 1970. Demand was entirely without precedent and it had run to a fifth edition by 1983. Twenty years later, it was still in demand and was republished with Friedman's outstanding IEA Paper *Unemployment versus Inflation?* (originally IEA Occasional Paper 44) in IEA Readings 57.

Based on long theoretical and empirical work, Occasional Paper 33 set out in little over twenty pages the definitive monetarist explanation of inflation, expressed in simple language, as may be judged by his conclusion: '… inflation is always and everywhere a monetary phenomenon in the sense that it is and can be produced only by a more rapid increase in the quantity of money than in output'.

I took the opportunity of Friedman's presence in London to arrange for him to meet various politicians, including the new Conservative

Prime Minister, Edward Heath. But any hopes that the Conservatives would prove better guardians of the currency than Labour were swiftly dispelled when, to the plaudits of *The Economist*, Heath's government pursued the mirage of full employment by means of a record expansion in the money supply above 25 per cent a year, which, after the customary time lag, yielded record inflation above 25 per cent in 1975. By then Heath's government had been swept from power as well-justified punishment for ignoring the power of Friedman's basic proposition. More encouraging was the later example of James Callaghan, whom we had spotted at the Wincott lecture. In 1976, as Labour Prime Minister, he announced the formal abandonment by the Labour government of deficit spending to promote full employment in well-chosen words that Friedman subsequently made a habit of quoting. His dramatic conversion has been attributed to the direct influence of Peter Jay, his son-in-law, who was then economics editor of *The Times* and had long been celebrated as 'the cleverest young man in England'.

Jay was undoubtedly our most spectacular early convert and one of the first journalists to seek a personal meeting with Friedman at the IEA office. Thereafter, his articles in *The Times* became like regular seminars on the continued mismanagement of the money supply, matched only by Samuel Brittan in the *Financial Times*. Yet it was this same Jay who had earlier publicly scorned monetarists as 'Friedmaniacs'. His turn-around gave us heart that 'clever sillies' were by no means beyond redemption. But it was getting late in the day. Inflation in the later 1970s was still well above 5 per cent a year, itself a rate sufficient to reduce the value of the pound to less than three pence over an average lifetime.

But there were plenty more publications to come. In the second of the half-dozen essays Friedman wrote for the IEA, *Monetary Correction* (Occasional Paper 41) in 1974, the master inveighed against the inequity and damage done by the fall in the value of money and concluded that, if politicians continued to indulge in the fraud of inflation (he described National Savings as a 'bucket-shop operation'), they should be required to bring in indexation of asset prices for the calculation of capital gains tax and index other tax thresholds as well as index-link payments on government bonds and encourage escalator clauses in wages, rents and other long-term private contracts.

The key issue that came to be endlessly debated was how far monetary expansion could reduce unemployment without the increased demand for labour pushing up money wages. In short, what was the safe limit to the pursuit of full employment policies? A confident answer was supplied in 1975 in Friedman's *Unemployment versus Inflation?* (Occasional Paper 44[3]), which developed the concept of a 'natural rate of unemployment'. This Paper had run into four editions by 1981, helped by Samuel Brittan, who popularised this important concept as the 'non-accelerating-inflation rate of unemployment', which became famous among the cognoscenti under the abbreviation of 'NAIRU'. It shifted the debate to ways of improving the flexibility of the labour market so as to reduce the unavoidable margin of idle resources. As has been noted, still in demand in 2003, it was then republished. Also important was Axel Leijonhufvud's brilliant critique of Keynes, *Keynes and the Classics* (Occasional Paper 30), which was reprinted seven times.

How much unemployment?

If there was a safe NAIRU, it would be necessary to have a better guide to the changing number of unemployed, which Arthur Seldon judged to be grossly exaggerated by the published statistics. So in 1971, when the Labour opposition, the CBI, the TUC and the National Institute of Economic and Social Research (NIESR) were again clamouring for 'reflation' to combat unemployment rising above a million, he persuaded our deputy director, John Wood, to subject the published figures to detailed analysis. The revealing result was published as Research Monograph 28 in 1972 with the title *How Much Unemployment?* After allowing for the

---

3   Occasional Paper 44 contained a commentary by David Laidler applying Friedman's analysis to the UK.

acknowledged unemployables, the short-term unemployed moving between jobs and the unfilled vacancies, he concluded that the headline of 'one million unemployed' might be close to the minimum compatible with avoiding inflation in our inflexible labour market. The favourable reception of this Monograph encouraged him to write in 1975 a full-length Hobart Paper (65) with the more challenging title of *How Little Unemployment?*, which reinforced the lesson that political and press panic about 'mass unemployment' was misguided and should not be exploited by the Conservative opposition to justify expansionary 'reflation'.

In addition to throwing light on the domestic inflation/unemployment issue, our ingenious editorial director found further celebrated authors, such as the brilliant, maverick Conservative politician Enoch Powell, and academic Harry Johnson, to discuss such related aspects of the international economy as the choice between devaluation, floating exchange rates and the discipline of the gold standard as alternative ways of avoiding the persistent cycle of boom and bust, which condemned Britain to recurrent balance-of-payments crises throughout those post-war years.

Hayek's competing currencies

F. A. Hayek – who ranks with his fellow Nobel Laureate, Milton Friedman, as our most distinguished author and mentor – chose the IEA to publish his most radical, even revolutionary, proposal in 1976. It involved nothing less than the removal from governments of the age-old state monopoly over the issue of legal-tender money. The logic was, as always, impeccable. Unlike producers of other goods, all national monetary authorities can compel citizens to hold their fiat notes and coins, however much they depreciate in value owing to over-issue. Hayek's simple solution was to deprive governments of their monopoly by abolishing the legal-tender laws and permitting competition from private issuers of money. In this way, people would be given a choice between currencies so that, by a reversal of Gresham's law, good currencies (i.e. those that best kept their value) would drive bad currencies out of circulation. Instead of governments profiting from inflating the currency, they would have the strongest conceivable incentive at all times to maintain the value of the currency. If they did not, the government would risk their currency being driven out of circulation by more successful competitors.

I remember standing in the board room at 2 Lord North Street when the great man outlined the theme of his manuscript, to which he had given a title along the lines of 'A proposal for concurrent currencies'. After a chuckle over its audacity, I recall hesitantly asking whether we would be accurate to render his message for marketing purposes as 'The denationalisation of money'. He astonished me by expressing instant enthusiasm for my title – by which his 1976 Hobart Paper 70 passed into a second edition in 1978 and became something of a cult text among our growing band of student acolytes. It was certainly the most advanced example of a free market solution to the ever present threat of inflation. Although no government has yet implemented such a dramatic policy within its own country, the abolition of Britain's wartime system of exchange control in 1979 (within months of publication of IEA Research Monograph 33, *Exchange Control For Ever?*, by John Wood and Robert Miller, urging repeal of exchange controls) enabled British citizens for the first time since 1939 to hold and transact in dollars or any other foreign currencies they might prefer to sterling. This was a reform that was long delayed by governments of all parties as 'politically impossible' yet, like many IEA-inspired reforms, would now appear unthinkable to reverse.

19 NOW FOR 'PLANNING'
Ralph Harris

It is easy with hindsight to see where post-war governments of all parties went wrong, leading to the incalculable damage of ever rising inflation, recurrent sterling crises, industrial unrest and flagging standards of living. Their combined effect was to bring Britain from the peak of international prestige as leading liberators of Europe in 1945 to the status of 'sick man of Europe', suffering from 'the British disease'. What can be claimed for the IEA is that, from its earliest days, under the editorial selection, direction and orchestration of Arthur Seldon, our growing band of authors consistently diagnosed the errors and pointed to remedies that were largely ignored – even mocked – until the election of Margaret Thatcher in 1979 following 'the winter of discontent'. Yet we had no access to special information, let alone the many millions of pounds of taxpayers' funds that should have conferred a huge research advantage on the NIESR, the National Economic Development Council (NEDC) and of course the Treasury, with its army of mostly Keynesian-trained economists. Nor would we, or our authors, have claimed to possess superior talents to all those 'clever sillies' trapped in the Keynesian collectivist consensus. The two critical advantages we enjoyed were a thorough grounding in classical market analysis and an independent station, which left us wholly free from the encumbrance of the party political pursuit of short-term electoral expediency.

Misled by the apparent success of wartime planning – with a comprehensive apparatus of coercion wholly inappropriate to a free society in times of peace – and a single national vision, the Labour Party after 1945 assumed there were no limits to the power of good intentions to solve every economic problem. Hence their reckless promises, not only of full employment, but of bigger and better welfare benefits, rising standards of living, a strong pound and stable prices. Despite Churchill's instinctive call to 'set the people free', the Conservatives before 1979 shrank from a head-on confrontation with unpalatable collectivism and settled for an unprincipled 'mixed economy'. It was the predictable failure to resolve these inherent contradictions which shifted the policy mixture cumulatively towards an increasing measure of confused collectivism.

On to 'growthmanship'

In addition to the distortionary effects and inequity – I would say fraud – of continuous depreciation of the value of money, inflation was used, as we have seen, to justify ineffective incomes policies and ever more piecemeal government expedients that were dignified by the name of 'planning'. A particular source of long-run damage was the increasing subsidisation of nationalised industries in the hope of holding down their prices. Such expedients had the unintended effects of removing the spur to efficiency, financing unearned wage increases and raising taxation to cover the resulting deficits, without keeping inflation in check. So if governments were not prepared to stop the 'too much money' which was 'chasing too few goods' for fear of violating the sacred cow of full employment, the soft option appeared to be to go flat out to increase the supply of goods.

Thus did the leading aim of policy shift to the single-minded cultivation of a new sacred cow, namely that of economic growth. Having nationalised the 'commanding heights of the economy' only to find they became bottomless pits for taxpayers' money, ministers set ambitious targets for their output. Instead of repeated failure bringing such expedients into question, it led to ever more strident demands for more or 'better' planning. It was a Conservative government which first launched a 'national exercise' by setting up the NEDC in 1961. The Chancellor, Selwyn Lloyd, was briefly able to bask in the euphoric support of the CBI, the TUC, the NIESR and what passed as the 'responsible' press and broadcasting commentators. In place of piecemeal planning, the big idea was an essentially corporatist attempt to bring together representatives of government, industry and trade unions to help guide the economy on to an agreed 'path' of faster economic growth, principally through Andrew Shonfield's superficial panacea of increased investment. Even before the NEDC had produced its first projections, Arthur Seldon had invited an internationally renowned economist from Oxford, Dr Colin Clark, to review the prospects.

The result was an outstanding Hobart Paper (10) published in 1961 with the simple title of *Growthmanship* and the author's subtitle: 'A Study in the Mythology of Investment'. He offered a damning definition of growthmanship as: 'An excessive preoccupation with economic growth, advocacy of unduly simple proposals for obtaining it, and the careful choice of statistics to prove that countries with a political and economic system which you favour have made exceptionally good economic growth ... '

That characterisation is worth pondering as the verdict of a leading economic statistician whose pioneering *Conditions of Economic Progress*, written 20 years earlier, had become a widely acknowledged student classic. In addition, sceptics might bear in mind that Clark was a former Fabian and his hint at statistical skulduggery is especially significant from a scrupulous analyst who was respected as a devout Roman Catholic. Rather than parade his superior technical skill, he identified the principal factors in economic growth as being not material but human qualities, including knowledge, effort, skill, organisation, education and enterprise. His list of recommendations constituted a radical programme of liberal reform, ranging from freeing competitive markets by reducing both union and business restrictive practices, to cutting taxation, imposing commercial criteria on state industries and encouraging the distribution of profits rather than ploughing them back. Above all, he scored a bull's-eye by warning against trying to force growth by means that created inflation, thereby distorting efficient investment that was the professed aim of the whole exercise.

Behold: the National Plan

So far from heeding such strictures from a former planning assistant to the austere socialist Sir Stafford Cripps, the Labour government that came to power under Harold Wilson in 1964, following his appeal against 'thirteen wasted years of Tory misrule', went hell for leather to create a whole new Department of Economic Affairs free from what Keynesians scorned as the cautious 'Treasury view'. Its senior minister – as full secretary of state, no less – was the trade union MP George Brown. His speciality was persuading and cajoling trade union and business leaders into paying at least lip-service to a fully fledged, comprehensive National Plan. This document was duly assembled on the basis of dubious company answers to a national questionnaire on such issues as production capacities and demands for labour and strategic materials, not forgetting corporate hopes for expansion. The imposing-looking document duly mocked nature by having a gestation period of one year followed by a frenetic life of only nine months before collapsing amidst yet another economic crisis. The whole charade was masterminded by the NEDC, which acquired the user-friendly nickname of 'Neddy'. Recalling the *Shorter Oxford* definition of a mule as 'the off-spring of a he-ass and a mare', I used to parade one of my favourite quips that Neddy, like the mule, 'had neither pride of ancestry nor hope of progeny'.

But the Conservatives in opposition were not to be left out of the launching celebrations. Proof of the all-party commitment to such nonsense was provided by a great Conservative swell and old Etonian baronet named Sir Edward Boyle, who joined enthusiastically in supporting a House of Commons motion welcoming the National Plan, adding the sneer that everyone now supported planning except the Oxford professor Jewkes. No doubt this well-bred Oxford man singled out Jewkes not only as an opponent of the truly egregious socialist Oxford don Thomas Balogh, but also as author of a brilliant exposure of wartime economic management published back in 1947 under the title *Ordeal by Planning*. Knowing John Jewkes well as a delightful, gentle, modest IEA trustee, I was not surprised by how hurt he was to have been exposed to public mockery.

Does planning never work?

The abject failure of the National Plan was predictable, and was indeed predicted. Several months before it was unveiled, portentously as ever by George Brown in September 1965, the IEA published an Eaton Paper (having moved from 7 Hobart Place to 66a Eaton Square) with the same title, exposing the emptiness of the sterile questionnaire to businessmen on which it purported to be based. The author, John Brunner, was another old Etonian, modest, scholarly and wholly free from party political delusions, but with good 'leftist' credentials, having worked for the BBC and the Treasury, before joining the *Observer*, from where he had helped respond to the Department of Economic Affairs questionnaire. That experience persuaded him how unreliable industry's answers would be as a guide to future investment and employment, based as they must be on a mixture of sheer guesswork, pious crystal-ball-gazing and optimistic hopes by companies of increased production, without any certainty of being able to sell the projected output. He warned against fabricating a statistical straitjacket for British industry and concluded: 'The more everything is reconciled with everything else, the worse the confusion when a particular forecast is confounded.' This verdict brings to mind a similar warning by Hayek in *The Road to Serfdom* that 'the more the State plans, the more difficult planning becomes for the individual'.

George Brown certainly took his Plan very seriously indeed, and we at the IEA positively relished the accolade of being denounced by him as 'weary willies'. We took more tangible satisfaction from Brunner's Paper going into three editions in as many years. Even *The Economist*, on this occasion, welcomed 'a corrosive examination of the ponderous questionnaire that the DEA sent to businessmen to help it prepare its plan'. Alas, John Brunner was so disenchanted with Mr Wilson's government that he emigrated to Western Australia, where, he said, politicians did not indulge in endless rhetoric about growth but rather created the freer market conditions that encouraged growth to happen.

However trenchant we may judge John Brunner's lucid Paper to have been, it cannot be claimed to have contributed to the collapse of the National Plan since such a mountain of make-believe did not require outside help to fail of its own absurdities. Suffice to report that by mid-1966 a renewed balance-of-payments crisis jolted the shell-shocked Mr Brown into declaring: 'Britain no longer has a Plan', and the economy limped on planlessly towards Labour's second unplanned devaluation in 1967.

So far from being discouraged by the apparent indifference of politicians to our warnings, Arthur Seldon's reaction was to redouble his search for authors in order to produce a positive barrage of high-powered literary shells against the entrenched position of the planners in government and academia. On the recommendation of Professor Jewkes, we appointed as staff researcher the industrious George Polanyi (son of the legendary polymath Michael), who drew on his experience as an economist in the gas industry to prepare a report published as *Planning in Britain: The Experience of the 1960s* (1967). Notice that, just as we produced our National Plan before the original was actually published, we could not wait until the end of the decade before pronouncing our requiem on the 1960s. Polanyi's exhaustive documentation and meticulous analysis left no room to doubt the failure of the NEDC and the Department of Economic Affairs to escape from the go-stop cycle. Most compelling was his demonstration that planning offered no rational criteria to guide investment and other decisions between alternative lines of production. In short, planning provided no substitute for 'the price and profit signals' of competitive markets.

Not content with such demolition, Arthur Seldon threw himself with gusto into assembling more and more economists to expose the fallibility of planning and forecasting in steel, electricity, nuclear power, science, medicine, imports, exports, national income (GNP) and even the revised estimates of population changes by no less an authority than the

Registrar General. Again and again, the errors were caused by extrapolating past trends, without allowing sufficient margins for unexpected changes. Always, the planners were backward-looking. The official forecasters were further inclined to incorporate an undisclosed element of wishful thinking in which the planners were encouraged to persist longer, so that eventual adjustments had to be all the more drastic and disruptive.

... even in France

Frustrated by economic crises at home, the 'clever sillies' took refuge in *la planification française* of M. Jean Monnet, which prompted our masterful editorial director to commission an appraisal by Dr Vera Lutz, an English economist living in Switzerland. Her meticulous report, published for us by Longmans in 1969, was called *Central Planning for the Market Economy* and showed that French planners were not immune to wide discrepancies between targets and outcomes. Dr Lutz's scholarly analysis identified the fundamental problem as nothing more than 'the prevalence of uncertainty and limited knowledge about the course of human affairs'. As an anonymous joker has said: forecasting is always difficult, especially about the future. The decisive merit of a market economy is that it acknowledges a central role for risk-taking and mitigates the problem of ignorance by dispersing judgement and initiative among entrepreneurs using their own or their shareholders' money.

When the failure of planning drove Galbraith and Shonfield to propose the great 'new' idea of a convergence between the collectivist and competitive models, Dr Lutz argued powerfully that compromise was impossible between the rival logic of two utterly distinct conceptions. Instead, the best prospect of progress was by purging such distortions as inflation, excessive taxation, bureaucracy and restrictive practices; and ending the political denigration of the profit motive.

Among further papers that followed in the 1960s, the persistent Professor John Heath followed Professor B. S. Yamey's earlier classic (and successful) demolition of resale price maintenance with Hobart Paper 11, entitled *Still Not Enough Competition*, in 1961. The wise economic historian Professor G. C. Allen wrote Occasional Paper 14, entitled *Economic Fact and Fantasy*, published in 1967, celebrating how vigorously competitive enterprise persisted in the teeth of inappropriate and inconsistent state interventions. In Research Monograph 5, *Private Enterprise and Public Emulation*, published in 1966, a young Italian journalist named Mario Deaglio compared another of Labour's pet ideas, launched with the usual fanfare of trumpets as the Industrial Reorganisation Corporation (IRC), unfavourably with its more thorough-going Italian model, renowned as the Industrial Reorganisation Institute (IRI). In more constructive mode, Professor Harold Rose of the London Business School drew on his combined experience in business and academia to launch in 1963 our new series of Eaton Papers with *Disclosure in Company Accounts*, which called for more information more frequently to enable shareholders, takeover bidders and managements themselves to assess the efficiency with which all aspects of their business were conducted. An interesting proposal, echoed by other IEA authors, was that companies should distribute profits to shareholders for reinvestment or spending, rather than retaining them for investment as the directors decided, which too easily led to 'the survival of the fattest' rather than of the fittest.

Not forgetting free trade

The lessons of both Dr Deaglio and Professor Rose were reinforced in 1970 by Dr Brian Hindley's Hobart Paper 50, *Industrial Merger and Public Policy*, which urged freer competition, including from imports, through tariff reduction. Against the meretricious fashion of growth through planning, many IEA authors consistently argued for the stimulus of international competition through free trade. In Research Monograph 17, entitled *The Shape of Britain's Tariff* (1968), Dr Sidney Wells attacked protectionism, which is after all a patchy form of partial planning. In

Hobart Paper 17, *UK, Commonwealth and Common Market*, 1962, another of our Nobel laureate authors, James Meade, welcomed the prospect of removing trade barriers while strongly opposing the Common Agricultural Policy and import levies, and warning of the possibility of the EEC becoming 'a tight parochial, European bloc'. Nevertheless, at that time the comparative success of post-war European economies appeared to offer disillusioned Keynesians and planners in all parties an escape from go-stop in Britain by joining the 'common market', as the European Economic Community (later EU) was then called.

To test this new fashion, Arthur Seldon commissioned Russell Lewis as a liberal economist and a 'good European' who had represented the Brussels Commission in London. His Hobart Paperback 3 shrewdly analysed the Treaty of Rome as incorporating the free market principles of Adam Smith, but operating through a strong bureaucracy in the form of an unelected Commission. My chosen title, *Rome or Brussels...?* (1971), exactly conveyed the author's anxiety that the benefits from widening competitive markets could be swamped by bureaucratic regulation from an overactive Commission. We can now see how that fear was realised by the nomination of a French corporatist, Jacques Delors, as President of the Commission. Instead of implementing the Single European Act to open up the market through 'mutual recognition' of national products, the Commission imposed crude standardisation in the name of 'a level playing field', which is no more than a textbook example of flat earth economics, since trade depends on differences rather than uniformities of products. It is primarily that collectivist impulse which explains why market economists have almost universally turned against such an apparently liberal project.

The verdict on 'planning'

Looking back on the prolonged collectivist experiment of those three post-war decades, the saddest reflection for an economist concerned with public as well as personal economy is the truly incalculable waste of time, talent and resources devoted to the project of planning the British economy. Is there anyone not personally caught up in these tortuous proceedings who would in retrospect dispute my verdict that it was all along an intellectually disreputable project? Despite the apparent sophistication of the civil servants, businessmen, leading commentators and at least some of the politicians involved, it amounted to nothing more than a succession of desperate expedients in a determined effort comparable to making water flow uphill. It is a wry reflection that most of the guilty men, especially from the Treasury, will by now be blissfully retired, some with knighthoods and all with comfortable pensions, the values of which were thoughtfully indexed on the very eve of Heath's reckless inflation after 1972!

Against such a sorry background of profound intellectual confusion and bewilderment, a mere handful of MPs stand out all the more memorably for their courage and clear thinking. Among Conservatives, such exemplars would include Enoch Powell, whose sophisticated advocacy of free market forces put his colleagues to shame, the young Geoffrey Howe from the Bow Group, who became one of our most principled and perceptive regular subscribers, and the scholarly Keith Joseph, who was conscientiously fighting his way from early agnosticism to crusading champion of competitive enterprise. All three were regular students of IEA papers and periodic visitors to Eaton Square and Lord North Street. For a brief interval we had hopes of intellectual support from a brooding Welsh Labour MP, Desmond Donnelly, who broke away from his party to launch an independent, anti-Wilson campaign for freedom of choice, which abruptly collapsed in the 1970 general election. The only Liberal MP from whom we drew the least indication of interest was its dashing leader for a while, Joseph Grimond, who totally failed to carry support among any of his followers.

It was not until the early 1970s, with the abject failure of Heath's latest version of 'economic planning' plain to all except Wedgwood Benn and a handful of hard Left MPs and trade union leaders, that we at the IEA detected unmistakable signs of keen interest among an emerging band of high-flying Tory MPs. Led by Margaret Thatcher, Geoffrey Howe and Keith Joseph, they now included a younger trio of lively economic journalists (Nigel Lawson, David Howell, Jock Bruce-Gardyne), a thoughtful stockbroker (John Biffin) and a delightful, sparky solicitor (Ian Gow). Both Arthur Seldon and I, impatient as ever for the anticipated awakening, might be forgiven for thinking it had seemed a long and lonely wait.

20 MARKET VERSUS STATE
Ralph Harris

The 'clever sillies' were perhaps at their silliest in their lofty scorn for 'market forces'. It is hardly too harsh to say that many sophisticated academic leaders of the Keynesian collectivist consensus never really got the hang of market pricing.[1] They seemed stuck in the early chapters of elementary textbooks that start from the highly abstract formal model of 'perfect (atomistic) competition' and go on to denounce such real-world 'imperfections' as consumer ignorance, salesmanship, branded products and other 'monopolistic' practices. The trouble was less with the real world than with their wholly unrealistic parody of perfection.

Incorrigible socialism

This is a large subject, but the assumption that every market 'imperfection' can be remedied by political intervention depends on the elementary non sequitur of perfect government. The best demolition of this fallacy was a masterly Occasional Paper by our editorial director, Arthur Seldon himself, for which, with his rare verbal felicity, he chose the title *Corrigible Capitalism, Incorrigible Socialism*. It was published as Occasional Paper 57 in 1980. It compared 'the relative perfectibility of competitive private enterprise and monopolistic government production'. Not only does competition disperse and diversify decision-making, its faults are 'largely incidental and removable', whereas the faults of monopoly government production are 'essentially integral and irremovable'. That

---

1 Their visceral hatred of market forces was vividly revealed by T. Balogh's confident but premature obituary on Erhard's post-war miracle in Germany, mockingly entitled *An Experiment in 'Planning' by the 'Free' Price Mechanism*, Basil Blackwell, 1950.

argument followed his old LSE mentor, Lord Robbins, who taught that the market was more democratic than government because it provided a process of election[2] in which consumers vote daily with their own money for the goods and services that best satisfy their (developing) individual preferences. Even imperfectly competitive pricing thus widens consumer choice and gives full representation to minority tastes.

Rather than joining the elaborate theorising of the 'clever sillies' on monopolistic competition, oligopoly and other variants, Arthur Seldon constantly sought out authors who could assemble and analyse empirical evidence from the practical operation of markets and non-markets in a wide range of goods and services both at home and abroad. Thus one of the earliest Hobart Papers, entitled *To Let?*, published in 1960 as Hobart Paper 2, by Norman Macrae of *The Economist*, showed how rent control exacerbated the housing shortage by increasing the demand and reducing the supply of rented accommodation, exactly as would be predicted by the elementary, commonsense theories of supply and demand. Similar lessons from other distorted markets were taught by, among others: Hallett and James in *Farming for Consumers* (Hobart Paper 22), published in 1963; a succession of devastating exposures of the contradictions and contortions of politicised fuel policy by Professor Colin Robinson, starting with *A Policy for Fuel* (Occasional Paper 31) in 1969; and from the different world of commodity markets in *Prices for Primary Producers* (Hobart Paper 24) in 1963 by Sir Sydney Caine, who drew on his unrivalled early experience in the colonial service to show the advantages of freer trade and market pricing.

When the spread of car ownership began to exacerbate road congestion, a transport economist named Gabriel Roth was discovered to write *Paying for Parking* (Hobart Paper 33, 1965), which showed how such then unheard-of devices as parking meters worked in other countries to check the problem of congestion. The following year, the same author produced Research Monograph 3 entitled *A Self-financing Road*

---

2   *The Economic Problem in Peace and War*, Macmillan, 1947.

System, which went well beyond tolls in charging for the use of scarce road space. The IEA's last Research Monograph (59) before this volume was published, *Pricing Our Roads: Vision and Reality*, by Stephen Glaister and Daniel Graham, also tackled this issue of road pricing. The politicians are catching up with sensible free market economics: but only slowly, with minor road pricing and private road schemes having been developed in London and around Birmingham! Turning to the supply side, John Hibbs was invited to write Hobart Paper 23, entitled *Transport for Passengers* (1971), in which he dismissed talk of excluding private cars from cities and urged freer, unsubsidised competition between roads, minibuses, so-called 'pirate' operators and rail transport to serve passengers. A major, early contribution to another debate that has since exploded – that of how to deal with environmental problems in a market economy – was Hobart Paper 66, *Pricing for Pollution* (1975), by Oxford professor Wilfred Beckerman.

What about the unions?

Evidence of the priority we gave to trade unions – as anti-market, rather than non-market, institutions – in the diagnosis of the British disease was the invitation in 1959 to Ben Roberts, Reader in Industrial Relations at the LSE and a former research scholar at Nuffield and lecturer at Ruskin, to write *Trade Unions in a Free Society*. His broad sympathy with the aspirations of the British labour movement informed this review of the history, organisation, law and economic consequences of trade unions. All the more weighty were his proposals, which, in addition to advocating the abolition of the closed shop and more local wage bargaining, went to the heart of the role of wage demands in the causation of inflation. Rejecting a 'central wages policy' as unenforceable in a free society, he challenged the Keynesians head-on by suggesting 'a more reasonable definition of full employment than an excess of jobs over persons available to fill them'. If that single, seasoned academic insight had been heeded, the boom-and-bust inflation of the following two decades under both Labour and Tory governments could have been avoided.

Two years later, another challenge was thrown down in Hobart Paper 12, entitled simply *A Market for Labour*. The author, Dennis Robertson, dared to analyse the labour market 'as a market and not as some kind of social institution'. It is indicative of the intellectual climate of those days that one reviewer was so shocked that he asked rhetorically whether the author was harking back to slave markets. Others expressed milder surprise that an economist should apply to human beings the same analysis of supply and demand that seemed more appropriate to groceries! Many later authors were to direct even more pointed analysis at the restrictive working practices of trade unions (as in *The Restrictive Society*, 1967, by John Lincoln, an assistant to Beveridge on his wartime reports, with a foreword by ex-Labour minister Sir Hartley (later Lord) Shawcross), and the abuse of 'peaceful picketing', by which these monopoly suppliers of labour routinely enforced strikes to support wage demands and closed shops.

Hayek and other IEA authors repeatedly called for repeal of the Trade Disputes Act of 1906, which, together with union closed shops, strengthened these labour monopolies and gave them immunity from claims for damages caused by their disruption of production. Most persistent was the irrepressible Professor W. H. (Bill) Hutt, an academic from Cape Town University, whose scholarly Hobart Paperback 8, published in 1975, *The Theory of Collective Bargaining 1930–75*, contested the popular view that unions were necessary to overcome the disadvantage of workers in bargaining with powerful employers and argued that restrictive practices kept wages down by discouraging investment in new technology – as forced on the print unions after the long-delayed reforms of union law in the 1980s. In 1975, when Ted Heath was asked what he thought of the usurpation of political authority by the unions, Hutt quoted him as accepting it as 'the reality of industrial life'.

That craven acceptance of impotence by a former British prime minister on an issue of such decisive importance for the survival of a free society stands in stark contrast to the persistence of IEA authors acting on the editorial injunction to 'think the unthinkable'. It also explains the reliance of the Keynesian collectivist consensus on mounting exhortation and successive incomes policies in a doomed effort to check continuing wage inflation accommodated by the Keynesian neglect of monetary policy. Indeed, wage inflation was aggravated by a rigged market in which the supply of labour was constrained by trade union restrictions while demand for labour was increased by a Keynesian full employment policy.

IEA authors hammered away on the advantages of competitive pricing in goods and services as varied as agricultural products, postal services, blood banks, foreign currencies, air transport, television, sport, telephones, water and local government services. An interesting experiment in 1967 suggested that some students had a firmer grasp of market realities than many of their teachers. Thus Arthur Seldon arranged a school essay competition in the name of a Labour MP of liberal economic views, Evan Durbin, who had died in tragic circumstances. The product was *Essays in the Theory and Practice of Pricing* (Readings 3, 1967), which included discussion of metering water supply, charging for private beaches and varying electricity tariffs by time of day to even out peak loads. The cumulative result was a powerful reaffirmation of the power of open markets to harness the energies of competing producers in the service of individual consumer choice.

Why not welfare?

There is insufficient space here to do justice to the enormous volume and variety of IEA studies of market alternatives to state services, especially in health and education. In both areas, the collectivist consensus in policy, though less so in public sentiment (see below), has prevailed with few, mostly superficial, concessions to the preferences of consumers, who, as taxpayers, continue to be required to pay the ever higher cost of 'free' services. The full extent of government failure has been brought home to me from my vantage point on the cross-benches in the House of Lords where, even after 1979, I have watched dozens of full-blown statutes on education and health forced through by the party whips, each purporting to provide lasting cures for the acknowledged failures of previous 'remedies'.

The failure of what Richard Cockett called Margaret Thatcher's 'counter-revolution'[3] to have any significant impact on the lingering dinosaurs of state medical care and education cannot be explained by any failure of IEA authors to demonstrate their need for radical reform. Indeed, one of our earliest Hobart Papers (14), *Health through Choice* (1961), by Dr Dennis Lees of Nottingham University, might be singled out as a classic model of diagnosis and prescription. Ponder deeply the following luminous extracts from Lees' conclusions in the light of all that has since transpired:

> The fundamental weaknesses of the NHS are the dominance of political decision, the absence of built-in forces making for improvement and the removal of the test of the market. These defects bring dangers for the quality of medical care that cannot be removed without far-reaching reform (p. 60).
>
> My verdict would be that a monolithic structure financed by taxation is ill-suited to a service in which the personal element is so strong, in which rapid advances in knowledge require flexibility and freedom to experiment, and for which consumer demand can be expected to increase with growing prosperity.

Rather than offering a detailed alternative blueprint, which has become the fashion for the multiplying number of modern 'think tanks', Dr Lees was modestly content to indicate lines of reform. His aim was 'to diminish the role of political decisions and to enlarge the influence of consumer choice'. Methods should include, first, moving away from taxation and free services to private insurance and fees, helped by tax concessions for those who can provide for themselves and direct assist-

---

3   *Thinking the Unthinkable: Think-tanks and the Economic Counter-Revolution 1931–1983*, HarperCollins, 1994.

ance to the dwindling minority who cannot; and second, part-payment for the cost of prescriptions with special provision for life-saving drugs and patients with low incomes.

On the other major, failing pillar of state welfare, *Education and the State* (1965) by E. G. West provided a no less powerful intellectual demolition of the case for political control. The author's meticulous study of nineteenth-century developments led him to the remarkable conclusion that in 1870, before compulsory state education was introduced, over 95 per cent of fifteen-year-olds were literate. Little wonder that Dr West's study prompted the generally aloof *Times Educational Supplement* to offer a rare eulogy: 'If his arguments cannot induce us to abolish state provision, they can surely open our eyes to the urgent need, on grounds of human dignity, for more parental choice.'

The same 'undemocratic' lack of choice and failing standards led a brace of heavyweight professors from the University of York, Alan Peacock and Jack Wiseman, to write Hobart Paper 25, entitled *Education for Democrats* (1964). With scrupulous analysis, they urged financing by loans for university students and, for schoolchildren, full-cost education vouchers paid to parents as taxable income so as to recoup part of the subsidy from better-off families.

Many more specialist studies amplified and reinforced the case for moving away from state monopoly of welfare services, to remedy the obvious defects of inadequate finance, poor quality and suppression of family choice and responsibility. With the welfare state accounting for a third or more of all public spending, the commonsense argument was repeated over and again: that rising incomes made possible direct payment by the majority in return for lower taxation, with more subsidy to the declining minority in need. To demonstrate the spread of support for radical reform, Arthur Seldon assembled a study group of a dozen academics, doctors and journalists, whose report was published as *Towards a Welfare Society* (Occasional Paper 13, 1966). The authors proposed a reverse income tax in place of means testing and offered evidence from opinion polls that a change in direction on health and education was 'politically possible' and, from foreign examples, also 'administratively feasible'.

A new opportunity presented itself with the resignation from Harold Wilson's government of a former, highly independent trade union leader, Douglas (later Lord) Houghton, who for two years had served as minister with special responsibility for coordinating social policy. He marked the occasion with a typically challenging speech which our watchful editorial director immediately sought his permission to publish as Occasional Paper 16 under the unassuming but radical title *Paying for the Social Services* (1967). His bold proposal of charges for the NHS was so startling from a serving Labour MP that his reasons deserve quotation as being even more valid 40 years later: 'What is in doubt is whether we in Britain will ever give medicine the priority given to it in some other countries (and America is not the only one) so long as it is financed almost wholly out of taxation …' Then came the blunt reason:

> While people would be willing to pay for better services for themselves, they may not be willing to pay more in taxes as a kind of insurance premium which may bear no relation to the services actually received … we are now getting the worst of both worlds. The government cannot find the money out of taxation and the citizen is not allowed to pay it out of his own pocket.

Alas, almost forty years later the Chancellor, Gordon Brown, is attempting to paper over the gap by lavishing huge sums of taxpayers' money on creating an ever larger state monolith.

Public choice

Politicians brush aside the painful, pervasive and perpetual failures of state welfare and other services by appealing to the holy grail of 'representative government'. A policy may not turn out well or may fall victim to the law of unintended consequences by achieving results different from, even opposite to, what was intended, but they say: 'It's what the people want', or at least 'what they voted for'. It becomes subsumed in that most question-begging of all phrases: 'the public interest'. But, as Robbins first asked, how can a single vote every four or five years, between two or three parties giving away a monstrous ragbag of several hundred assorted services listed in cunningly compiled political manifestos, stand comparison with the 'daily referendum' of competitive markets? None of the individual promises can be voted on separately, except by referendum. None indicates costs. None carries the money-back guarantee increasingly offered by leading producers or retailers. Politicians at elections say, in effect, 'a vote for me means a vote for every item in my party's programme'. In the economic analysis of business, it is called 'full-line forcing' and is branded as an anti-competitive practice that prevents consumers comparing costs and values for separable elements of the product mix.

It has taken the development of 'public choice', more descriptively known as 'the economic analysis of politics', to expose how representative government has been transformed into misrepresentative government, catering not for broad majorities but captured by organised, often small, minorities. Thus doctors, teachers, nurses, other public sector workers, farmers, motorists, cyclists, conservationists and hundreds of other groups, sharing a cohesive, common (sometimes arcane) interest, can each organise themselves to lobby MPs for subsidies or other special privileges. As many IEA authors have pointed out, their success depends on their members having a larger, more concentrated stake in gaining their ends than the widely dispersed individual taxpayers or consumers have in resisting (even noticing) the costs.

Leaving aside the European farm lobby's racket of the EU Common Agricultural Policy, examples from social policy would certainly include the defeat of Keith Joseph's effort to introduce student loans or education vouchers in the 1980s, and Michael Howard's recent opportunistic opposition to university top-up fees, all in deference to organised lobbying by the unions of teachers and students, backed up for good measure by the self-serving bureaucrats in the national and local education establishments.

It was another example of the genius of Seldon that he was among the first in Britain to spot the importance of this new American academic development of public choice, associated with two fellow Mont Pèlerin Society members, James Buchanan and Gordon Tullock. His first major blow was to publish an exposition by Tullock in Hobart Paperback 9, entitled *The Vote Motive*[4] (1976), which compared the politician's drive to maximise votes with the businessman's aim to maximise profits. He then organised the first seminar in Britain on the subject and assembled a symposium of British, American and European academics, publishing their lectures as an IEA Reading entitled *The Economics of Politics* (Readings 18, 1978). A general conclusion was that the democratic process does not merit the widespread presumption of moral superiority over the economic marketplace. Elsewhere, Arthur Seldon has summed up the operation of the political market by rewriting Lincoln's definition of democracy as: 'Government of the Busy, by the Bossy, for the Bully'.[5]

A related editorial initiative was to combine the businessman's market research with the politician's opinion polling to discover people's preferences between state and private provision of health and education. The party men like to quote periodic polls showing large majorities in favour of the ('free') NHS, and to point to the small minorities who chose to support BUPA or private schools, as proving satisfaction with state provision. The twin fallacies in all such arguments arise from conveniently neglecting two facts: first, that approval of state services ignores their (unknown) 'price' both in terms of alternatives forgone and the high taxes levied even on families with low incomes; and, second, that private provision paid for out of net income involves double payment, in insurance or fees on top of taxes for the state service they do not use.

---

4   Editor's note: this title was the inspired choice of Ralph Harris himself. Gordon Tullock once said that *The Vote Motive* did more to spread public understanding of public choice economics than any other single publication as a result of its multiple editions and twelve translations.

5   *Capitalism*, Basil Blackwell, 1990, p. 235. Although it is not published by the IEA, I commend it as an unsurpassed exposition of the anti-statist case from a combined economic, political and ethical standpoint.

Accordingly, we had lengthy discussions with a leading professional market researcher to find out whether he could compile a questionnaire that would present a more balanced choice between public and private health and education services. The result was a series of four reports published between 1963 and 1979[6] on employing the device of the voucher. *The Economist* at last redeemed itself in my eyes by printing a well-aimed review of the last of these reports: '... the ideas adumbrated so readably in this book do have the most plausible application ... The IEA's splendidly anti-bureaucratic principles are an invaluable antidote to public sector Toryism as much as to socialism'.

In bald summary, a national quota sample of some two thousand men and women of working age were invited to say whether they would accept vouchers for education and medical care amounting to two-thirds or one third of the (stated) cost and add the balance to make up the full cost of private provision. The number accepting the larger voucher was in both cases naturally higher than those accepting the smaller, and rose for education to just above 50 per cent in 1978 and for medical care to 57 per cent. Even allowing for the standard margin of error of around 3 per cent, these and other findings of our *Choice in Welfare* researches left little doubt that the universal provision of 'free' tax-financed welfare was very far from satisfying the public's underlying taste for choice in medical care and education.

It must be admitted that our repeated findings of wide support for radical reform in welfare have so far foundered on the misplaced prejudices of the modern 'levellers': if all cannot have the best, none shall have better. They ignore the evidence from everyday markets that competition works ceaselessly to transform today's minority luxuries into tomorrow's necessities – videos, CDs, DVDs, mobile telephones ... Instead of welcoming such creative competition, Labour and Tory spin masters now engage in offering make-believe competition within the public

---

6   *Choice in Welfare*, 1963, 1965 and 1970; and Harris and Seldon, *Over-ruled on Welfare*, Hobart Paperback 13, 1979.

sector, both sides shrilly claiming to have solved the illusion of conjuring real choice for parents and patients from the unyielding, entrenched, monopoly bureaucracies of state education and healthcare.

21 BEHIND ENEMY LINES
Ralph Harris

How can any observer under the age of 50 recapture the hostile, even intimidating, intellectual atmosphere of the post-war national debate on British political economy? The reigning Keynesian collectivist consensus, though less oppressive than the KGB, scornfully dismissed dissenting opinion and, albeit with diminishing confidence, prescribed what passed as 'sophisticated' discussion of public policy. Those of us who dared persist with stubborn doubts only gradually overcame what I might call a shared sense of isolation. A little fancifully, I have, in retirement, come to liken my experience travelling round the country to address some unknown student audience – say at Essex University at the time of student unrest – to that of a wartime British agent infiltrating hostile territory in the vanished era of Attlee, Macmillan, Wilson, Heath. With few exceptions, most notably the *Daily Telegraph*, the mainstream media, including the BBC and commercial television, paid little attention to critics of the new collectivism. Even the prestigious *Financial Times* confined itself to a brief note on most of our Papers but, with the exception of individual writers such as Harold Wincott and later Samuel Brittan, never rose to an expression of approval in its staid leaders. Elsewhere, critics of the received wisdom were regarded as lacking in patriotism, even as engaged in mildly treasonable activities.

Throughout the 1960s and into the 1970s, whenever the general run of commentators deigned to notice our Hobart and other papers, they invariably described us as 'the right-wing IEA', whereas the National Institute of Economic and Social Research – which was both government-funded and Keynesian-inspired – was always respectfully referred to as 'the independent NIESR'. We consoled ourselves by privately mis-naming them the 'National Institute of Economic and Social*ist* Research'.

Cool reception

The reception for IEA speakers was distinctly cool when addressing audiences of people who accepted the prevailing economic opinion of the age. There was of course little chance of convincing a conference of earnest social workers in my favourite Cambridge one overcast Saturday morning that increasing unconditional cash benefits for the unemployed must risk actually increasing unemployment so long as income tax was levied on earnings below benefit levels. Here was another example of the law of unintended consequences. Elementary market economics predicts that the higher you pitch social benefits, especially for families with children, the more you risk making benefits more attractive than net take-home pay from a full week's work. Yet to meet their swollen budgets Chancellors of both parties thought nothing of starting to levy tax on incomes below social benefits paid to families with children. I recall press gossip of beneficiaries saying they could not afford to take a job – unless it was in the 'cash' economy. And how could I hope to get the secretary of the Engineering Employers' Federation to grasp that successive incomes policies were no shield against an inflation stoked up by monetary excess?

As for a trade union audience in Tunbridge Wells of all places, no fallacy was too crude for some hecklers to deploy in favour of ever-rising wages. But then the likes of such trade union barons as Jack Jones and Hugh (later Lord) Scanlon never tired of telling their members that wage increases could actually increase employment – by raising the public's spending power and thereby stimulating demand for unemployed labour. Such myopic Keynesianism was blind to the effect of higher wages (unmatched by higher output) in raising unit costs so as to cancel any stimulus from monetary demand and pricing marginal workers out of jobs.

Then again, was I wasting time travelling to Oxford for a seminar – presided over by Roger Opie, who was a dashing leader in the Keynesian collectivist consensus? Could his students really be expected to display much sympathy for my warning against the neglect of monetary discipline against inflation, when Opie had long preached the opposite? In the event I found I had not entirely wasted my journey when two or three students quietly sidled up after the meeting to express interest in what I had said and to enquire about the work of the IEA.

Again and again at such meetings, the chairman would read a formally polite introduction – Cambridge economist, double first, general director of the IEA, author, etc. – before I found myself rising to confront an impassive audience. To break the ice, I would ring the changes on endlessly repeated opening quips against the whole tribe of economists: 'Six economists, six opinions – or seven if Keynes was present'; 'If all economists were laid end to end, they would still reach no definite conclusion'; 'Economists, those chaps who know the price of everything and the value of nothing'. I would ask rhetorically how many economists – or for that matter politicians – would be prepared to back their confident forecasts with their own money, or even with that of their spouses. These and rather better topical jests would often be received in frozen silence, and I would soon be running a practised eye along the rows of impassive faces for the odd trace of a nod or knowing smile.

Planning again

There seemed no escape from hostility. I remember welcoming at last the prospect of allies in addressing a sober audience of business economists on the folly of George Brown's 1965 National Plan. Here was no parachute drop into enemy territory. These were, after all, people paid to think about future changes in their companies' markets and the impact of government policies on them. They should have been the first to grasp the dangers of centrally planning the entire economy by official extrapolations of past trends. They should have been especially wary of such Keynesian macro-magnitudes as total demand, investment, employment and, most elusive of all, forecasts of the vagaries of foreign trade. Among what I supposed to be friends, I launched into my demolition of national economic planning by inviting the audience to agree that all such exercises were backward-looking, 'like steering a ship by its wake' while calling for full speed ahead. This analogy came into its own when, as Chancellor of the Exchequer, Jim Callaghan (a former naval man) used to boast that he would avert the next sterling crisis by a timely 'touch on the tiller'.

But surely an audience of business economists might be expected to be highly receptive to my commonsense warning against unforeseeable rocks in an uncharted future? Alas, most of them appeared no more perceptive than those CBI worthies whom I later came to upbraid for accepting the routine incantations about a mixed economy without foreseeing that inevitable setbacks would risk progressive dilution of the mixture by more party politics and less private enterprise.

It was this perennial phantom of central planning or 'better planning' to which the Keynesian collectivist consensus endlessly appealed, despite mounting evidence of economic disorder and failure. Picture me being ushered into a bare sixth-form classroom for a debate on the National Plan, some time in the brief interval between its enthusiastic launch in September 1965 and its collapse in June 1966. My opponent on this occasion was a large, imposing, pukka public school man, like me in his early forties. He had been seconded, by a top firm, to the NEDC with a specific brief to promote George Brown's National Plan. Almost forty years later I have not forgotten his opening sentences along the following lines: 'The purpose of the Plan is to raise economic growth to four per cent a year in the gross national product and associated parameters. And I would add, as a practical businessman, how proud I am to be using this kind of technical language.' Practical businessman?! Technical language?! Bah! What was I, as a mere academic economist, to say? I suppressed the wicked retort that some businessmen who had been seconded to the NEDC were duds the sponsoring companies were glad to see the back of.

My adversary was eventually to vanish whence he came, but at that school debate I was momentarily encouraged to detect that the sixth-form audience were not much impressed by his pompous, pseudo-technical mumbo-jumbo. My cheerful response had attempted to explain the crucial difference between a central plan devised by party politicians to impose a single, fixed blueprint for action on everyone, and a business plan that is shaped by competitive market realities ('price signals') but remains sufficiently flexible to accommodate prompt revision in the light of ever changing relative costs and prices, consumer demand, foreign trade, advertising, new products and, not least, new entrants into the market. Even a rather dim 'practical businessman' could hardly dispute there was something in that distinction.

Though short lived, the long-forgotten National Plan provided plenty of opportunities for me to advertise the IEA's teachings on the role of the entrepreneur. A favourite theme was the ubiquity of uncertainty in the rapidly changing post-war world, especially for Britain, with almost a third of national output devoted to the vagaries of foreign trade. As an old *Glasgow Herald* leader writer with a penchant for a good headline, I liked to commend the guidance of business investment decisions by 'profits' rather than by 'prophets'. So when invited to address the Ashridge Management College on the subject of planning, I waxed lyrical on the contribution of the entrepreneurial drive to the transformation of our well-equipped kitchens and centrally heated and carpeted homes, no less than to widespread motoring and foreign holidays. It went down well enough, but I was astonished when the director of the college wound up thanking me especially for introducing the word 'entrepreneur' for the first time he could remember in his years at Ashridge. For some time thereafter I feared the worst about the new fashion of 'management training'.

Enter *bête noire* Shonfield

One of my most miserable memories in the Wilson years was of an encounter in a cramped BBC radio studio with no room to sit down and – more serious – no 'hospitality room', where victims were introduced to each other over a welcome drink. My antagonist turned out to be one of my least favourite *bêtes noires*, Andrew Shonfield, then economics editor of the *Observer* and author of an influential Penguin Special called *British Economic Policy since the War*, published in 1958. I recognised him as an outstanding *FT* journalist and found him an even more fluent talker, who pontificated impressively with an unmistakable aura of authority. The interviewer shuffled forward deferentially and addressed Shonfield by his Christian name as an old friend before briefly turning to me and reading my name from his script. The subject was incomes policy, which gave Shonfield the opportunity to hold forth magisterially on the important role of trade unions and the need to win their leaders over to moderation in their ceaseless demands for higher wages. When my turn came, I got no farther than beginning to explain how market forces must in the end set limits to the level of wage increases that could be afforded without causing either inflation or unemployment. With barely concealed impatience, the interviewer cut me short and turned back to Shonfield, who almost pityingly dismissed talk of market forces as 'laissez-faire extremism irrelevant to the real world …'. I remember crawling home and vowing to avoid, whether on radio or television, any further such unequal encounters, which allowed no time to develop a coherent argument. It was a vow to which I resolutely stuck thereafter, preferring a live audience whose reactions, favourable or not, I could see and judge and respond to as I went along.

For all his reputation as a savant, Shonfield's Penguin paperback revealed an almost religious faith in political intervention to boost economic growth. His universal panacea for policy, guided by something he dignified with the title of the 'capital-output ratio', appeared always to require more and yet more investment, although, in the absence of the despised profit motive, without any clear guidance about what exactly the new machines and equipment were supposed to produce. His ideal was later mocked in the *Daily Telegraph* by Colin Welch, a marvellous literary writer with no pretensions of economic expertise beyond what he had learned from the IEA. He summed up Shonfield's panacea as: 'investment in machine tools, to produce machine tools, to produce machine tools ...'. It was a turn of phrase I used to good effect in many subsequent lectures.

Shonfield loved to mock concern about the Bank Rate as primitive worship of a totem pole to appease the gods of the City of London. He displayed the standard Keynesian preference for continued inflationary pressure, rather than using interest rates to moderate the booms. It was no mere technical dispute about alternative economic theories. Not only did the go-stop cycle severely disrupt industrial production and investment, it led to wildly fluctuating inflation from between 1 and 10 per cent a year in the 1950s to 25 per cent in the 1970s. In addition to cheating people living on pensions and other fixed incomes, the erratic rises in price undermined national budgeting as well as good domestic housekeeping. Above all, they created the new post-war practice of annual trade union wage demands, the escalation of which provoked a succession of incomes policies leading to the further disruption of strikes and civic disorder. The final indictment of the Keynesian era is that so far from inflation warding off unemployment, the jobless total rose remorselessly over the economic cycle from a peak of around 300,000 after the war to above a million in the early 1970s, before hitting 3 million in the early 1980s.

Such was the price, or part of the price, paid for the appalling hubris of the 'clever sillies'.

Et tu, William!

At least I knew of Shonfield as a deeply committed socialist intellectual, super-confident in the power of planning to transform Britain's flagging fortunes. But what was I to expect when, around 1970, a Conservative women's organisation invited me to share the platform at Caxton Hall with William Rees-Mogg, whom I then knew of only as the rather aloof, highbrow editor of *The Times*. He had a reputation for studious sophistication of manner combined with a quiet profundity of matter which had already carried him effortlessly from president of the Oxford Union to chief leader writer of the *Financial Times* and City editor of the *Sunday Times* before becoming successively political and economics editor then deputy editor and finally editor of *The Times* in 1967. In those days the 'top people's paper' was still a touch too Establishment-minded for my taste, but I was attracted by the topic, which was 'The Responsible Society', and looked forward to a constructive exchange of views in a friendly atmosphere. I might have been warned when 'madam chairman' greeted Rees-Mogg warmly by his Christian name and turned to me, briskly announcing that I would speak first.

I recall setting out my standard case that a free society founded on a market economy gave the widest scope for individual and family freedom and responsibility, which, I always added, was thrice blessed by economic, moral and political advantages. If governments would turn from dispensing universal free benefits, they could provide more generous support for the declining minority in poverty. When Rees-Mogg's turn came, he was formally perfectly polite but made no reference to my arguments, beyond saying that although he had thought of a number of possible interpretations of the term 'responsible society', the case I presented had not been one of them. How was that for a lofty put-down? There followed an eloquent exposition of the paternalist case for the welfare state with plenty of references to compassion and other civilised values.

This story is worth telling only because a very few years later Rees-Mogg, and *The Times* under his direction, was among the leading apostles of the best of the ideas that came to be known as 'Thatcherism'. Indeed, in 1974, after the collapse of the Heath government, he wrote a marvellous slim volume assailing the evils of inflation under the title of *The Reigning Error*, which he exposed as a manifestation of the pervasive human tendency to push everything, including the money supply, to excess. His nicely chosen word was 'inordinacy', which I have since often pressed into service to drive home arguments against excessive government (I like to believe he would now agree that the neglect of individual responsibility has been carried to inordinate lengths in the welfare state, as in many other paternalistic policies).

Keep smiling

I sometimes began to wonder why I should expose myself to such mostly hostile encounters. But of course it was an essential part of my chosen work at the IEA, as a kind of missionary in a pagan land preaching the gospel according to such intellectual giants as Adam Smith, Hayek and Friedman. After all, our Keynesian tormentors were hardly to be feared as dangerous cannibals. Furthermore I could often work up my notes into articles for the *Daily Telegraph*, the *Director* or the *Spectator*.

But beyond economic motives, I must admit I mostly came to enjoy such jousts and increasingly encountered allies and, most rewarding of all, new younger converts, especially at my alma mater of Cambridge, and even at Oxford, the home of so many lost Labour intellectuals. My favourite meetings were undoubtedly at St Andrews University, where I had earlier spent seven years lecturing in the political economy department. Despite the long journey, involving an overnight stay, I seldom refused an invitation to return to address the students and was amply repaid when the *Scotsman* reported that they received every new Hobart Paper as 'an additional chapter of the Bible'. It was an added reward when that beautiful medieval university produced two very modern, enterprising graduates, Eamonn Butler and Madsen Pirie, who in 1977 created the lively Adam Smith Institute, whose work in spreading the free market message was very much complementary to that of the IEA. St Andrews also produced half a dozen young Conservative MPs to support Margaret Thatcher's free market crusade, including the outstanding Michael Forsyth, who became an impressive Secretary of State for Scotland under John Major.

Lighter relief was regularly provided in the 1970s and 1980s by debates at the Oxford and Cambridge Unions, to which circuit I came to be regularly invited. Once I had witnessed how casually the ayes and noes were sometimes counted at Oxford, I took less interest in the final vote, which was just as well since, in the pre-Thatcher era, the announced verdict usually went against my free market side. Instead, I came to relax and enjoy the high-spirited student rough-and-tumble, with constant good-natured interruptions and often hilarious 'points of order'. From the handbills of debates that I have kept, I am reminded that other participants over the years included a succession of trade union leaders, including Ray Buckton, Alan Sapper and David Lea. There were also plenty of livelier adversaries, including Tariq Ali, Peter Shore, Bernard Williams and Lord Soper, and a growing list of doughty allies, including Kenneth Minogue, William Hague, Geoffrey Howe, Norman Lamont, Bill Deedes, Lord (David) Young, Patrick Cosgrave, Sir Ian McGregor and John Wakeham.

The first Oxford Union debate that brought hope that the IEA view was coming into the ascendancy was the year before Margaret Thatcher won the general election of 1979. The terms of the motion could not have been more explicit: 'That a return to a free market economy would be the best solution to the British crisis'. I immediately took heart when I saw that the bumbling Lord Balogh was the main speaker on the other side, but could hardly believe the vote when it was announced by the president as: 230 in favour and 128 against. Even if the counting tended to be a little irregular, there was no disputing our overwhelming victory. From Cambridge, among the many outstanding allies I best remember were David Prior, the charming son of one of my most jolly but sceptical sparring partners, James (now Lord) Prior, and Simon Heffer, since author of many fine political biographies as well as star columnist of the *Daily Mail*.

Honourable defeat

Another enduring memory was of a less happy encounter with students at Exeter around 1968, though it had a happier twist some years later. After a cold train journey from London with the prospect of returning after midnight, I had to propose the motion that 'economic planning is a form of necromancy'. After verifying the dictionary definition of the key word as 'prediction by means of communication with the dead', I had leapt at the chance to instruct serious students in my established view that national planning was essentially backward-looking, being based on extrapolating past trends, and was doomed to fail. Instead of the antici-pated victory, I was comprehensively trounced by around twenty-odd votes to nearer two hundred. It was an honourable defeat in so far as my tormentor was an exceptionally persuasive debater, a trained barrister, and unfailingly pleasant to boot. He was the youthful Dick (later Lord) Taverne, then a confident, well-briefed Treasury minister under Harold Wilson.

The memory of that defeat is softened by recalling my next encounter with the still-youthful Dick Taverne around 1980, when he had accepted an invitation to lunch at the IEA. Greeting him ceremoniously at the door, I cheerfully confessed shame at the memory of my total defeat at his hands. His smiling reply was along the lines of: 'No, there's no need for shame. I won the vote, but I now see you won the argument'. It is also worth noting that he courageously resigned and fought his constituency as an independent candidate. When freed from the Commons, he was able to do far more good, first building up the Institute for Fiscal Studies, then developing the Social Democratic Party, becoming a director of many businesses, and finally joining the Lords. My only lingering regret is that, instead of joining me and the other mixed bag of independent peers on the cross-benches, he joined the Liberal Democrats, who have always struck me as not particularly liberal and too inclined to look to government as the answer to every problem.

Valediction

From comfortable and contented retirement, these hard-fought battles over Keynesian inflation and collectivist planning seem a vanished era. In 1995 Tony Blair won the leadership of a 'new' Labour Party under the brave banner of 'a dynamic market economy', which even some of Margaret Thatcher's more Tory followers might have found a touch stark. In 1997 they swept John Major's government from power. Today, both main parties vie with each other in lauding choice, competition, enterprise and avoidance of higher income tax, though not (yet) lower total taxes. It is now accepted that lower inflation, though not (yet) stable money, comes before reducing unemployment. It is perhaps less widely understood that its recent achievement has depended entirely on restoring to the Bank of England the very control over monetary policy which Labour had reck-lessly swept away after their electoral victory in 1945.

Since the Thatcher counter-revolution, the central economic battle-ground has shifted – first, to the extent of Westminster and Brussels regulation and control compatible with Blair's 'dynamic economy'; and second, to the ability of the British government to manage effectively its inflated range of functions, and to finance the mounting cost of devel-oping welfare services, on top of a host of new 'initiatives'. The smallest budgetary setback must now risk still higher direct, indirect, central and local (and concealed) taxation that would further weaken and distort incentives to individual effort and enterprise.

As a non-economist without business experience, Tony Blair may be forgiven neglecting the probability (I would say 'certainty') that the gargantuan NHS, even under the masterful direction of John Reid, will eventually prove impossible to adapt to ever changing opportunities and requirements – for some of the same reasons that recently prompted Bill Gates to question whether Microsoft will survive another ten years of ceaseless global competition. Likewise, rising incomes and frustrated parental aspirations are likely to overwhelm the ill-performing state schools, presided over by a combination of self-serving teachers' unions and a complacent and bloated educational bureaucracy. Like the drab council housing into which I was born almost 80 years ago, the welfare state must fail increasingly to satisfy what Adam Smith diagnosed as: 'The uniform, constant, and uninterrupted effort of every man to better his condition ... ', and, I would add: to better the condition of his family, community and other freely chosen causes.

It is central to my philosophy that no one can be certain about the precise direction of the changes ahead. This uncertainty prompts two further questions that overhang our future: first, the pace and scale of this transformation, and second, whether its progress will be eased or obstructed by what passes as modern representative government, which finds such difficulty in restraining its incessant itch to interfere.

Meanwhile, debate has moved away from the clear-cut issue of dispersed versus centralised initiative, which has been largely won – at least in principle though not yet in practice. We are still faced with the crucial judgement of how much government regulation is consistent with continuing economic success in a global economy faced with totally unprecedented economic, social and political change. Having watched the interplay between professed political idealism and crude election-eering since 1945, I have been repeatedly reminded of Adam Smith's description of: '... that insidious and crafty animal, vulgarly called a statesman or politician, *whose councils are directed by the momentary fluc-tuations of affairs*' (my emphasis). And that was written in 1776, long before MPs turned professional!

We can now appreciate the huge benefit of removing monetary policy from the opportunistic control of party politicians. The signal success of this bold act of depoliticisation demonstrates the urgent need to remove schools, universities, health services, pensions and other social benefits from the present unchecked, daily electoral vote-grubbing. Since govern-ment controls inevitably grow like Topsy and bring with them more party political administration, I believe experience will increasingly demonstrate that the less we have of both the better for the true welfare of our families, the flexibility and vigour of the economy, and the health of British democracy, with individual freedom at its heart.

APPENDIX

THE DEVELOPMENT OF THE IEA'S ACADEMIC REPUTATION – A PERSONAL REFLECTION
Arthur Seldon

The chain of events that led to my becoming Joint Founder President of the Institute of Economic Affairs began when, as a humble state scholar, I entered the portals of the London School of Economics and inadvertently opened the door of Professor Arnold Plant's room. When I seemed about to retreat he called, 'Don't go, stay,' and that is how I became his student and reinforced my already keen interest in the tenets of classical liberalism.

Soon I was attending some of Professor Lionel Robbins' lectures and, later, those of the newly arrived Professor Friedrich Hayek from Austria. I was relieved when his command of English improved and his lectures became inspiring, especially to graduates. It was not surprising that I became interested in student politics, and with fellow new 'Liberal' friends Stuart Waterhouse, who came from an old Liberal family (his father knew Lloyd George) and Douglas Allan, who became Head of the Civil Service as Lord Croham, formed the Liberal Society of the LSE.

I became fascinated by Professor W. H. Hutt's new 1936 book *Economists and the Public – a Study of Competition and Opinion*. He later became a leading author of IEA writings, attacking excessive trade union power. One, entitled *The Strike-threat System: The Economic Consequences of Collective Bargaining*, sold especially well. Hutt was one of the IEA's pioneers in advocating the value of competition. At the time when I read his book at the LSE, John Strachey's *The Nature of Capitalist Crisis* had just appeared, advocating economic and social policies that would curtail the freedom of the individual. I was inspired to write a strong critique in the LSE students' journal, *The Clare Market Review*, in March 1937.

After graduation I was appointed Plant's research assistant, to assist his advisory services to growing firms, an appointment that was interrupted by the outbreak of war in 1939. I continued to exchange letters with him from North Africa and Italy, noting the waste and inefficiency involved in providing food and clothing without pricing. I have never forgotten the debt I owed to Arnold Plant, who soon after I was demobbed recommended that I write a report for the Liberal Party Committee on the Ageing. This enabled me to study state pensions, and in 1957 I used some of the material for my first publication for the IEA, *Pensions in a Free Society*.

My colleagues on the committee were Lord Amulree, a Liberal peer, and Dame Barbara Shenfield, who with her husband, Arthur Shenfield, became most faithful supporters of the early Institute.

While writing the report on ageing I interviewed Lord Beveridge and noted his emphasis that the post-war state pension should not be paid in full until a fund had been built in the succeeding 20 years. Doubtful of this proposal, I later wrote in my early IEA publication that the National Insurance Fund would be misused by government and that the taxpayers would have to pay the pensions.

I was recommended to the Institute of Economic Affairs by Lord Grantchester, one of its early supporters. The IEA was reorganised in 1957 with Ralph Harris as General Director. I then joined as part-time editorial adviser, becoming full-time editorial director in July 1961. Plant had suggested my name to Grantchester, and I hope that Arnold was pleased later when I assembled an IEA book containing four of his most prestigious essays.

Installed in the Institute, which had very little money to finance publications, I thought of neglected subjects which would yield to economic analysis and solutions and, second, of authors who would share my philosophy. That philosophy, also that of the IEA's founder, Antony Fisher, was that people would spend their own money more wisely than the state would spend it. Authors would have to ignore political pressures, give no precedence to what was 'politically possible' and write as academics seeking truth.

My first choice as author was an old friend from LSE days, Professor Basil Yamey. I asked him to write on the consumer-unfriendly resale price maintenance, which prevented retailers from lowering prices. Basil responded as a good friend, ignoring the fact that the publication would be by a then unknown Institute, and produced a splendid text which hit the headlines and changed government policy.

Another early publication was by Norman Macrae of *The Economist*, who accepted my invitation – against the advice of his friends – to write on rent control (*To Let?*, Hobart Paper 2, 1960).

Through the 1960s and the 1970s I invited some very well-known economists to write for us. To name a few of a veritable galaxy of intellectual talent: (from the UK) Professor Alan Prest (purchase tax), Professor James Meade (the Common Market), Professor Alan Peacock and Jack Wiseman (education), Professor Paish (incomes policy), Professor Denman (land use planning through the market), Professor F. G. Pennance, my co-author of Dent's *Everyman's Dictionary of Economics* (housing and town planning), Professor Alan Walters (money), Professor Brian Griffiths (competition in banking), Professor Colin Robinson, who succeeded me as editorial director, and Eileen Marshall (the future for British coal); (from the United States) Professor Geoffrey Brennan and Professor James Buchanan (monopoly of money), Professor William Niskanen (bureaucracy), Professor Gordon Tullock (the vote motive), Professor Armen Alchian (the economics of charity), Professor James Buchanan with Professor Charles Rowley (from the UK), Professor Albert Breton (Canada), Professor Bruno Frey (Switzerland) and Professor Martin Ricketts (the UK) (the economics of politics).

All accepted my critical editing. Many of my prefaces were reproduced in *The Making of the Institute* (Economic and Literary Books in association with the IEA, 2002).

The IEA's publications were praised by Hayek in 1983. As he put it, 'It has taken the IEA a long time to prove its success. I think it has now become the most powerful maker of public opinion in England. By now book shops usually have a special rack of Institute of Economic Affairs pamphlets. Even people on the Left feel compelled to keep informed of the Institute's publications.'

Academic attention was quickly followed by attention from journalistic and political specialists. I recall with pleasure two cogent attacks on the welfare state: on the National Health Service by Professor Denis Lees (*Health through Choice*, Hobart Paper 14, 1961) and on state education by a hitherto unknown protégé of Professor John Jewkes, Edwin West. West had studied the history of education in the nineteenth century, particularly the gradual stifling of private provision by the state. It enlightened many people, not all on the left, who had believed that the state had to intervene in order that all should receive schooling. The book was widely discussed and reviewed. West was subsequently offered a chair at Carleton University, Canada, where he continued his educational research.

I knew that some Labour politicians were interested in the IEA's work and in 1966 persuaded Douglas Houghton, a former minister in Wilson's government, to write *Paying for the Social Services* (Occasional Paper 16, 1967).

The Institute's work was reinforced by many articles I wrote in the *Daily Telegraph* and other broadsheet newspapers. Its features editor, Colin Welch, had much sympathy with the IEA's free market philosophy.

My last word must be an accolade for one of the greatest thinkers of the twentieth century: F. A. Hayek, Nobel laureate in 1974. I was privileged to produce and publish some of his work. Hobart Paper 87, *1980s Unemployment and the Unions*, was an analysis of the stubborn obstacles to the efficient working of markets in the British economy. In 1990 he wrote *Denationalisation of Money*. After this publication he wrote: 'Against all my habits, after completing the first chapter of this paper, I left most of the exacting and time consuming task of publishing the exposition and preparing it ready for publication to the sympathetic endeavours of Arthur Seldon whose beneficial care has already made much more readable some of my shorter essays published by the Institute.'

My old friend Ronald Coase, who was at the LSE when I was a student, wrote a few years ago that he believed 'Arnold Plant would have been proud of your work'. But it is Hayek's commendation which gives me lasting satisfaction.

ABOUT THE IEA

The Institute is a research and educational charity (No. CC 235 351), limited by guarantee. Its mission is to improve understanding of the fundamental institutions of a free society with particular reference to the role of markets in solving economic and social problems.

The IEA achieves its mission by:

- a high-quality publishing programme
- conferences, seminars, lectures and other events
- outreach to school and college students
- brokering media introductions and appearances

The IEA, which was established in 1955 by the late Sir Antony Fisher, is an educational charity, not a political organisation. It is independent of any political party or group and does not carry on activities intended to affect support for any political party or candidate in any election or referendum, or at any other time. It is financed by sales of publications, conference fees and voluntary donations.

In addition to its main series of publications the IEA also publishes a quarterly journal, *Economic Affairs*.

The IEA is aided in its work by a distinguished international Academic Advisory Council and an eminent panel of Honorary Fellows. Together with other academics, they review prospective IEA publications, their comments being passed on anonymously to authors. All IEA papers are therefore subject to the same rigorous independent refereeing process as used by leading academic journals.

IEA publications enjoy widespread classroom use and course adoptions in schools and universities. They are also sold throughout the world and often translated/reprinted.

Since 1974 the IEA has helped to create a world-wide network of 100 similar institutions in over 70 countries. They are all independent but share the IEA's mission.

Views expressed in the IEA's publications are those of the authors, not those of the Institute (which has no corporate view), its Managing Trustees, Academic Advisory Council members or senior staff.

Members of the Institute's Academic Advisory Council, Honorary Fellows, Trustees and Staff are listed on the following page.

The Institute gratefully acknowledges financial support for its publications programme and other work from a generous benefaction by the late Alec and Beryl Warren.

Other papers recently published by the IEA include:

WHO, What and Why?
Transnational Government, Legitimacy and the World Health Organization
Roger Scruton
Occasional Paper 113; ISBN 0 255 36487 3
£8.00

The World Turned Rightside Up
A New Trading Agenda for the Age of Globalisation
John C. Hulsman
Occasional Paper 114; ISBN 0 255 36495 4
£8.00

The Representation of Business in English Literature
Introduced and edited by Arthur Pollard
Readings 53; ISBN 0 255 36491 1
£12.00

Anti-Liberalism 2000
The Rise of New Millennium Collectivism
David Henderson
Occasional Paper 115; ISBN 0 255 36497 0
£7.50

Capitalism, Morality and Markets
Brian Griffiths, Robert A. Sirico, Norman Barry & Frank Field
Readings 54; ISBN 0 255 36496 2
£7.50

A Conversation with Harris and Seldon

Ralph Harris & Arthur Seldon
Occasional Paper 116; ISBN 0 255 36498 9
£7.50

Malaria and the DDT Story

Richard Tren & Roger Bate
Occasional Paper 117; ISBN 0 255 36499 7
£10.00

A Plea to Economists Who Favour Liberty: Assist the Everyman

Daniel B. Klein
Occasional Paper 118; ISBN 0 255 36501 2
£10.00

The Changing Fortunes of Economic Liberalism

Yesterday, Today and Tomorrow
David Henderson
Occasional Paper 105 (new edition); ISBN 0 255 36520 9
£12.50

The Global Education Industry

Lessons from Private Education in Developing Countries
James Tooley
Hobart Paper 141 (new edition); ISBN 0 255 36503 9
£12.50

Saving Our Streams

The Role of the Anglers' Conservation Association in Protecting English and Welsh Rivers
Roger Bate
Research Monograph 53; ISBN 0 255 36494 6
£10.00

Better Off Out?

The Benefits or Costs of EU Membership
Brian Hindley & Martin Howe
Occasional Paper 99 (new edition); ISBN 0 255 36502 0
£10.00

Buckingham at 25

Freeing the Universities from State Control
Edited by James Tooley
Readings 55; ISBN 0 255 36512 8
£15.00

Lectures on Regulatory and Competition Policy

Irwin M. Stelzer
Occasional Paper 120; ISBN 0 255 36511 X
£12.50

Misguided Virtue

False Notions of Corporate Social Responsibility
David Henderson
Hobart Paper 142; ISBN 0 255 36510 1
£12.50

HIV and Aids in Schools

The Political Economy of Pressure Groups and Miseducation
Barrie Craven, Pauline Dixon, Gordon Stewart & James Tooley
Occasional Paper 121; ISBN 0 255 36522 5
£10.00

The Road to Serfdom

The Reader's Digest *condensed version*
Friedrich A. Hayek
Occasional Paper 122; ISBN 0 255 36530 6
£7.50

Bastiat's *The Law*

Introduction by Norman Barry
Occasional Paper 123; ISBN 0 255 36509 8
£7.50

A Globalist Manifesto for Public Policy

Charles Calomiris
Occasional Paper 124; ISBN 0 255 36525 X
£7.50

Euthanasia for Death Duties

Putting Inheritance Tax Out of Its Misery
Barry Bracewell-Milnes
Research Monograph 54; ISBN 0 255 36513 6
£10.00

Liberating the Land

The Case for Private Land-use Planning
Mark Pennington
Hobart Paper 143; ISBN 0 255 36508 x
£10.00

IEA Yearbook of Government Performance 2002/2003

Edited by Peter Warburton
Yearbook 1; ISBN 0 255 36532 2
£15.00

Britain's Relative Economic Performance, 1870–1999

Nicholas Crafts
Research Monograph 55; ISBN 0 255 36524 1
£10.00

Should We Have Faith in Central Banks?

Otmar Issing
Occasional Paper 125; ISBN 0 255 36528 4
£7.50

The Dilemma of Democracy

Arthur Seldon
Hobart Paper 136 (reissue); ISBN 0 255 36536 5
£10.00

Capital Controls: a 'Cure' Worse Than the Problem?
Forrest Capie
Research Monograph 56; ISBN 0 255 36506 3
£10.00

The Poverty of 'Development Economics'
Deepak Lal
Hobart Paper 144 (reissue); ISBN 0 255 36519 5
£15.00

Should Britain Join the Euro?
The Chancellor's Five Tests Examined
Patrick Minford
Occasional Paper 126; ISBN 0 255 36527 6
£7.50

Post-Communist Transition: Some Lessons
Leszek Balcerowicz
Occasional Paper 127; ISBN 0 255 36533 0
£7.50

A Tribute to Peter Bauer
John Blundell et al.
Occasional Paper 128; ISBN 0 255 36531 4
£10.00

Employment Tribunals
Their Growth and the Case for Radical Reform
J. R. Shackleton
Hobart Paper 145; ISBN 0 255 36515 2
£10.00

Fifty Economic Fallacies Exposed
Geoffrey E. Wood
Occasional Paper 129; ISBN 0 255 36518 7
£12.50

A Market in Airport Slots
Keith Boyfield (editor), David Starkie, Tom Bass & Barry Humphreys
Readings 56; ISBN 0 255 36505 5
£10.00

Money, Inflation and the Constitutional Position of the Central Bank
Milton Friedman & Charles A. E. Goodhart
Readings 57; ISBN 0 255 36538 1
£10.00

railway.com
Parallels between the Early British Railways and the ICT Revolution
Robert C. B. Miller
Research Monograph 57; ISBN 0 255 36534 9
£12.50

The Regulation of Financial Markets
Edited by Philip Booth & David Currie
Readings 58; ISBN 0 255 36551 9
£12.50

Climate Alarmism Reconsidered
Robert L. Bradley Jr
Hobart Paper 146; ISBN 0 255 36541 1
£12.50

Government Failure: E. G. West on Education
Edited by James Tooley & James Stanfield
Occasional Paper 130; ISBN 0 255 36552 7
£12.50

Waging the War of Ideas
John Blundell
Second edition
Occasional Paper 131; ISBN 0 255 36547 0
£12.50

Corporate Governance: Accountability in the Marketplace
Elaine Sternberg
Second edition
Hobart Paper 147; ISBN 0 255 36542 X
£12.50

The Land Use Planning System
Evaluating Options for Reform
John Corkindale
Hobart Paper 148; ISBN 0 255 36550 0
£10.00

Economy and Virtue
Essays on the Theme of Markets and Morality
Edited by Dennis O'Keeffe
Readings 59; ISBN 0 255 36504 7
£12.50

Free Markets Under Siege
Cartels, Politics and Social Welfare
Richard A. Epstein
Occasional Paper 132; ISBN 0 255 36553 5
£10.00

Unshackling Accountants
D. R. Myddelton
Hobart Paper 149; ISBN 0 255 36559 4
£12.50

The Euro as Politics
Pedro Schwartz
Research Monograph 58; ISBN 0 255 36535 7
£12.50